THROUGH OTHER EYES

Essays in Understanding 'Conscious Models'
—Mostly in Hong Kong

BARBARA E. WARD

The Chinese University Press
Hong Kong

Westview Press
Boulder, Colorado

Published jointly in the United States of America in 1985 by

The Chinese University Press
The Chinese University of Hong Kong
Shatin, New Territories
Hong Kong

Westview Press
5500 Central Avenue
Boulder, Colorado 80301
Frederick A. Praeger, Publisher

Library of Congress Catalog Card Number: 85-50396
ISBN (Westview) 0-8133-0257-9

Printed in Hong Kong by New Island Printing Co. Ltd.

Contents

Foreword vii

Introduction ix

I. CHINESE FISHERMEN: STUDIES AMONG THE BOAT-PEOPLE OF HONG KONG

1. A Hong Kong Fishing Village 3
2. Chinese Fishermen in Hong Kong: Their Post-Peasant Economy . . 23
3. Varieties of the Conscious Model: The Fishermen of South China 41
4. Sociological Self-awareness: Some Uses of the Conscious Models 61
5. Folk Models, Decision, and Change 79

II. SOCIO-ECONOMIC PAPERS

6. A Hakka Kongsi in Borneo 105
7. Cash or Credit Crops? 121
8. A Small Factory in Hong Kong: Some Aspects of Its Internal Organization 139

III. ASPECTS OF SOCIALIZATION

9. Temper Tantrums in Kau Sai: Some Speculations upon Their Effects 173
10. The Integration of Children into a Chinese Social World: A Preliminary Exploration of Some Non-literate Village Concepts . . . 187

IV. MODERNIZATION AND THE STATUS OF WOMEN

11. Men, Women, and Change: An Essay in Understanding Social Roles in South and South-East Asia 201
12. Women and Technology in Developing Countries 271

Foreword

My appreciation of the work of Barbara Ward may be expressed in the words of Chuang Tzu, the famous Chinese philosopher of the fourth century B.C., when he observed, 'Those who have fled into deserted valleys . . . will rejoice in the sound of human footsteps'. It is my hope that Barbara Ward's steps, her penetrating studies of Chinese society in Hong Kong and in the overseas Chinese communities of southeast Asia, will similarly be warmly received by readers of this collection of her essays.

Hong Kong is a community composed of highly diverse elements. Local traditions and external influences form sharp contrasts. Local boat-people, Hakka peasant women, Chinese temples, and other picturesque features have become the objects of tourism and are used to promote this activity. Anthropologists, of course, have made much more serious efforts to understand the reality of such phenomena. But there have been few expeditions into the basic dynamics of the community as serious as those conducted by Barbara Ward. She devoted herself continuously for thirty-two years to researching the facts of social life in Hong Kong and communicated to all who came in contact with her the enormous sense of joy which she gained from these studies.

It was on the basis of her ethnography of the boat-people in Hong Kong that Barbara Ward developed her interpretations of 'conscious models' in the Chinese context. Although historians have made important contributions to our understanding of certain Chinese ethnic groups such as the Hakka, it is an unfortunate fact that the bitter past of the boat-people has not been nearly as well served. The boat-people are the indigenes of the region around the present city of Canton, and were the original inhabitants of the area now called Hong Kong. It is recorded that when the region was brought under the sovereignty of the Chin government (A.D. 265-420), there were 50,000 households of boat-people and other local inhabitants who refused to submit to the new rulers. It was only after several centuries, during the T'ang dynasty (A.D. 618-917), that they paid tribute to the imperial government. Largely as a result of their rebellious activities these floating people have never been treated as equals with other subjects of Chinese states. For much of Chinese history they were driven by usury, forcible seizures and so on into piracy. In 1792 an imperial edict allowed them to settle on land, but their despised condition continued with little alteration. This troubled history is surely an important part of the background necessary to understanding how the boat-people's particular pattern of a conscious model of Chineseness was formed.

Barbara Ward's friendship and sympathy with the fishermen of Kau Sai made a deep impression on me when I visited that small island in 1979. She was quite definitely not one of those anthropologists who treat their informants merely as instruments and as material for their monographs. During my visit the head of the village told me on more than one occasion how grateful to her the villagers were for helping them acquire their first generator. What struck me most from this visit was my experience of seeing how these semi-literate boat-people, sitting in a room full of clay idols and mah jong tables and employing the symbols and ideographs of Chinese writing, were able to plan and organize all their modern fishing operations. This experience made me realize that the much-vaunted modernization of the 'underdeveloped' is not so hard to achieve once some aid or assistance is rendered. Perhaps it is in such assistance that anthropologists should seek wider scope for their work, in conjunction with the people they study. Barbara Ward's death came too soon for the full report of her thirty years' work to be completed. Nevertheless, I am certain that she will always be remembered by the people of Kau Sai.

TIEN JU-KANG

Introduction

Both for sociology . . . and for history, the object of cognition is the subjective meaning-complex of action.

—Max Weber[1]

Evidence in sociology must always be framed in terms of meaning. . . .

—Peter L. Berger and Hansfield Kellner[2]

When I first came to Hong Kong, the tallest building—and one of the only three public places with air-conditioning (the other two were cinemas)—was the Hong Kong and Shanghai Bank, and sharp bets were being laid on how many storeys higher the new Bank of China building, then going up next door, would rise. By day most of the streets were lined with shoe-shine boys, by night with street sleepers. The date was 1950.

At that time it was still quite normal to travel about by rickshaw. There were even a few green sedan chairs in Wyndham Street waiting for customers. Street life was also marked by seasonal changes in colour, for most men still wore Chinese suits—black in summer and soft bluish grey with wide white turned back cuffs in autumn and winter. For women, *cheung shaam* 長衫 (with three inch collars) were everyday wear for the well-to-do, and everyone else wore *shaam-fu* 衫褲 and wooden slippers (*khek* 屐) which clattered as they walked. Television did not exist, and very few people owned private radio sets, but cinemas did good business with hair-raising serial stories, and Cantonese opera played to packed houses on both sides of the harbour nearly every night. In the harbour itself, all the local craft were under sail; in the New Territories every particle of flat or terraced land was under rice; and the beach at Repulse Bay was almost empty—even at weekends.

[1] Max Weber, *The Theory of Social and Economic Organization* (New York: Oxford University Press, 1947), p. 101.

[2] Peter L. Berger and Hansfield Kellner, *The Homeless Mind: Modernization and Consciousness* (Harmondsworth, 1974).

All that, and all that it implies about the economic, social, and cultural structure of Hong Kong at the time is still only half a life-time away.

The dozen or so papers collected together here were all written at different dates during that half life-time. They fall fairly naturally into four groups. A group of essays on the boat-people of Hong Kong and South China, a second group on different socio-economic topics and third, two somewhat tentative papers on socialization. Finally, there are two papers on the position of women. In one fashion or another, most of them touch upon the central sociological problem of meaning.

They do this in a modest, not to say simplistic way which derives, I suppose, from the particular set of intellectual and practical experiences that came my way as student, fieldworker, and teacher over much the same period of time. As an undergraduate at Cambridge just before and at the beginning of the war that broke out in 1939, I read history, concentrating with most enthusiasm on the social history of the Middle Ages in Europe. In 1941, rejected by the uniformed services for reasons of health, I was 'directed' into teaching and spent the next twelve months learning my job at the Institute of Education, University of London. There I was introduced, both formally and practically, to sociology, social anthropology, and intercultural interaction by three of the greatest teachers of their day: Karl Mannheim, Margaret Read, and John Fairgrieve. It is scarcely surprising that an imagination already fascinated by the differences in mentality between mediaeval and modern Europe should have been eagerly receptive to the more general messages about the sociology of knowledge that all three were transmitting.

In Mannheim's lectures, of course, the main interests were in ideology; Margaret Read examined the social organization of education in different societies and its relevance for cultural differences; Fairgrieve, in the classroom, taught us that successful teaching only begins when a teacher is willing to accept that his pupils already have a great deal of knowledge and that he must build on that whatever it may be. 'Start where they are,' he used to say, 'not where you or your textbooks think they ought to be.' It was a precept I was to rely on during the next few years of school teaching, first in a small village primary school in southwest England and later at a prestigious secondary boarding school in West Africa.

The war over and freedom of occupation restored, I was able to go back to University for graduate work—not now, however, to the mediaeval studies that had previously absorbed my attention, but, after the Institute's theoretical introduction and the last few years' practical induction, to social anthropology instead. I was not yet sure what I was looking for, but I knew that my interests lay somewhere in the area I had learned to call the sociology of knowledge. I knew, too, that this meant a great deal more than simply accepting that peoples from other cultures and societies have 'other points of view'. After all, although shifting my stance to your position will, indeed, show me the world from your angle, nevertheless, if I cannot also 'get behind your eyes' and look out with your mental equipment, I shall not see the view that you see, for it is not just that our angles of view are different but rather that you and I actually construe the objects 'out there' differently.

The first British Anthropology Department to reopen after the war was at the London School of Economics. Accordingly, that was where I went. I have described the post-war scene in that Department elsewhere. It was exciting and puzzling. Some part of the time one felt astonished at what seemed to be the embarrassing simplicity of the subject matter; most of the time one was embarrassed by its astonishing complexity. We spent many hours discussing the existential status of 'social structure'. Did it really exist 'out there' as Radcliffe Brown was insisting in his most natural science moments.[3] Or was it all in the mind, as Leach seemed to be arguing?[4] It seemed to me obvious that it was both, but I was too insecure to push this idea at the time, and it was not until many years later that I read Berger and Luckmann's *Social Construction of Reality*[5] and found myself saying: Why, yes, of course!

In the meantime, as I started to write about my own fieldwork among fishing communities in Hong Kong and one or two other matters, and as I began University and extra-mural teaching, I almost insensibly discovered that what I wanted to try to put across was the view that social institutions and structures are the outcome of repeated actions[6] and that unless done under compulsion, human action, in its turn, is always ultimately the outcome of mental processes (decisions) in which the significant factors are the actor's own considerations of (*a*) costs and benefits and (*b*) morality (both of which

[3] A. R. Radcliffe Brown's papers 'On Social Structure', 'The Study of Kinship Systems', and 'Religion and Society' were published in the *Journal of the Royal Anthropological Institute* (London) in 1940 (Vol. LXX), 1941 (Vol. LXXI), and 1945 (Vol. LXXV) respectively, but owing to the closure of anthropological teaching in Britain during the war years they were not widely discussed in British anthropological circles much before 1940. Meyer Fortes' compilation, *Social Structure: Essays Presented to Radcliffe Brown* (Oxford: Clarendon Press) appeared in 1949.

[4] At the time of which I am writing, Leach was a Lecturer in the London School of Economics Anthropology Department. His Highland Burma book was published a few years later (E. R. Leach, *Political Systems of Highland Burma: A Study of Kachin Social Structure*. University of London and Athlone Press, 1954).

[5] Peter L. Berger and Thomas Luckmann, *The Social Construction of Reality*, was first published in the United States (Doubleday and Co.) in 1966.

[6] Following in this respect the argument of Frederick Barth, *Models of Social Organization*. Royal Anthropological Institute, Occasional Papers No. 23 (London, 1966). Barth's paper was originally delivered as a series of three lectures at the London School of Economics in 1963.

can only be understood by him in his own local 'cultural' terms) in the light of (*c*) his own appreciation of the situation (equally inevitably derived from his own local 'cultural' socialization and other experiences as a member of a particular set—sub-set, or whatever—of his own society).

The germ of this simple idea is already present in the earliest of the papers in this collection, the essay on a Hakka kongsi in Borneo in Section II below, which was originally written to be an appendix to *The Chinese of Sarawak* on which I worked with T'ien Ju-k'ang in 1949-50.[7] The late eighteenth and early nineteenth centuries saw the creation in Borneo (and elsewhere in South-East Asia) of a number of small enclaves of Chinese immigrants. Most of them were engaged in one or other of the extractive industries, including panning for gold. Isolated in what was in effect usually unadministered territory, these groups necessarily ran themselves as independent units. Inevitably as time went on the increasing penetration of the central government would put an end to their independence, but while they lasted these were successful little 'republics', tiny Chinese local structures on Bornean soil. The article describes the best documented of them, and argues that the form of its social structure was the predictable outcome of the fact that the only model the immigrants 'had in their heads' was the Hakka variant of the village/lineage community back in northern Kwangtung Province in China. This does not mean that the home model was, or could have been, reproduced in the totally different, natural, economic, and political environment of the Bornean jungle as it was two hundred years ago, but that the actions taken there by the Hakka Chinese and their leaders were necessarily the result of the decisions they made in the local circumstances as they understood them and for what they perceived as their own advancement in the light of the only knowledge they possessed about the organization of local community life, namely, the villages they had left in China.

The paper on Cash or Credit Crops, which follows the Borneo paper in Section II, was published in 1960 and written two or three years before for a seminar at the Institute of Commonwealth Studies, University of London, shows something of the same approach. The paper deals mainly with cash crop economies in the then still colonial territories, but explicitly claims a wider application as well. Again, the point made is a very simple one: namely, that in many situations where credit is required but modern institutionalized methods of making loans (banks etc.) are either not present or not relevant, the number of creditors in the population is likely to be relatively large because (*a*) no one has a great deal of capital anyway and/or (*b*) no one is

[7] T'ien Ju-k'ang, *The Chinese of Sarawak: A Study of Social Structure*. London School of Economics Monographs in Social Anthropology No. 12 (London: Athlone Press, 1953).

willing to lend cash or sell goods or services on credit except to individuals who are personally well known to him. As the number of individuals any one person can know well enough for this purpose is likely to be fairly small so, assuming a high demand for credit, the number of lenders is likely to be fairly large.

The third paper in Section II was written in 1969. In describing the organization of a small factory which I had studied in Hong Kong in the previous year, it makes use of the expression 'the Chinese way' which was constantly on the lips of one of the managing directors at the time. The article considers to what extent organization and management in this factory was or was not 'Chinese'. The upshot of the investigation is that whereas the major part of the organization was dictated by purely technological and economic considerations unaffected by cultural differences, there were some aspects which were, or were believed by the actors to be, peculiarly Chinese. Here again, the interest turns on the actors' own mental constructs, their perceptions of how things were and ought to be.

The first two papers on Chinese fishing communities in Hong Kong (Section I), written in 1952/3 and 1964/5 respectively, provide background data for the three following essays on 'conscious models' which were written between 1960 and 1980. Were I writing the first two today, I feel fairly sure that I would make a number of changes, but the general argument would be the same. As before, the main idea is to try to 'get at' some of the differences between the ways actors and observers see the same situations and, also, to distinguish the views of different actors. Because it would be difficult to outline the arguments of these three essays without repeating almost the whole of each, it seems wiser not to attempt to summarize them in this brief introduction but to let them speak for themselves. I would like to point out, however, that the rather tiresome proliferation of terms in these essays was made for purely heuristic reasons. There was no intention of trying to create a new technical vocabulary.

Something must be said, however, about the use of the term 'conscious model' which I adopted from an article by Lévi-Strauss entitled 'Social Structure', published in *Anthropology Today* in 1953,[8] since at least two reviewers of the volume in which the first of my three papers appeared[9] took exception to my usage and argued that the term 'model' was inappropriate

[8]Claude Lévi-Strauss, 'Social Structure', in Sol Tax and others (eds.), *Anthropology Today* (Chicago and London: University of Chicago Press, 1953), pp. 524-53.

[9]Percy S. Cohen, 'Models, a Review Article', in *British Journal of Sociology*, Vol. 17 (1966), p. 74, and J. Littlejohn, Review of M. P. Banton (ed.), *The Relevance of Models for Social Anthropology* (A.S.A., Monographs in Social Anthropology, Vol. 4, London: Tavistock Publications, 1965), in *Sociological Review*, Vol. 14 (1966), p. 357.

for what I was writing about. Of course they were right, or right at one level. They claimed that 'model' as commonly used in social science at the time (and certainly as used by Lévi-Strauss in the article from which I had adopted it) did not refer to content but to underlying pattern. Given that restricted use of 'model', then what I was writing about would have been more aptly given the label 'cognitive map', or some similar term. There is a clear conceptual distinction and the point was well taken. Since then, however, one or two other developments have occurred which have made me unwilling to change the term originally put forward. First, the word 'model' itself has taken on in social science some of the wider, vaguer connotations it has in everyday usage. The recent Association of Social Anthropologists' volume on Folk Models is sufficient evidence of this but there are many other instances.[10] Then there are questions of personal preference (linked, no doubt, with a general Humpty Dumpty view of the use of words, anyway). I do not myself like to use the word 'folk', which for me has an unacceptable smack of condescension, *de haut en bas*, about it. In Hong Kong journalism, for example, the easy alliteration in the term 'fisherfolk' no doubt explains its constant use which contributes, in my opinion, to the persistence of a derogatory image of the Boat-people. On the other hand, the two-dimensional image conveyed by the term 'cognitive map' seems to me inadequate as a description of the depth and wealth of content, imagery, and values—in fact the whole knowledge of their own society—which all human beings carry in their minds. Finally, and perhaps most tellingly, there is the consideration that the term 'conscious model' as used in these three essays has now been in circulation for some time among Chinese social scientists and colleagues who appear to find it useful. The translation they have given to the term carries connotations very close to those I had in mind in using it in the first place, and I have therefore decided to retain it.

Section III contains two short papers on socialization. Both were originally given in response to requests from local associations of social workers and psychologists in Hong Kong. There is a gap of some twenty-five years between the two papers, but the discussion in each centres on observations made in the same fishing village. In each I wrote as a social anthropologist with the same major object—namely, to try to convince my non-anthropological audience of the essential importance of accepting that 'the people themselves' (their 'clients' or 'subjects') have their own concepts and that both successful social work and meaningful cross-cultural analysis necessarily

[10] L. Holy and M. Stuchlik (eds.), *The Structure of Folk Models*, Association of Social Anthropologists Monograph No. 26 (Academic Press, 1981). The essay on 'Folk Models, Decision, and Change' (pp. 79-101 below) was to have been published in that volume, but was delayed in transit from Hong Kong.

depend upon understanding what these are and then, as old Mr. Fairgrieve would have said, 'starting there'—in other words one has to begin by trying to see *through other eyes*.

Finally, in Section IV there are two papers on the status of women. Both were commissioned by Unesco following a conference held in Calcutta in 1958 to discuss the contribution the social sciences could make to a Unesco Major Project on Mutual Understanding of Eastern and Western Cultural Values. In general terms this contribution had already been delineated as 'the task of acquainting the general public with the contemporary evolution of these values, and of clarifying the new conditions of relations among peoples'. The conference was convened in order to recommend particular areas of study in South and South-East Asia which could most usefully be selected for special emphasis in fulfilling this threefold task.

One such area was quickly agreed upon. It was undeniable that in the past half century almost every country in the world had enacted legislation to improve the position of women. What did these formal changes amount to in practice? Of course the members of the conference were well aware of the steady monitoring carried out by the United Nations Special Committee for the Status of Women. There was no need to duplicate that. What was wanted, they decided, was something both more general and more intimate; namely, a study, or series of studies, of the impact of the new public status of women upon the everyday lives of both sexes. In 1959 I was commissioned to direct such a project and edit the resulting book. With the title *Women in the New Asia*, it was published by Unesco in 1963. Paper No. 11 below is the Introduction to that volume, and paper No. 12 a follow-up paper written for the Unesco journal *Impact of Science on Society*. The second, a short piece on modern technological changes, is a summarizing article of the kind one might find in almost any of the so-called serious weeklies. Paper No. 11 on 'Men, Women, and Change' requires rather more explanation.

The Unesco project covered eleven countries in all: Burma, Ceylon (now Sri Lanka), India, Indonesia, Laos, Malaya (now the western part of Malaysia), Pakistan, the Philippines, Singapore, Thailand, and Viet-Nam. It is not surprising that neither time nor funds permitted undertaking new research over such a wide area, so it was necessary to rely on existing data and experience. I decided to invite two kinds of contribution: first, a number of special papers of a general nature written by professional social scientists who had already been working on the same or similar topics in the area, and, second, a set of personal, autobiographical accounts written by women nationals from each of the countries on the list. Inevitably, despite strenuous efforts by all concerned, the resulting articles were diverse, and the long introductory essay included here was an attempt to clear the ground and systematize a little, while at the same time warning against oversimplification.

These two papers on the status of women differ markedly in approach and style from those which precede them. These are more or less orthodox essays in comparative sociology written at a rather low level of abstraction and sophistication (especially in the kinship sections) for the general educated reader. In other words they are not directed at a specialist or academic audience, nor are they in any way attempts at constructing anybody's conscious models. However, the main body of the book on *Women in the New Asia* contains, as I have already said, articles written by women nationals of all the countries on the above list. Each contributor was asked to write a descriptive account of the changes that had occurred in her own society from the days of her grandmothers through those of her mother, herself, and, if possible, her daughters. The result is a series of fascinating reports of authentic social experience more vivid and compelling than anything an anthropologist is likely to produce out of the slow analytical process of building up a so-called 'conscious model'. But the one kind of report complements the other, and ideally, I suppose, both would be required by anyone who seriously hoped really to see 'through other eyes'.

But even if it were possible to develop such a degree of alternate vision (and I do not believe that it is), it must be clearly understood that, despite a good deal of popular misconception, the endeavour to do so is not what social anthropology is all about. An anthropological book on conscious models, even as is this one, on the conscious models of one sub-section of one highly differentiated society, is not ultimately directed at providing a descriptive analysis of how the people under consideration see their own social world (though it should try to provide just that), but must also have the wider aim of furnishing data and insight for the comparative analysis of human life in general. As an individual living in a Chinese fishing village, what I loved most was the (undoubtedly largely illusory) feeling that I really was beginning to understand how 'they' saw the world they lived in, but what I have tried to produce as an anthropologist (in the first Section of this book) is a certain kind of ethnographic analysis which attempts both to describe the conscious models idiosyncratic to these particular fishermen and to show, by exemplification, that any understanding of human action requires an appreciation of the fact that all people everywhere have their own conscious models and inevitably, necessarily, can only act in respect of them. Here, rather than in the personal enjoyment of the exercise which is the pleasure of some—but not all—anthropological fieldworkers or the inculcation of empathy for its own sake (good though that may well be), lies the sociological and social anthropological justification of trying to understand, and explain, how the world looks 'through other eyes'.

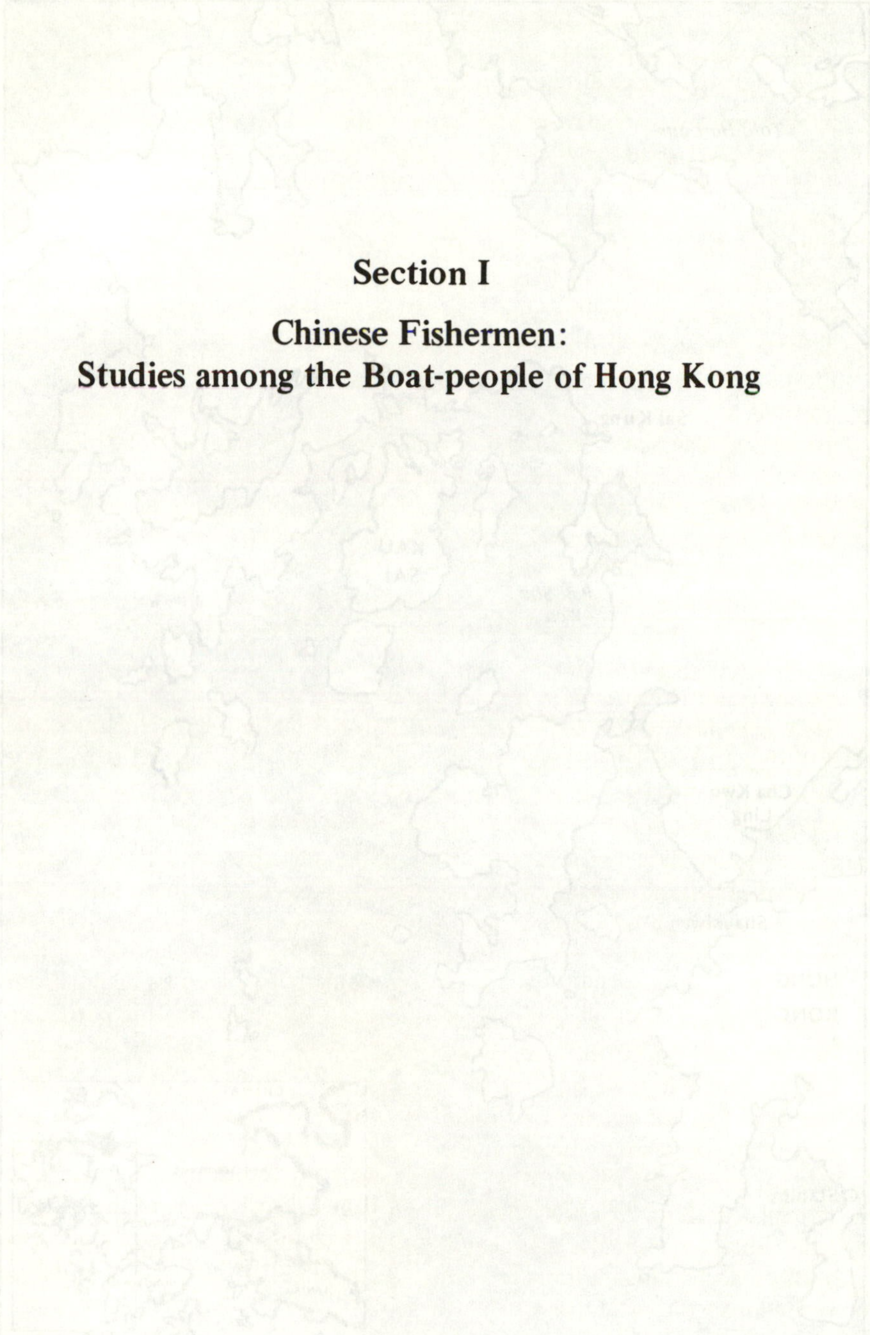

Section I

Chinese Fishermen: Studies among the Boat-people of Hong Kong

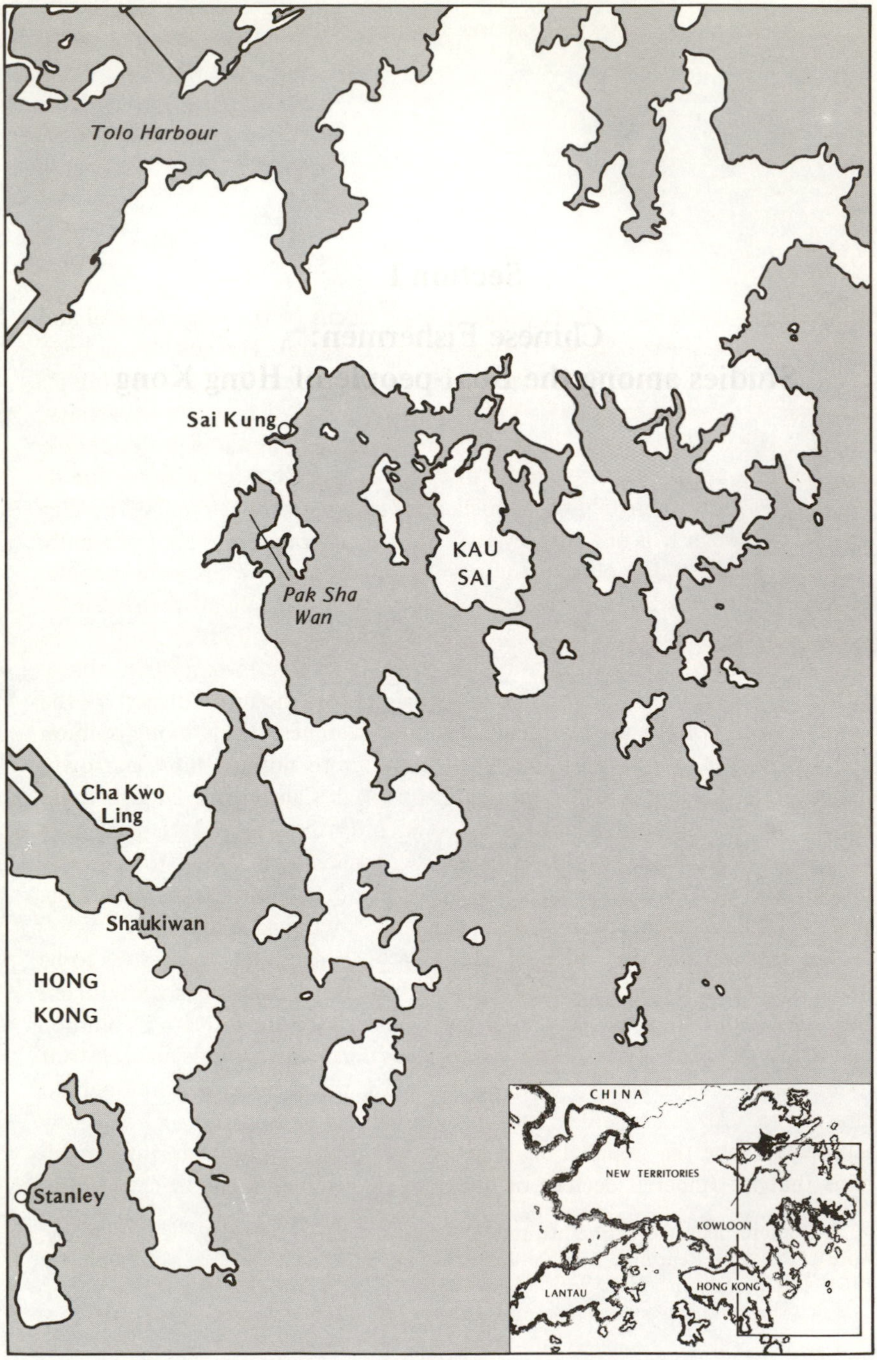
Tolo Harbour
Sai Kung
KAU SAI
Pak Sha Wan
Cha Kwo Ling
Shaukiwan
HONG KONG
Stanley
CHINA
NEW TERRITORIES
KOWLOON
LANTAU
HONG KONG

1. A Hong Kong Fishing Village*

It is not my intention to discuss here the problems of the origins, racial and cultural, of the boat-people of Kwangtung in general. The matter has been gone into very thoroughly by others far more competent than I—notably by Professor Ch'en Hsü-ching 陳序經, formerly President of Lingnam University, in his '蛋民的研究'—but it is relevant to recall that those water-people have usually been considered to be distinct. They have a particular name—'Tanka' 蛋家 † or 'Tanman' 蛋民, which is interpreted as 'Egg families' or 'Egg people'—though it is not unlikely that the 'egg' character was used originally to represent the sound only of the term used to designate the water-people. In any case the term 'Tanka' is definitely resented by them when used by outsiders; and though water-people will often use it both seriously and jokingly amongst themselves, they think of it as a term almost of abuse, rather in the same way that coloured people resent the term 'nigger'. If the word 'Tanka' is to be used with any scientific exactness it can, in my opinion and in Hong Kong at least, be taken to refer to nothing more narrowly defined than 'people who live on boats and speak Cantonese'. Though there are certain peculiarities of the dialect spoken by the Tanka water-people in general, though there are certain peculiar customs which they follow, and though it is usually easy to recognize a boatman on sight, these distinguishing traits are, I am convinced, all of a cultural, and not a racial, nature.

The fact remains that the boat-people in general still feel themselves to be looked upon as a distinct group, and a despised one. Landsmen quite often tell tales about their alleged moral and physical abnormalities—a common one is that they are all supposed to have been born with six toes on each foot—and it is always related how in the old days they were forbidden to intermarry with landsmen or (along with barbers, actors, and such like low fellows) to take the Imperial examinations. Professor Ch'en Hsü-ching maintains that no Imperial decrees or other legislation mentioning such prohibi-

*A lecture delivered at the Institute of Oriental Studies, University of Hong Kong, April 15th, 1953. Reprinted from the *Journal of Oriental Studies*, Vol. 1, No. 1 (January 1954) with permission.

†The character for '*tan*' is sometimes written '蜑'. *JOS* Ed.

tions can be found, but he agrees that in fact few, if any, boat-people ever could have reached even the lowest official positions. The consequences of such a disability under the old regime would naturally be profound, and the attitudes it generated still largely remain. Whatever the actual legal position it is true that the Tanka were, as to a large extent they still are, a despised group, and, because of their ways of life, a largely illiterate one. These facts, and the water-people's own recognition of them, are important to bear in mind in any closer consideration of their ways of living and their general psychological make-up.

Hong Kong has a floating population, which, unlike that of almost any other great city, literally floats. They get themselves born, they marry, they die, on their junks and their sampans. The overwhelming majority of them only go ashore to stay after they are dead. There has been no census of Hong Kong since 1931, and estimates of population figures are necessarily mere approximations: there may possibly be around 100,000 water-people here altogether. Of these perhaps about one half are fishermen, the rest being engaged mostly in trading and in various kinds of transportation, including, for example, the small, bright sampans which take passengers out to the fish restaurants in Aberdeen and the large class of lighters, the *kam sing teng*, to be seen every day clustering round the steamers in port, like sucking pigs around their mother.

There are, therefore, about 50,000 odd souls engaged in the Hong Kong fishing industry, which is undoubtedly one of Hong Kong's major industries, for more fish per year are caught and landed here in Hong Kong than in the whole of Australia. Of these 50,000 or so perhaps nearly one half, more or less, are engaged in small-scale inshore fishing of one type or another—that is, roughly about 20-25,000 people (including women and children). A very large number of these are based upon small villages in sheltered bays around the coasts and islands of the New Territories.

These small fishing villages are, sociologically speaking, of a type quite different from the larger fishing towns such as Cheung Chau, Aberdeen, and Shaukiwan, which are the bases of the deep-sea fishing craft, trawlers, and longliners, and whose populations, together with land-people, run into tens of thousands. Examples of fishing villages are many. They exist on Hong Kong Island—for example, at Stanley, at Tai Tam, at Chai Wan, on the Po Toi and So Ku islands, and on Ping Chau, and they are characteristic of the New Territories with examples at Tap Moon, Kat O, Po Tu O, Tsun Wan, and elsewhere. All these places are essentially little dual communities, with a wooden floating section lying just offshore from a stone built land section. Usually the water section has been there longer than the land section, which is in a sense parasitic upon it. Usually, though not always, the land people are

Hakka-speaking and do some farming. The men are often working away from home in Hong Kong or elsewhere. They may also fish a little or work on collecting boats, but there are to the best of my knowledge no Hakka-speaking water families. These dual villages are usually small, land and water populations together totalling a few hundreds or at most a few thousands. Sai Kung and Tai Po I should also class together as essentially villages of this type, at least from the fisherman's point of view.

THE VILLAGE

The village I have been living in is, or rather was, a village of this type, though its character has recently undergone a rather drastic change as a result of a decision to remove the land-people to another site. Up to July 1952 the village—Kau Sai—which lies on an island in the Port Shelter area, consisted of a simple line of houses built just along the shore, which contained about seventeen Hakka families, and several lines of boats anchored just off the shore, which contained between three hundred to four hundred Tanka people . Now the fishermen remain, but the land-dwellers are at present reduced to one Hakka family, and two ex-fisher families—one of whom runs the village shop while the other acts as caretaker for the village temple.

This shop and this temple are the most significant buildings in the village. The shop is run, as I have said, by an ex-fisherman. On the whole this is a rare thing; it is much more usual to find the village shop run by a Hakka landsman, even in what are otherwise purely Tanka fishing hamlets like Kiu Chui or Kolauwan. Recently in Kau Sai a second shop, run by the remaining Hakka family, has been gaining in importance, but the ex-fisherman's shop still remains the real centre of village activity. It sells all sorts of miscellaneous goods: torch batteries, cigarettes, matches, incense-sticks and paper goods for religious purposes, toothbrushes, soap, rice, beans, sugar, oil, cakes, biscuits, sweets, and aerated water, as well as some of the lesser fishing requirements such as wire, twine, hooks, and the glass globes and mantles for the purse-seine fishermen's bright lights. Much of its trade is done on credit. It acts also as a general store-house where many of the floating people can keep spare nets, rope or *shue leung*, or store their winter bedclothing during the summer months. For dwellers on small craft this is an important service indeed. No charge is made. Finally the shop also serves as a general meeting place, a resort for recreation, talk, gambling, sleep, and listening to the wireless. It thus fulfills in almost every particular the joint functions of village-hall, village-post-office-cum-general-store, and village pub (as we know them so well) in England. At the time of the village festival or at other crises the shop is the centre of all organizational activity.

In all this the shopkeeper—whose brothers and cousins are all local fishermen and who took to his present land job only at the end of the war—plays a quiet, cheery, and rather self-effacing part. He keeps open house, but he does not attempt to organize the groups and individuals who wander in and out of his shop, sleep on his tables or his beds (or even in the rice bins), listen to his wireless, gamble with his cards and mahjong tiles, and now and then even buy his goods. Very often people simply help themselves to what they want and then hand over the cash to the shopkeeper or his wife, or whoever happens to be around, or see that their debt is entered in the ledger. It is a common sight to see a three-year-old clutching a fistful of biscuits and butting his way among the legs of a group of mah-jong playing adults until he can find the shopkeeper and hand over his five or ten cent piece. The shopkeeper exacts no interest on credit sales, nor does he charge a higher price for them—though his prices in general are a bit above those on the mainland. His business depends upon the goodwill of his customers—nearly all of whom are the local fishermen he has worked and played with for the last forty years and to most of whom he is related by kinship or by marriage; and these fishermen in their turn depend very largely upon him—his shop provides in fact a sort of second home ashore for them, an indispensable local land establishment.

Another is the temple. This temple is one of the most prettily sited, and certainly one of the best kept in the New Territories. It used to house the village school, but since last summer when the landsmen moved over to the mainland there has been no school. The temple is administered by fishermen, and an ex-fisherman is employed as temple keeper, with the job of keeping the place clean and performing the obligatory morning and evening 'services' of gong beating and incense lighting. Five times a year the temple is the scene of festivals and great activity. At most other times it is deserted—providing a cool place for resting in the hot summer days—though it is often visited by individuals on occasions of commemoration, or for thanksgiving or seeking spiritual guidance by divination. The visiting individuals may be anyone at all: landsmen, Hoklo, or Tanka water-people, all go from time to time—visitors and locals alike. If you want to get a proper priest to perform ceremonies for you, however, you must go to Sai Kung or Shaukiwan—priests only come to the village once a year, at the time of the festival in the Second Moon. Then they perform rituals on behalf of the community as a whole, at the same time a company of players is engaged from Kowloon, a large matshed theatre is erected, and operas are performed for five nights and four days. The usually quiet bay is filled with well over 300 boats including up to a dozen of the big longliners from Shaukiwan—the aristocrats of the Hong Kong fishing fleets.

The close links with the shop and the temple are accompanied by others. After all there are certain things which must be done on land. Water and firewood come from the hills and the streams and the village wells. Clothes are usually washed on shore and boat boards scrubbed, aired, oiled, and dried there—all by women. Then nets and sails have to be dyed from time to time, and boats careened. The dyeing is done over on the other island in the dyeing pits and steaming vat, both of which are the property of the (Hakka) ex-village headman, who charges $3.00 a time for their use.* Careening is done, twice a month as a general rule, in the shallow water of the straits at low tide. The bottom of the boat is scraped, the marine growth burned off with burning grass, and the hull then rubbed all over with tung oil. The legs which prop the boats up during this process are left on land near the careening spots, or in the shop.

Most important of all the shore jobs, however, is the drying of nets and fish. Except in continuously rainy weather or when there are no catches this is a daily task for all the purse-seiners and accounts for much time, energy, and planning. For a local purse-seiner fisherman the importance of having suitable places for net and fish drying can hardly be exaggerated. Not only must the nets be dried out every day, but also the bulk of their catch is sold dried—mostly small stuff. (Incidentally, it is interesting to note the wealth of terms these fishermen have for naming different kinds of fish, many of which the landsmen—even the local villagers—lump all together as just 'small fish'. One of the favourite ways the fishing children have for teasing me is to hold up a minute silverish scrap of something and ask what kind of fish I think it is. Yet if I ask them in my turn the name of a flower or bird they usually reply with an indifferent: 'Oh, that's just a flower' or 'That? Isn't that a little bird?')

The shore, then, is the place for shopping, storing things, meeting friends and discussing matters, and for recreation. It is also the place for major items of worship, and above all indispensable for certain essential parts of everyday economic activity—the drying of nets and fish, the dyeing of nets and sails, the making of rope and string, the collecting of firewood and water. The fishermen themselves often stress another aspect, and over and over again I have seen them point to their obviously very bonny children and heard them explain that their health and development depends much on their freedom to spend their days largely ashore rather than cramped up in the boats, like the children in more crowded, more urban, or less safe and less familiar places.

Leaving the land now, let us look at the boats. Though moving at times

*All dollars referred to in this lecture are Hong Kong dollars (HK$1.00 = 1s 3d).

to less exposed positions, according to the direction of the wind, these never lie very far off the shore. Farther or nearer, however, makes little difference. Indeed, the strong antithesis between land and water, which we as land-dwellers tend automatically to make, does not, I think, exist for these villagers. Here in the bay, in their own environment, ashore or afloat they are equally at home—and this applies almost as much to the Hakka as to the Tanka. It is true that going from, say, the shop to the boat requires two kinds of movement: the one provided by the legs—walking—the other by the arms—*yu loh*; but to them there is little significant difference. Any six-year-old can *yu loh* with ease and skill; by the time he is ten it is every bit as much 'second-nature' as walking. The water passage is thus but an extension, as it were, of the land (or perhaps from the Tankas' point of view it might be even less misleading to suggest that the land here in the village is but an extension of the water).

This is perhaps rather a difficult point to grasp. As landlubbers we automatically think of water-dwelling as something essentially other, essentially different. But the more I see of water-dwelling in Hong Kong, and especially in the village where I know it best, the more I find myself forced to realize that this is not entirely so. Differences there are, of course, but they are differences explicable more in terms of the size of the dwelling space and the rhythm of economic activity than in terms of water-dwelling as such. It is true that the skills in boat handling which are developed by cargo-boat dwellers and sampan people are very similar to those developed by the village fishermen or the trawlermen based, say, upon Cheung Chau, and many of the customs, especially those connected with avoiding the perils of water life, are the same, but in other respects, some of them at least as basic if not even more basic to the culture and social structure are absent. I would venture to suggest that the cargo-boat people of the harbour have more in common with land-dwelling business men and transport owners than they have with mainland purse-seiners or island-based trawlers and longliners, and vice versa.

Thus the fisherman going down to his boat in the village, goes down to it in just the same spirit as the landsmen going along to his house. At this level of thinking the boat is just another dwelling place.

FISHING METHODS

Yet it remains true, of course, that these people are fishermen, and the most important thing about fishermen is that they fish, and therefore they have certain peculiar skills and certain peculiar rhythms of living which set them apart from the land-dwellers, just as fishermen all over the world are set apart from the rest of us.

Let us take the skills first: from Kau Sai four or five main kinds of fishing are practised; purse-seining, which mostly takes place by night, is the major activity but there are also about twenty-five small longliners, handliners, and trappers. Purse-seining and longlining are specialist activities, but almost all fishermen from time to time will engage in handlining and trapping. Specialists in trapping and handlining also exist, however; they are usually amongst the poorest, sometimes just able to make ends meet, sometimes failing altogether. In the spring some varieties of fish are caught by spearing on a sort of trident, though it has four prongs. This is done as much as a sport as anything else. Fish are also caught by diving in the summer.

Handlining, of course, need not be described. The trapping most commonly practised is done by means of beehive-shaped traps of various sizes into which the fish, attracted by a bait usually of crushed fish, enter through a non-return valve at the side. Traps are laid in suitable waters and usually collected the next day. All traps are made by the fishermen themselves. Longlining is a method of catching fish on hooks dependent from a series of short lines attached to one or more long lines which trail out behind the junk or sampan.

Purse-seiners, *ku chai* 罟仔, are those chunky-looking little boats with, usually, two masts, main and for'ard. There is a wooden shelter (cabin) amidships, and a projecting wooden platform at the stern where cooking is done and firewood stored. Most purse-seiners are about 27-35 feet in overall length, and about 9-11 feet in the beam. A new one made of teak and fir costs today about $4-4,500 in Shaukiwan. Just about eighteen months ago the first of these small boats to be mechanized installed a small, two-cylinder 15 h.p. diesel engine—today over twenty of them have such engines—the buying and installing of which costs between $8-10,000. Kau Sai is proud of the fact that despite its small size it was a Kau Sai purse-seiner who first put in one of these engines and that today Kau Sai, with six pairs of purse-seiners mechanized, still leads the way—definitely ahead of all those large places like Aberdeen and Shaukiwan.

Purse-seiners are the most numerous of the local craft; there are possibly about two thousand of them based in local waters. Kau Sai has about thirty. They do their fishing in pairs and usually by night—being in fact the bearers of those bright cat's-eye lights to be seen all around the coasts, especially for instance off Repulse and Deep Water bays in the summer. The method of fishing is called purse-seining because the net, or seine, is drawn in or pulled in to encircle the fish by a line called the purse-line running through the bottom meshes. The bright kerosene lights are used to attract the fish in the first instance—usually being placed in a sampan for that purpose. The pair of purse-seine junks then proceeds to encircle the sampan with the net, the boats moving first away from each other and then converging again on the other side of the sampan, paying out the net as they go moving rather slowly by means of the long sweeps—*yu loh*. The net is thus laid in a kind of circular wall around the sampan with its bright light. The workers on the two junks then begin to haul in on the purse-line, which runs through the bottommost meshes of the net wall, and so the net is gradually gathered in at the bottom—at the same time it is hauled in from either end and the circular purse thus gradually narrows. The sampan glides out over the top of the narrowing circle, the fish, flipping and leaping silvery in the light, are scooped out into the holds of the fish junk with a hand-net, and the whole operation is ready to be repeated again. It takes about thirty-five minutes, more or less, altogether each time. The drawing in of the purse-line is often accompanied by loud shouting, beating the surface of the water, and other noise to scare the fish which may be escaping back into the net. Because the motive power for the whole operation is provided only by hand propulsion, it is very slow, and most local purse-seiners maintain that they would not be able to catch enough fish if they did not quite often use dynamite to stun them first. This, which is quite illegal, sometimes leads to appalling accidents.

RHYTHMS OF LIVING

For the purse-seiners the real work of the day begins some time before sunset —the evening meal is at 5.30 p.m. or so in summer, earlier in winter. It is cooked usually by the youngest wife in the boat family, and eaten *en famille* in the for'ard shelter or in summer on the open bows. Immediately it is finished and cleared away, faces and bodies are washed, and with the minimum of fuss the boat with its partner boat is off to sea. The further afield they plan to go, the earlier they start—but by sunset as a rule all the purse-seiners have cleared off, and only a few liners and perhaps a few Hoklo visitors are left in the bay. The landsmen have their meal a little later, their children play—a much diminished group—until it is too dark to see, the wireless in the shop provides open entertainment for all, particularly on Monday and Friday evenings when programmes are relayed from the Po Hing or Ko Shing theatres and the shop is therefore open till midnight. Talk, bed, sleep—and mosquitoes.

On the purse-seiners there is a rather excited, very wakeful passage out to the chosen fishing ground, where the two boats stop, set their kerosene pressure lamps and wait. If it is calm and there are fish about they may angle for them—but mostly they sleep then, to be wakened at about midnight by an alarm clock. Actual fishing is usually done in two separate periods—around midnight and just before dawn—with sleep in between. Altogether they may get about four to five hours sleep if they are not lining all the time. The small children, of course, get more, but a ten-year-old is already a useful hand. During the fishing time, especially during the dawn period, fish-collecting boats call around to buy, and a few small liners too may come around to buy bait for their activities next day. As dawn comes up the purse-seiners are on their way back to base.

Meanwhile the landsmen have slept, but they wake up at dawn, or just before, and the first purse-seiners arrive at an already busily working village —clothes already being hung out to dry, pigs being fed and fields tilled. The liners and Hoklo junks are getting ready to go out with bait, purchased usually from the returning purse-seiners. As each pair of purse-seiners comes in, the sampans are launched, the wet net, piled high in the bows of the net-boat, is bundled into one of them, and carried off at once with about ten people to spread it out to dry. No time is lost at all. Back on the boat, washing and teeth-cleaning has probably already taken place, children are wakening, breakfast is being cooked; the returning net spreaders are fed—rice and fish as usual. The land-people have their breakfast perhaps a little later—not much. Then on the boats there is sleep, there are jobs to do, there is play for the children—these come ashore on any fine day at about nine-thirty or ten o'clock. And they play there most of the day—the school ones go to school of course, and so do the land children.

The grown-ups' main jobs are concerned obviously with the nets, making and mending, and making rope; with the fish, drying and sorting; and with boats and gear, careening, mending up, and cleaning. Net mending is mostly done by men, and so is most net making, but women can and do knit nets as well, and certainly always take part in the fish drying and sorting, careening, etc. In addition women do all the boat cleaning—turning out and scrubbing right through usually two or three times a month; cooking and food preparation, including the cutting and collecting of firewood and water, are also their jobs, as, of course, are clothes-making, washing, and mending. When it is realized that in addition they have all the chores for the young children to perform, it is not surprising to learn that they have little free time ashore—that is, away from their homes. A woman with free time is either young and unmarried with efficient sisters-in-law, or old with efficient daughters-in-law; the third possibility is that she may be childless. The men have a little more chance for recreation; they gamble (at poker, Russian poker or mah-jong), they listen all over again to a repeat performance of last night's opera, they talk and they sleep and they play with the children, especially the babies. Sometimes they even fish, for fishing remains a sport as well as a source of livelihood. At times they buy snacks—sweets, cakes, aerated water; and, if they are working on the dried fish or nets, for instance if it is a net-dyeing day, they will also eat a lunch, maybe of cakes or biscuits bought from the shop, maybe something special cooked on the boat and sent across to them, or which they are called back to eat.

By four o'clock the dried nets and fish are being gathered in, the boats are ready to go off again, the children wander back or are collected by older brothers or fathers or uncles or cousins, the evening meal is eaten, and after washing once more the fishermen are off for the next night's business. At sunset each evening, as at sunrise each morning, incense is burned for the ancestors and at the bows. On land the land-children now play where the boat-children have played all day, the evening meal is also eaten, the bath taken, and the doors are shut for sleep. The liners have mostly returned, and they too settle down to sleep; so does the crew of the collecting boat which sometimes comes in the evenings ready to pick up fish when the purse-seiners return again first thing next morning.

And so it goes on; round and round—the daily rhythm of production, consumption, recreation, and ritual. Not very exciting in itself, but enlivened always by the excitement of fishing and during the long days by the interests of gambling and gossip and children. Every now and then, too, there come the recurring items in the patterns of the larger rhythms of living: monthly, seasonal, annual.

Every month, usually twice, the boats must be careened; every month on the first and fifteenth mornings special worship is paid to the ancestral figures on the boats and at the prow; nearly every month some dyeing of nets or sail cloth is performed.

Seasonal rhythms naturally vary with the type of fishing: for the small liners the main season is during the first four months of the lunar year, but the purse-seiners are then in their slack season; they are busiest in the sixth, seventh, and eighth lunar months. At present they do well if they can just make ends meet—this year so far has been a bad one and many are already in debt. From the sixth to ninth month they hope to make a surplus: extra money that can go into boat building or to repairs, net buying, marrying off a son or a daughter, or, best of all in popularity at the moment, installing an engine. Men's talk in the village constantly comes back to talk of engines, the different makes and their varying merits. Were there enough engines on the market, and enough money in the fishermen's money belts, almost every small junk in Hong Kong would be mechanized tomorrow.

The annual rhythm of living in Kau Sai, as in most other parts of the world, is marked especially by the pattern of annually recurring ritual. The fishing people of Kau Sai are essentially religious in outlook—by this, I mean that they are constantly adjusting their lives and their thoughts to the presence of an unseen world, a world of spiritual power, which they believe they can contact and influence by certain special kinds of behaviour. This behaviour I call ritual. Kau Sai people observe many of the usual annual rituals of non-Westernized Chinese families everywhere, but there are some differences. At New Year, for instance, it is not the spirits of Heaven and Earth but the spirits of Heaven and the Waters that are worshipped on their boats, and at New Year too or after a death or a birth on the boat or at a time of bad fortune many people go off to Sai Kung or Shaukiwan and employ a priest to come down to the boat and perform a ceremony called 'changing the gods'. This, which involves spilling the blood of a chicken, is believed to bring about a kind of cleansing from bad fortune and a bringing of new, live, good fortune. A similar sacrifice is made on the Dragon Boats before the start of their races on the 5th of the Fifth Moon—it is said to be 'to open the Dragon's eyes'.

Kau Sai nowadays has no Dragon Boat, though it used to run one in the twenties, and on one memorable occasion even came in first in the 'regatta' attended by the Governor, in those days held in Aberdeen, they tell me. Nowadays the Dragon Boat festivals of other places are attended by Kau Sai people only as spectators, in their private capacity. The same is true of most other festivals, for instance the annual celebrations in Shaukiwan or Cha Kwo Ling, the biennial festival for the Queen of Heaven in Lung Suen Wan across the bay, and the annual Koon Yam (Kwan Yui) festival in Pak Sha Wan near Sai Kung. To the latter, as also to the festival which is a movable feast in Sai Kung, they usually contribute fair sums of money. They may go much further afield, to Cheung Chau or Tap Moon for instance. All these festivals are attended by individuals, family groups or in informal friendly groups. They are not village concerns as such. Twice a year, however, the village has public rituals to perform—on the 15th of the Twelfth Moon near the end of the year and at the annual festival of the temple, which falls on the 13th of the Second Moon. On both these occasions a pig is slaughtered and offered in the temple on behalf of the village as a whole. Later the meat is distributed. The annual ritual cycle therefore begins with the New Year and its family offerings and proceeds through the temple festival in the Second Moon—these are the two high lights of the year. Quickly in their wake comes Ching Ming and the festivals in other villages, which may be attended both to visit the temples and to see the plays. There is at least one of these festivals in each of the Third, Fourth, Fifth, and Sixth Moons. In the Seventh Moon comes the young women's festival and immediately after it the occasion for burning paper clothes and money to feed the hungry ghosts of those who have died by drowning or other accident and so had no proper burial. The Eighth Moon sees the Moon Feast, the Ninth once again brings visits to the family graves.

On the 10th of the Tenth Moon there is a small offering in the temple—a little pork and/or fish—to one of the lesser gods there. The Eleventh Moon brings the winter solstice and again a visit to the temple, and the Twelfth Moon sees once more the public offering of a pig in public thanksgiving for the successful completion of another year, while the preparations for New Year once again get under way.

The essentially religious outlook of the people is strikingly apparent at Chinese New Year. At New Year there is virtually no fishing. From noon on the 30th of the Twelfth Moon until a selected lucky day in the New Year—in 1953 it was the 5th—the junks may not move from their anchorages. At the selected lucky time on the selected lucky day all make a token move, to the accompaniment of a vast noise of firecrackers, and after that the prohibition is lifted. In 1953, therefore, there was a more or less complete immobilization for about a week—a week's holiday in fact. Now fishermen get few holidays and like to make the best of them. New Year is a time when the larger villages, like Sai Kung, and towns, like Shaukiwan, Yaumati, and Hong Kong, have endless attractions, as attractive for fishermen as for others: shops, plays, cinemas, bright lights, the Tiger Balm Garden, and Luna Park—all the excitements of city life. The pull is very great, and there are not wanting Kau Sai boats who go off to Causeway Bay or Shaukiwan for this period every year. In Kau Sai there is only the everyday scene, just the same old shop and broken down houses where the Hakka land-people used to live. It can be very cold and there are no bright lights. Yet no less than thirty boats came back for New Year in 1953, and their owners claimed to have done so for as long as they could remember. The reason is simply that they feel they owe a duty to their god—he resides in the temple; he has protected them throughout the years; they must return to give him thanks and implore his continued blessing.

The stories that are told of the power of this god, Hung Shing Kung, are convincing enough. On two separate occasions two fishermen who disobeyed the rule that during Kau Sai's festival Kau Sai boats should not put to sea met with disaster: one had the sampan from which he and his wife were fishing destroyed by fire—the kerosene lamp flared up, and his wife was terribly burnt, almost blinded (she is still in the village, where the husband is now the temple caretaker); the other had his boat overturned in a sudden squall, and, though he lost no lives, he did lose nearly all his property, including the whole roast pig he was in process of carrying to offer to a different god on another island. This very year, at the festival, power and omniscience were shown again when torrential rain threatened to ruin a part of the celebrations which must be held out of doors—the usual time for this was about noon, but rain poured down from eleven thirty onwards, seemingly relentless. At about one forty, when it was thundering, the organizing committee repaired to the temple to ask Hung Shing Kung what should be done. The divining blocks were cast and the answer came not to worry because by three o'clock the rain would cease. At two forty-five it began to clear; at two fifty, umbrellas were hardly needed; at two fifty-five the ceremonies began in a few fitful spots of rain only; at three o'clock it was completely fine, and it stayed so, too, till about four thirty—just long enough for all to be decently finished.

It is a commonplace of sociological thinking that one of the functions of ritual and ceremonial in any society, one of the things it actually does, is to reflect the social relationships and, therefore, the social structure of that society. A marriage ceremony, for instance, is a ritual which, amongst other things, publicly affirms a newly created social relationship; a family group gathered to worship its common ancestors is both expressing its cohesion as a group, and reinforcing that same cohesion by its corporate act of worship. So in Kau Sai if we look at the rituals and take note of the people who perform them, we can see fairly clearly what are the significant relationships and groupings in the social structure. These, broadly, are the family and the Kau Sai group of water-people as a whole.

ECONOMIC AND SOCIAL STRUCTURE

As in all known communities to date the basic structural group in the village is the simple family—that is father and mother and children—and as in all Chinese communities to date this simple family is often extended to include other patrilineal kin. This means in practice that on most boats are to be found living together a man and his wife and their children, often with the wives and children also of their married sons. Only two or three Kau Sai men have two wives, and one of them lets his second wife live ashore in Shaukiwan, where he goes to visit her now and then—he slipped off once, for instance, when he had a chance during the festival and when his Kau Sai wife had just lost $20 at cards and was very bad-tempered as a result. The usual complement of a purse-seiner is about ten, more or less, and purse-seiners work in pairs. Every pair of purse-seiners in Kau Sai is manned by a single extended family group, usually headed by a pair of brothers or a father and son. The numbers may be made up by hired hands, but these too are often also patrilineal kin (i.e. relatives having the same surname) of the owners. Hired men are housed and fed with the rest of the family on the junk, and usually receive as wages a share of four per cent of the catch. To have enough sons to be able to dispense with hired help is a very general ambition, but it is an ambition which increasing mechanization is going to make increasingly unlikely of fulfillment, for engines tend to require larger boats and larger boats require more hands—at least in the present stage of development.

A measure of the difference in wealth between the purse-seiners and the liners and trappers is afforded by a glance at the composition of their crews. It is a commonplace in the sociology of traditional China that the poorer the family, the smaller its numbers, and vice versa. Hardly one small liner or trapper contains more than a simple family—father, mother and children—and none has any hired men.

Each boat group forms a single 'household' that is a single unit of consumption, for eating and for sleeping. For the liners and trappers the single boat group is also the unit of production, but for the purse-seiners the unit of production is not the single boat, but the pair. In some very closely knit family groups the pair of purse-seiners is also the unit of consumption, but this is not so common: the money coming in is most usually divided equally between the two junk owners, and spent by them separately on things like food, clothing, cigarettes, sweets for the children, wages for the employees, and so forth. Money is usually kept by the boatmaster in a belt at his waist and doled out by him. Larger sums are put away in locked boxes in the holds with household goods, bedclothes, etc., and the keys are nearly always left in the care of the boat-owner's wife. When money is to be taken out she is asked to unlock the box. Savings that are not simply hoarded in this way may be used to buy gold ornaments, or go into loans to others, but even the more relatively prosperous Kau Sai fishermen do not keep their surplus profits long: there is always some item demanding expenditure; there is very often debt.

This is not the place to go into the problem of debt in detail, but the outline of what happens is in any case a familiar one. This is an economy short of ready money and dependent upon a fluctuating natural resource—fish. It is also an economy in which the necessary capital expenditure, on boats, gear, engines, is relatively very high, and a society in which certain necessary social expenditures, especially on marriages, are also high. From time to time almost all fishermen are in need of cash loans for particular items of expenditure, and very many indeed need loans not just for special expenditures now and then but almost all the time just to keep themselves going at all.

Loans may be acquired in three or four different ways, but the most usual is to secure an advance from a fish dealer. In return the fisherman sells his fish to that dealer who then collects it and dispatches it to the official markets for him. This saves the fisherman a good deal of extra time and trouble in any case, especially if he is living in an outlying village. The dealers usually take a six per cent commission on the sale price of the fish, which, with the official Market's commission of six per cent, means that the fisherman himself receives (or should receive) the wholesale price less twelve per cent. There is said to be a good deal of cheating over the price but it is not easy to say to what extent this is actually so. The usual dealer's commission of six per cent is not a fixed rate. Those heavily in debt may have to pay considerably more; close friends may pay less, and so on. There is at least one dealer connected with the village who charges six per cent for his debtors but only three per cent for those who have not borrowed from him.

The obverse side, as it were, of this loan relationship with the fish dealer (who is at the same time often a fish collector, usually, in the New Territories, a fish dryer too, and quite often himself a fisherman or ex-fisherman) is the credit relationship with the retail shops. This I have already touched upon in describing the position of the shop in the village. Every fisherman in the village (the landsmen too, for that matter) has a credit account—it may run up to $500 or even more. The debts are probably hardly ever completely paid up. You pay what you can, when you can. The shopkeeper, who knows all his debtors personally, does not chase them to pay.

Now the important things to notice about this system of loans and credit are: first, without some such system production would come to an end, and quickly. The situation in which a credit system acts as a kind of lubricant to the whole economic structure without which it would seize up is now well known, and not only in the Far East. Second, it is almost necessarily a localized system. By this I mean that firstly because of the small size of their capital resources and secondly because of their method of doing business neither the fish dealers nor the retail shops can have a very large clientele, while at the same time that clientele must be local and more or less permanent.

The significance of the small-scale capital here is obvious. The fish dealer most patronized by the villagers (he is himself an ex-purse-seiner from the village and is related to most of the others) lends out something over $15,000, according to his own estimate. Lending even such low sums as $100 a time would give him debtors amounting only to 150 at any one time—and most loans are likely, I think, to be larger than that. At the same time business is done entirely on a personal basis—money is lent, or credit given, not because of any bank or other guarantee but simply on personal knowledge. There is, naturally, a limit to the number of people whom a creditor can know in this way, and there is thus a limit to the scale of his business, which must be not only fairly small, but also localized. It is these two factors, the small capital and the need for personal, face-to-face relationships in the organization of the system of loans and credit, that I think explain in great measure the multiplication of small firms of apparently identical type which are to be found everywhere in this part of the world, and by no means only in the fishing villages.

I suggest, too, that they also help to explain the point which I have been labouring all through—the relative stability of these fishing communities, which in my opinion are far indeed from the unattached, unpredictable wanderers they are sometimes picturesquely described as being. Without a home base fishermen would be unable to obtain the loans and credit which are essential to them. They are themselves usually perfectly well aware of this. In the village, recently, there has been difficulty because firing practice from the neighbouring army camp interfers quite seriously with the small liners' fishing. Most of them have decided to stay on, nevertheless—one major reason, as they say themselves, is that they know they can obtain credit from the shops there and in Sai Kung. Elsewhere, may be, they would not fare so well.

Kau Sai has, in general, a very good name. If the Kau Sai boats return regularly to Kau Sai, as they do, it is because the *fung sui* is good there, the god is powerful and benevolent, there are water and firewood and good drying grounds, the bay is sheltered and above all extremely conveniently placed for reaching the fishing grounds, but it is also because they are known to be Kau Sai people. It is not an accident that this particular very small fishing community should be relatively so prosperous, and that it should be foremost in the race to mechanize. The dealers and shopkeepers in Sai Kung and Shaukiwan are well aware that Kau Sai fishermen are a good risk, and they themselves are proud of their good name.

But to return to the two main social groupings mentioned before: the family and the village group itself. The families are the economic units, these relationships with fish dealers and shops—nearly all of which lie outside Kau Sai itself, mostly in Sai Kung and Shaukiwan—are their concern and are controlled by the heads of the boat households. The village as a whole is not a single economic group but a group of families living in the same place and requiring organization, therefore, for purposes of law and order, and for social and ritual occasions. Kau Sai's good reputation for honesty in business is paralleled by a good reputation for general peaceableness and for successful festivals—and these are the concern of the village group as a whole.

The striking thing about the social organization at this, the village level, is its extreme looseness. Since the departure of the land-people last year there has been no officially recognized village headman. But even when there was such a one he had little authority in fact in community matters except as regards the land-people, of whom he was one, and in matters when it was necessary to use him as the channel of communication with Government. The annual festival, for instance, was in fact run entirely by a committee of fishermen, but arrangements for getting the necessary official permits were made by the officially recognized headman. His departure is not missed, however, rather the contrary.

If you ask the fishermen who their leaders are, they will tell you the names of three or four elder boat-owners whom they call their representatives, one of whom is considered senior to the others. If you observe village organization closely, however, you will find that although those individuals may take the lead in discussion or at crises, yet they are almost as likely not to do so. Indeed discussion is nearly always completely general, the voice of anyone who cares to join in having equal weight, according rather to his personal qualities than to what might be called his status—excepting only that women, because they are busy on the boats, are usually not present at all in general discussions of village business and that sons and employees who are not boat-owners tend to keep quiet in the presence of their fathers and employers. The main function of these fishermen's representatives seems to be in connection with the technical departments of Government, the Fisheries and the Marketing Departments for example, who use them as contact men. The small liners and trappers also have two representatives of their own who are used in a similar way.

Even in contacts with officials, however, other boat-owners, or even the shopkeeper, may take the place of any representative without any fuss at all. If it is a matter of calling in at the Marketing Department office in Kowloon, for instance, anyone who is going in will do. It is all the same, they say. Equality between boat-owners is complete, and it is usually impossible to predict exactly who will take charge.

The one occasion in the year which demands community organization is, of course, the annual village festival—which among other things requires the collection and disbursement of some $10,000, the engagement of a matshed, players, and priests, and the responsibility for law and order among 3-4,000 people, mostly strangers on holiday. I waited eagerly for this occasion—expecting that here at last the accepted hierarchy would emerge. It did nothing of the sort. Instead, on the 15th of the First Moon all proceeded to the temple and lots were cast to decide who should be this year's festival leaders and office bearers. Last year's chairman was at the bottom of this year's 'ballot'. This year's chairman was a young man not yet thirty, and later I learnt that he had been chairman also some three years before. The matter is decided by chance, or, in their belief, by the will of the god. There is no accepted hierarchy. All one can say for certain is that the community leaders consist of all the boat-owners, the purse-seiners being the most important, for only purse-seiners appeared on the list of names among when the lots were cast.

This looseness of organization and the extreme equalitarianism among boat-owners is, I think, to be ascribed to various causes. First, there is the fact that so much of life is looked after in the family groups on the boats themselves that there is little to be seen to outside; secondly, there is the fact that this is a community where everybody knows everybody else so well, having lived all their lives together, that the behaviour of each is fully predictable to all and unprecedented crises demanding leadership are therefore unlikely to arise; thirdly, there is the fact that situations which do require detailed organization—the running of the village festival for example—are usually regularly recurrent situations, which take traditional forms which everybody has known and understood almost ever since he first attended them as a baby on his mother's back, and in any case, as they are ritual situations they are backed by ritual sanctions which hardly any one would dream of questioning. There is no room for innovation. The management of the internal politics of small communities with an accepted tradition requires no highly developed organization or closely defined system of leadership.

The rub comes when situations arise for which tradition does not cater—when, for example, administrative requirements affect the fishermen's interests, or when relationships with landsmen prove refractory, as they often do. In such circumstances the fishermen are nearly always at a disadvantage, having no close organization, little education, and no self-confidence away from the sea. Again and again they themselves will say, '我哋漁民好怕事嘅' (we fishermen are desperately scared of trouble), and 'trouble' means almost any kind of altercation, but especially any conflict with, almost any contact with Authority and Officials. Out of dozens here is one story: last August some of the Kau Sai fishermen had occasion to receive from Government payment of $400 per boat. The money was brought to the village and distributed there. Collecting the money in their own village was a simple matter, but one of the poorest of these fishermen was found to have a mistake on his Identity Card which had to be put right first. This meant that he would have to go to Hong Kong to have the card altered at the Office for Registration of Persons, and then to the District Office to collect the cash. This was explained to him, and I have seldom seen a man so utterly appalled—he went really grey under his sunburn, trembled all over and begged with tears to be excused this ordeal. He was a man of about forty-eight years. It took several hours to calm him down and to persuade him not to forgo the money. In the end he only agreed because his widowed sister-in-law had a claim on part of it and he did not want to deprive her, and because the Fish Market's officer in Sai Kung, whom he knew and trusted, offered to take him and do all the talking for him. Now the point is that this was not considered at all extraordinary behaviour—the general attitude was that it was just very bad luck that this should have happened, that the man would be a fool to forgo the money (as he actually suggested he should), but that to have to do all this for it was really hardly worthwhile, for it was right and proper to keep away from officers and so avoid trouble.

This accent on avoiding trouble stems I think from three sources: in part it comes from the positive teaching that the avoidance of trouble has in itself a high value, this is common to most Chinese training; in part it can be ascribed to the fact that the water-people, being mobile, can in fact very often avoid trouble simply by going away until it is all over; but thirdly, and, I think, at least in the fishermen's own consciousness, most importantly, is the feeling they have of being members of the despised Tanka class, unfamiliar with the things that go on on land and fearful of being cheated by landsmen, who look down upon them. There is a saying that a Tanka who on the water is a veritable dragon, on land is only a miserable worm (水上一條龍，陸上一條蟲). Unfortunately, they tend to believe it themselves.

2. Chinese Fishermen in Hong Kong: Their Post-Peasant Economy*

Kau Sai is a village situated on the shores of a narrow strait between two small islands in the Port Shelter area of the waters of the British Crown Colony of Hong Kong (see McCoy, 1965; Ward, 1954, 1965, and 1966). In 1952 its total population was about 390, made up of 17 Hakka and 45 Cantonese speaking families. The Hakka all lived in small grey stone houses built parallel to the water front. Most of their men were away from home, earning wages in a variety of employments in the cities of Victoria and Kowloon; the women added to the family income by rearing pigs, for whose fodder they cultivated groundnuts and sweet potatoes on patches cleared by themselves on the hillsides, and cutting firewood and grass, which they sold to the fishermen for fuel. One Hakka man ran a small shop. All but two of the Cantonese men gained their livelihood from fishing and dwelt with their entire families on board their fishing boats. They owned no house property on land. Their boats (on average about 30 feet long and 10 feet in the beam) were moored in regular lines at permanent moorings, each man's boat in its accustomed place, which was usually said to have been occupied by his forebears for several generations. Two ex-fishing families lived ashore: one running the main shop (cf. King, 1954), the other, a very old man, paid a small wage to act as caretaker for the village temple.

In that year, 1952, Kau Sai had a village school of a kind. Its one all-age class, which met in a section of the temple, had to be dismissed on rainy days because the dogma of temple architecture decreed the existence of a large rectangular opening in the unceiled roof. Its one teacher was barely qualified. Most of the eighteen or so pupils were children of Hakka speaking landsmen. Only four fishermen's children went to school at all, all of them intermittently, and all of them boys.

In 1953 all the Hakka families were moved, at the government's initiative and expense, to a newly constructed village on the mainland. Their subsequent history does not concern us here. The schoolmaster went with them. All

*Reprinted from Maurice Freedman (ed.), *Social Organization: Essays Presented to Raymond Firth* (London: Frank Cass & Co. Ltd., 1967), pp. 271-88, by permission of the publisher.

teaching stopped.

By 1962 Kau Sai boasted a purpose-built school house with three separate, well-equipped, and entirely waterproof classrooms, a concrete basket-ball pitch, and a magnificent latrine; there were three well-qualified schoolmasters, two of them fluent in English; there were 118 pupils, most of them attending regularly and all of them fishermen's children—including all the fishermen's school-age daughters (even three who were upwards of sixteen years old). The total population of the village was now 404. This was divided into 59 families, all but one being Cantonese speaking. The single Hakka family was that of the temple caretaker newly employed by the fishermen to take the place of the old man who had died. Three of the Cantonese families were those of ex-fishermen now running small shops and living ashore. The remaining 55 Cantonese families all gained their livelihood from fishing, but at least eight of them owned house property on land, and lived in it. More were planning to follow their example.

Contrasts between the fishermen's standards of living at the beginning and the end of the ten years 1952-62 could be multiplied almost indefinitely. Speaking generally, food was better, clothing more, hygiene and health had greatly improved. Most families were in fact richer, but a few were poorer—or appeared to be so, perhaps because they had not shared the improvement in the lot of the majority. There were other changes too. Despite the removal of the Hakka, the population was larger. This was partly because Kau Sai, like most other fishing settlements in Hong Kong at the time, had received an influx of fishing families from China, but as the number of immigrant fishing families just about balanced the number of land families who had been moved away, the net increase in the population is to be explained in terms of a reduction in infant and child mortality. By 1962 most Kau Sai babies were being born in a government-sponsored clinic at the nearest market town and not on board the fishing boats, and most of them now lived. Whereas in 1952 there were about 70 children under the age of sixteen, in 1962 there were between 170 and 180—and their heads were not covered with the suppurating boils upon which a fieldworker had felt obliged to expend so much of her limited knowledge of first aid only ten years before.

These were all measurable changes. 1962 showed organizational and structural changes in Kau Sai as well: the village now had a regularly elected Representative—a fisherman.[1] Two co-operative societies had been formed.

[1] Village Representatives are the officially recognized spokesmen of their communities. They act as channels of communication with the administration, and can be called upon to advise. The methods by which they are selected are not uniform, but it is the administration's intention that they should be as 'representative' as their title in English implies. Like most Hong Kong boat people, the Kau Sai fishermen had previously

Several marriages were described as having been made by free choice—an impossible example of immorality by 1952 standards. Several young men had left fishing to take up shore jobs in the big cities or the nearest market town. Several girls had married non-fishermen and gone to live ashore. Already those few fishing families with their own houses on land had adapted themselves to a new organization and division of labour. Even among those who still lived on board their boats there were noticeable alterations in the relationships between parents and children.

Most striking of all, however, and obvious even to the most casual observer, was the one outstanding change which the people of Kau Sai themselves would certainly have placed first: namely, that whereas in 1952 all but one of their boats had been wind-driven, by mid-1963 only one was not mechanized. In other words, what had been going on was a technological revolution in microcosm, and most of the above changes (which continue in full swing at the time of writing) were closely connected with it.

Fish has always been Hong Kong's most important primary product. By 1950 the industry provided a livelihood for about 60,000 people (men, women, and children), almost all of whom lived their whole lives aboard the fishing boats, which numbered at that time about 6,000 in all. This was probably the largest fishing fleet in the whole of the then British Commonwealth and Empire. It is the more remarkable that this production was almost entirely in the hands of local men, owning and operating their own craft with the help of family labour and in many cases hired hands. By 1950, thanks in part to the strenuous efforts of the Colony's administration which had set up a satisfactory method of marketing fish, and in part to the hard work and natural resilience of the fishermen, the Hong Kong fishing industry was well on the way to total recovery from the startlingly low condition to which it had sunk during the Japanese occupation. In that year the marketing of more than 30,000 tons of fish was recorded, representing a wholesale value of more than \$H.K.38,000,000. This is not small-scale business.[2]

Nevertheless, the general attitude of the non-fishing public in Hong Kong, when it thought about the fishermen at all, was that they were an economically depressed section of the population, and largely deservedly so because of the

---

had to be content to be 'represented' by a landsman in whose appointment they had taken no part.

[2]*Hong Kong Annual Report* 1950, p. 41. These figures include both fresh and salt marine fish. Ten years later the fishing fleet numbered over 10,400 and the fishing population about 86,000. The quantity of 'fisheries products' sold through the wholesale markets in 1960 was 47,229 tons with a total value of \$H.K.53,904,468 (*Hong Kong Annual Report* 1960, p. 381). Since the Second World War the exchange value of the Hong Kong dollar has varied very closely around \$H.K.16 to £1 sterling.

feckless ways which were considered inherent in their 'gypsy-like' boat-dwelling mode of existence and their consequent lack of education. The fishermen, for their part, though hotly contesting these landsmen's views when expressed by landsmen, yet largely shared them—or rather that section of them which described their own general poverty and conservatism. That same year 1950, which followed immediately on the final success of the People's Government in China, saw the first beginnings of large-scale industrial development in Hong Kong. It is probably true to say that no one would have predicted that the fishermen would take part in it.

It is well known that the rapid industrial development in Hong Kong which has occurred since the Second World War was largely a by-product of political change in China. It would be possible to argue that this was also conducive to at least an increased overall income for Hong Kong's fishermen, for the swollen population and (despite the quite genuine and much advertised poverty) its rising standard of living necessarily entailed a bigger demand for their products. However, the immediate closing of Chinese markets for all Hong Kong's salt fish—up to that time the major export product—meant that in fact the first effect of the 1949 revolution in China was deeply depressing to the Hong Kong fishing industry.

Nevertheless, at the beginning of 1950 there were already as many as fifty-five mechanized fishing vessels in operation. Ten years later the figure had jumped to 3,329. Today (1965) it stands at between 6,000 and 7,000—more than sixty per cent of the present-day total number of fishing craft.

There are obviously a great many questions that one could ask about so profound and rapid a change. Those with which this paper is concerned fall broadly under two headings: first, how was it that in this free enterprise economy, without coercion of any kind, these so long believed to be ultra-conservative peasants were so eager to adopt such a revolutionary technological innovation; and second, what are likely to be its economic and social consequences?

Let us first consider the somewhat contentious term that has just been used: peasants. It was, of course, Professor Raymond Firth who first proposed including certain kinds of fishing community along with certain kinds of agricultural community in one broad 'peasant' category. His criteria for such a category were essentially economic and structural (Firth, 1946, especially pp. 22-27). They included: primary production, with usually some self-subsistence; limited specialization; a limited dependence upon markets external to the community itself, which are usually not fully integrated into the world market; a considerable amount of home production of capital equipment; a general lack of wage labour, and dependence upon family labour; a common dependence upon credit, but not usually upon a specialist class of moneylenders. These broad economic criteria are undoubtedly as applicable to the mixed farming and fishing communities of the east coast of Malaya, with which Firth was primarily concerned, as they are (with variations of degree and emphasis) to many entirely land-based agricultural communities in the Orient and elsewhere. It does not follow, however, that all Oriental primary producers except those engaged in plantation agriculture must be similarly classified. On the contrary, the very insight which can be gained from studying Firth's brilliant recognition of the similarities between fishing and agricultural communities in Malaya leads us to remark the numerous dissimilarities between fishermen and traditional peasant farmers in Hong Kong.

It is true that the Hong Kong fishermen are, in effect, and have long been, producers of a cash crop, part of which goes to provide for their own subsistence. But although fish is their most frequently consumed protein, and essential for their nutrition, only a very small portion of their diet is fish. And everything else has to be purchased. So does almost every other item of consumption—clothing, personal equipment of all kinds, even fuel. The experience of the Japanese occupation showed how quickly these fishermen could be reduced to starvation when they could no longer market their fish. Theirs is much more than a partial dependence upon the market.

Moreover, even long before mechanization, the level of their technology was such that the necessary capital equipment had become highly specialized. Different types of fish require different methods, different gear, and different boats, and most Hong Kong fishermen specialize not simply as fishermen (none of them owns land or performs any agricultural work) but as, say, trawlermen, longliners, seine-netters, gill-netters, and so on. Such a degree of specialization and technical sophistication is inevitably expensive. With the exception of sails, which are now rapidly going out of use, some (nowadays very few) nets, and fish traps, virtually all capital equipment is acquired by purchase from specialist craftsmen or stores in the market towns. By peasant standards (which are seldom capital intensive) the amount of capital required in relation to annual income is particularly large. In 1960, for example, a new medium-sized junk used for inshore purse-seining cost about $H.K.6,000, and an appropriate marine diesel engine to go with it about $H.K.10,000 more. The gross income of the most successful purse-seiner pair in Kau Sai that year was between $H.K.25,000 and $H.K.30,000, of the least successful around $H.K.7,000. It is obvious that one result of this situation is that loans have to be obtained. Apart from a few fairly small sums, these are nearly all negotiated outside the fishing communities themselves. The traditional source of loans was the fish-dealer; and the overwhelming majority of fish-dealers were, and are, specialists in their own turn, living on land in the market towns and often belonging to a different language group from the fishermen who are their clients.

Thus these southern Chinese fishermen have long been almost completely dependent not only upon a market that is external to their communities, and one which (it must be added) has for more than a century been linked with the world market, but also upon a specialist class of similarly external moneylender-middlemen. When to these facts is added the further point that on the larger fishing craft (trawlers and deep-sea longliners) wage labour is the traditional, universal, and essential supplement to family labour, and that even on the smaller inshore craft it has long been far from uncommon,[3] the usefulness of placing these fishermen in a general 'peasant' economic category of the kind put forward by Firth becomes increasingly doubtful. Nevertheless, until mechanization has taken place and brought with it full modernization in at least some of the ways discussed below, they remain both structurally and culturally distinct enough from the local traders and other 'non-peasants' to make it useful to class them in a separate category, for which the term 'post-peasant' will serve our present purposes well enough.[4]

The value of distinguishing such an intermediate category, between, for example, the traditional peasant rice farmers, on the one hand, and the local traders and others, on the other hand, becomes clear when we turn to comparison. We have seen that these post-peasant fishermen have long been fully enmeshed in a money economy. They have also long been familiar with such calculations as are necessary for planned saving towards capital investment, giving and raising credit, and so on. They are far indeed from being economically unsophisticated subsistence producers, and it is reasonable to suppose that their relative economic 'know-how' is one of the significant factors explaining the readiness with which they are modernizing their technology. Yet the Kau Sai fishermen regard their own economic sophistication as being considerably less than that of other Chinese. They deplore this

[3] Deep-sea trawlers, which stay at sea for sometimes as many as ten days or more, employ an average of about thirty wage earning fishermen; a longliner sometimes employs as many as fifty. Both types of deep-sea craft often carry women employees as well as men. By no means all the inshore owner-operators achieve their ambition of managing with family labour alone. Many carry one, two, or even as many as four or more hired men—and this on boats which double as family homes and have an overall length of about thirty to thirty-five feet.

[4] Since I wrote this paper my attention has been drawn to an article by Ernestine Friedl (Friedl, 1964), in which, quoting Foster (George M. Foster, *Traditional Cultures and the Impact of Technological Change*, New York, 1962) and Geertz (Clifford Geertz, 'Studies in Peasant Life: Community and Society', in *Biennial Review of Anthropology*, edited by B. J. Siegel, Stanford, 1962), she postulates a similar intermediate (transitional) post-peasant category.

state of affairs, and frequently mention it in explanation of their (in their own eyes) relative poverty, saying that they can easily be cheated because landsmen are more knowledgeable. There is some truth in their complaint, but it should be noted that the landsmen of whom they complain are not peasants but traders and middlemen. The fact that fishermen have less economic expertise than these should surprise no one; they could still be better equipped in this respect than local peasant agriculturalists. Whether or not they are so, I am not in a position to say, but certainly it is a fact that the indigenous rice farmers of Hong Kong have been much slower to accept change than the fishermen.

Closely connected with economic 'know-how' is the prevailing set of values, which gives the highest esteem to the man who makes good in the economic sense. This is a widespread attitude among present-day Chinese in Hong Kong and overseas. The fishermen are by no means the only Chinese of whom it can be said that no one really expects behaviour other than that directed towards the rational pursuit of self-interest, and it would be very difficult to contrast them with others on this count. On the other hand, it might be arguable that the fishermen are especially likely to manifest this particular facet of Chinese values because—like their thrusting compatriots overseas—they are relatively free of the restraints which might have been imposed by certain other Chinese values which were embedded in what is usually known as 'the gentry tradition'. As a rule, southern Chinese fishing villages contained no gentry. Moreover, Chinese fishermen, unlike many even very poor landsmen, had no ties with gentry kinsmen or affines, nor did they have much, if any, opportunity of ever rising to the ranks of the gentry through the examination system. Their ideas of gentry values—which undoubtedly, if they were asked, they would describe as 'best' and 'truly Chinese'—were in fact culled largely from the Cantonese operas they saw several times a year: dramatic tales which are much loved and usually known by heart, but which are little more directly relevant to their own daily life than are the tales of traditional pantomime to ours in England. If there is anything in the argument that the vigorous business methods of, say, the overseas Chinese may partly be ascribed to their freedom from both external and internalized gentry controls, it could equally apply to the fishermen of Hong Kong—but not, presumably, to the same extent to many Chinese peasants.

There is another feature which the south Chinese fishermen and the Chinese overseas have in common. Both are relatively free of clan and lineage obligations. For reasons probably mainly connected with their potential spatial mobility and the lack of land, these fishermen do not have a developed lineage system, nor any real concept of one. This is not the place to enter into the argument whether or not lineage ties and the claims of poorer members upon richer ones may act as a deterrent to economic enterprise, but if they sometimes do have a restraining influence, then these fishermen were in this respect also less restricted than most of the land-based peasants of south China. Their kinship structure has in fact far more in common with that of Chinese townsmen in, say, Hong Kong or Singapore (and overseas Chinese in general).

Their economic groupings reflect this situation, as, no doubt, they also contribute towards its development. In Kau Sai the labour units are all family units with or without the addition of one or two (sometimes more) hired men. Each family (man, wife—occasionally wives, children, including often married sons and daughters-in-law and grandchildren, but excluding married daughters and their offspring) lives on board a fishing boat and engages as a unit in both production and consumption. The boats are all owned by their operators, and licensed in the name of the family head who is also captain, so to speak, of the crew. In day-to-day matters, each boat-household (or, for those engaging in operations requiring two boats, each pair of boat-households) is an independent unit with full freedom to take decisions on its own account.

The fishermen are free in other senses too. They pay no rent, the resources they tap are theoretically unlimited, and with their sea-worthy floating homes they are potentially more physically mobile than almost any other human group. In all these ways their situation appears to contrast favourably with that of most other primary producers, certainly with that of any ordinary land-based Chinese peasants.

Everything put forward so far would apply with equal force to the sea fishermen of the rest of the south China coast and to the fishermen of Hong Kong—and would have applied also for at least the last century, probably much longer. One might ask, therefore, why it was that, the socio-economic circumstances being apparently so similar and so favourable, rapid technological change did not occur among these fishermen before 1949, and even after 1949 did not occur with the same rapidity outside Hong Kong.

There is one very simple answer which is glaringly obvious: it is that suitable engines for mechanization were not available anywhere in the Far East much before 1949. Nevertheless, obvious, and indeed crucial, though this fact is, it does not supply the whole answer. As so often, the truth is not necessarily the whole truth, and if we rest content with the obvious we may fail to take account of other equally significant factors. For one thing, mechanization is not the only technological change that has occurred; for another thing, even when engines were becoming available they were not adopted immediately everywhere at the same rate.

One of the other technological changes was connected with the night-time bright-light fishing which is practised by the (pair) purse-seine fishermen. The lamps in use today are almost exclusively kerosene pressure lamps, with incandescent mantles inside specially made glass globes. These have been standard since the early thirties. Before the War of 1914 flaring torches of burning pine wood were used, and had a long history. During that war the carbide lamps which were then in use on most road vehicles first appeared in Hong Kong. They were not readily available until after 1918, but as soon as they were, the bright-light fishermen seem to have snapped them up. In about two years, so my informants told me, flaring pine torches had disappeared from the local scene entirely. They reappeared for a time during the Japanese occupation. The early thirties, so I was assured, showed a similar rapid change-over to kerosene lamps.

But carbide and kerosene lamps, and another technical innovation that was taken up almost overnight in the mid-fifties—nylon nets and lines—have qualities which engines large enough to power Chinese fishing junks do not. They require little or no special technical skill, they are cheap, and their introduction brings with it no significant technical or organizational changes. Marine engines, assuming them to be available, require of their operators a certain standard of education and of their owners a considerable outlay of capital, and inevitably entail either a change in methods of fishing or in methods of organizing the fishing enterprise, or both.

Before about 1930 virtually no fisherman in either Hong Kong or south China received any education at all. In Kau Sai in 1950 one could assume that most of the men over fifty were illiterate, many of those over thirty were just literate, and many of the younger ones rather more so; no women could read or write. Under Hong Kong law sea-going vessels fitted with mechanical propulsion must carry a licensed coxswain and a licensed engineer. To obtain the licences it is necessary to pass special written examinations and, of course, receive the necessary preliminary instruction. Unless a fisherman owning and operating his own craft is willing to employ an already qualified man (and because of the expense few are so willing; moreover few qualified men are available), it is necessary to have at least one family member educated enough to take the courses and pass the examinations. From about 1940 onwards this would probably not have been beyond the bounds of possibility for at least a fair number of fishing families in Hong Kong. Evidence from China is not complete, but there is reason to believe that the situation there was rather worse (at least up to 1949). But at that time, in any case, there were no engines on the market, and from 1941 of course nearly all children ceased to attend school for a few years. There is thus a real sense in which mechanization could not have 'caught on' much before 1950, even if the market had been overflowing with cheap engines, because of the educational block.

Furthermore, the educational difficulty having been at least partially met, the economic difficulty remained. I listed earlier several social factors which appeared theoretically to make it possible for these sea fishermen to be economically more enterprising than other Chinese peasants. But in fact they were not in a position to exploit their theoretical advantages in practice. It was implied above that fishermen were more fortunate than farmers because the resources they tapped were theoretically unlimited. This is true in the sense that sea fishing grounds off these coasts are open to all without legal or customary restrictions. But at least four sets of circumstance limit their actual exploitation: natural fluctuations in the fish populations and their movements, which can only very partially be predicted; hazards of weather, especially in the typhoon season which lasts from May to October inclusive; technical limitations of boats and gear and methods of fishing, including the distances that can be travelled in a given time and the positioning of markets —because fish, even now when ice is available, is a highly perishable commodity and the south China waters are tropical; and, finally, limitations in the skill and knowledge of the fishermen. The former two considerations, being limitations inherent in the nature of the product and the local climate, lie outside our present sphere of enquiry, but the latter two concern us directly.

As far as technical and technological matters are concerned, it is clear that, while they were still using wind-driven craft, the geographical limits within which all but the largest deep-sea going vessels could work were narrow, and even the deep-sea fishermen—who could go much further afield—were closely limited as to the seasons they could operate in, for fear of bad weather. Mechanization was a prerequisite to the fuller exploitation of the theoretically unlimited resources. This particular economic advantage in being a fisherman (and not a farmer) therefore did not apply before the moment of technological change, and so must be discounted in any comparison with land-based peasants.

The skill and knowledge of the fishermen are likewise limited to certain types of fishing and certain localities. At least for the inshore fishermen, such as those of Kau Sai, skill depends upon the fairly slow building up of knowledge about the fishing grounds, knowledge of this kind coming only from personal experience. Only one thing limits its scope: the opportunity to learn about new areas. But opportunity is hard to come by. Some time at the height of the inshore longlining season in 1952, Ma Yao-Foon and three other Kau Sai longlinermen decided to try their luck on a different stretch of the coast. They were away about six weeks. When the four little boats came sailing in to Kau Sai again everybody wanted to know how they had fared. The answer was a dismal one: they had come back to Kau Sai because it was the only place they could make a living. No, there had been no objection from the local fishermen up the coast, and the fishing grounds were probably good, but they had not been able to spend enough time there to discover their full potentialities. Once their savings had been used up they had had to return. In other words, they had had to give up their exploration of new fishing grounds because they were unable to tide themselves over the initial period of trial and error. Their savings were insufficient, and no shopkeeper in the strange district would give them credit.

Here we arrive at the economic crux of the matter. We argued earlier that these fishermen are potentially completely mobile; in fact they are anchored. We stated also that they paid no rent, and implied by this that they enjoyed an economic and legal freedom very different from the situation of most ordinary land peasants in south China. But in fact the fishermen too are tied. Like so many producers of cash crops, they are involved in most cases much less in a cash nexus than in a credit nexus. Very few of them ever have much cash in hand; instead they stand in a more or less complicated series of credit relationships, taking loans for capital expenditure on the one hand and running up credit accounts at a shop or shops, for everyday current expenditure, on the other. Almost any capital outlay requires a loan, and, as we have seen, loans have traditionally been obtained from the middlemen-dealers in the wholesale trading of fish. The result has been the setting up of long-term personal creditor-debtor relationships between dealers and fishermen, which have frequently been held to be the source of all the fishermen's one-time poverty. Today, at least, few Kau Sai fishermen are willing to agree that 'their' middlemen are the wicked parasites they are sometimes declared to be, but there is no doubt that in the past the opportunities for cheating the fishermen were many and that by no means all middlemen resisted temptation.

Immediately after the Japanese war the government of Hong Kong stepped in for the first time. A government-controlled wholesale marketing organization was set up, and it was made illegal to sell or buy marine fish wholesale anywhere else than in an authorized market. In this way fishermen were assured of fair weights, public auctions, and published prices, and if they wished they could themselves handle their own fish on to the auction floor. At the same time the Fish Marketing Organization launched the first of a number of loan schemes which were to ensure a fixed rate of interest and open accounting. By 1950 the advantages of mechanization were patent for all to see and suitable diesel engines were beginning to be available. Accordingly, the loan schemes were increased, partly from an allocation from the Colonial Development and Welfare Fund, and a revolving fund instituted specifically for the purpose of helping mechanization.

A Kau Sai man was one of the first two inshore fishermen to take advantage of this scheme. That was in 1950. Since then several thousand other fishermen have followed suit, and several thousand more have mechanized their craft with the aid of loans taken in the traditional way from middlemen, and in some cases other outsiders. The middlemen-dealers, whatever their position in the past, are now in competition with the official loan schemes with their fixed rates of interest, and, as they no longer themselves control the wholesaling of fish, their potential stranglehold on the industry has been broken. The Hong Kong Government claims that without its intervention the rapid mechanization of the fishing fleets would have been impossible; it may well be right.

The argument so far, then, is that this rapid technological change was possible because the economic attitudes of the fishermen and the social structure of the fishing communities were already so favourable that when the opportunity to adopt useful technical change was offered it was likely to be seized upon, unless blocked by something else. By 1950 the opportunity to mechanize did appear—engines were available. By then, too, the possible educational block had been partly removed, and governmental action in freeing the market, injecting money, and providing training courses and encouragement was all that was required to set a revolution in process.

What of the consequences of this rapid mechanization? Most of the more obvious social changes have already been listed: better education, improved standard of living, greater self-respect for a hitherto despised group, and so on. Figures of actual *per capita* income range up to, and in some cases beyond, twice the pre-mechanization income in money terms. Certainly there is clear ocular evidence of greater affluence. There is also evidence of the beginning of certain predictable economic and further technical changes which in their turn will inevitably have social concomitants.

The industry as a whole may be roughly divided into (*a*) deep-sea fishing, and (*b*) inshore fishing. The former requires a much greater capital outlay than the latter, and a much larger labour force. The capital requirements are already beginning to go beyond the limits possible for a single owner-operator, even with official (i.e. Fish Marketing Organization) assistance, or even, probably, in co-operative organization. It is predictable that this section of the fishing industry of Hong Kong will show a fairly rapid change-over to land-based capitalist ownership, employing hired crews at all levels on the fishing craft. A few Japanese-owned and British-owned trawler companies have been operating from Hong Kong for some years, using more or less modern fishing craft; the local type boats are likely to fall under similar capitalist—but Chinese—organization very soon. This will inevitably result in the full proletarianization of the deep-sea fishing industry, though a few existing owner-operators who have been exceptionally fortunate in recent years will set up as capitalists themselves. Women and children will very soon be absent from these capitalist-owned boats, and will live ashore. This in itself will give the opportunity to change the design of these craft to more definitely functional lines (from the point of view of both mechanization and propulsion) and make possible the introduction of further technological advances in fishing methods—echo-sounders, mechanical winches, refrigeration plants, for example. The present longliners are already going out of business, largely because of over-capitalization on the one hand and labour troubles on the other. In five years from now there may well be none left, and in another five years there will be hardly any owner-operated trawlers either. Fewer fishing firms, with a much smaller and more highly specialized labour force, will be at work. The displaced fishermen will have to find other employment. Probably very few will remain at sea at all. When it is remembered that almost every one of these fishermen has been a water-dweller all his life, and most of them descend from generations of water-people, it becomes clear that this will be a revolution indeed.

(It has already begun. Quite a number of the waiters who work in the new Chinese restaurants which have sprung up all over the British Isles in the last dozen years, and are now spreading on to the Continent as well, are ex-fishermen from Hong Kong.)

Even the present-day longliner and trawler owners (particularly the former, who have been the virtual aristocrats of the local fishermen) will mostly become wage-earners, probably as officers on the boats if they stay on the boats at all. A few will, as we have said, become capitalist employers. A third section, also few in number, is likely to set up in retail business, dealing in fishery goods of all kinds, as ship-chandlers and so on, and probably engaging in money-lending too. This type of business already exists, of course, though few ex-fishermen have managed to break into it. The larger-scale business firms of this kind are likely gradually to acquire their own deep-sea fishing boats. In other words, they are likely to supply the major part of the shore-based capitalist ownership predicted above. This is already happening.

The following story of one particularly successful fishing family illustrates one possible set of processes. Lau Kam-Ch'ing of Cheung Chau is the eldest of several brothers who in 1950 owned and operated a pair of wind-driven deep-sea trawlers. A series of good seasons gave them the chance to consider mechanization, and with the help of a loan from the Fish Marketing Organization they duly installed engines and refitted their junks. Lau Kam-Ch'ing himself seldom went fishing. It was believed in the family that he brought bad luck, and after consulting a suitable oracle, in the form of the god at his local temple, he decided to move ashore to live. He was well able to afford to do so. Thereafter he acted as the shore-based manager of the trawling business. His brothers operated the junks, and all profits were pooled and shared. Lau Kam-Ch'ing then decided to educate his son to prepare him for his future role as business manager. The boy was intelligent and hard-working and ultimately was sent to one of the fishery colleges in Japan—the first Hong Kong fisherman's child ever known to have received higher education. On his return his father set up as a ship's supplier, the boy's Japanese contacts proving very useful for this business. Lau Kam-Ch'ing and his brothers with the now grown-up second generation still work as a family business, owning between them three pairs of mechanized trawlers, with which they are currently experimenting with more modern techniques, as well as the shop. They are also known to be ready to lend money to fishermen who require it. Few of the deep-sea men will succeed to this extent; most will become hired men or give up fishing and look for employment ashore. A few will maintain their independence at the cost of becoming smaller-scale fishermen in the inshore branch of the industry.

There it is unlikely that change will be quite so rapid or radical. There will probably remain for quite a long time a fairly large number (possibly some thousands) of medium-sized craft, fishing the inshore and nearer waters, owned and operated by independent men, employing still their own family's labour with perhaps one or two hired hands. As things are at present, it seems likely that these independent owner-operators will survive and flourish at least for some time, provided only that the waters are not overfished (there is a real and mounting danger of this) and that the demand for their products remains high (there seems to be no foreseeable danger of it decreasing, rather the reverse). The period of their survival as what might be called independent 'yeoman' fishermen may be quite long, but the ultimately necessary adoption of new techniques, which will certainly prove expensive, will probably force them out in time. Individuals have already shown the course which the forcing out process is likely to take—through over-capitalization to subsequent failure. Chung Fuk-Shun, of Kau Sai, for example, already saw the writing on the wall in 1963. Three years earlier he had invested in a new boat with a more powerful engine. His only son operated the boat with the help of the son's wife, a brother, and his wife and two hired men. The venture prospered so well that by the end of 1961 he was determined to repeat the process and build an even bigger boat with a still more powerful engine. This done, he found he now had to employ at least six hired men, and although fuel bills were almost twice as heavy as before, catches remained much the same. Half way through 1963 he realized that he was only just breaking even, and that his chance of fully paying off the loans he had had to raise for the capital expenditure was slight. He is still in business but only just.[5]

Although this class of independent fishermen, depending still mainly on family labour, is likely to continue to exist for some time, it does not follow that the traditional customs and social structure of the fishing communities will also survive. Women, or some of them, and children are already beginning to move ashore to live. Increased affluence has made this possible; increased comfort and safety and above all the insatiable demand for schooling, make it desirable. No fisherman now fails to see the need for education. Coxswains' and engineers' certificates, successful marketing, coping with government regulations, all depend on it. Educated daughters are at a premium as wives, too, and the fact that one by-product of educating a daughter is that she may marry out of the water communities is often seen as an advantage rather than the opposite. So, for the nearish future, say thirty to fifty years, one can foresee this middle class of fishermen remaining economically independent, becoming gradually smaller, and beginning socially to merge more and more with the land population with which it will have increasing cultural and structural links.

What of the present-day poor fishermen, the smallest independent owner-operators and those who are already hired labourers, whose wives usually run small ferrying or hawking businesses on sampans? These men will either go out of the industry altogether, or become hired men on other boats; the women and children will remain as now on their sampans, but will do all they can to move ashore. This may not be too difficult if their husbands can get any sort of shore employment. In any case, the wives of hired men, living on their own sampans, do not usually move far afield and their children as a result have often been better educated than the sons and daughters of their husbands' employers.

So much for the emergence of a clear three-class stratification which I predict will be the immediate and direct effect of the current technological revolution which is sweeping the Hong Kong fishing fleet. Two points seem to require a little further notice: the movement to land dwelling and the changing position of women. The evidence on both these matters is already perfectly clear, as also is the connexion between them. Chung's daughter, for example, married a non-fisherman in 1958 and moved to live with him in an apartment in a large new tenement block on Hong Kong island. It was a free

[5]The following extract from a letter received from Chung Fuk-Shun in July 1966 shows that even this is no longer true. It was written in English for him. '. . . my family life is not so well. In the last few month I have been sale my fishing boat. . . . Would you please to make the voucher for my son Kam Ho. Do you remember him? He like to go over to England to work. If you can make the voucher for him please don't worry the job, because I had a Chinese friend in England, he had a Chinese restaurant. . . .'

choice marriage. The girl had her third baby a few months ago, and for a time had to give up her job in a factory which makes electric torches. She is the envy of every woman in Kau Sai, and nothing that she has done would have been possible even ten years ago. Going ashore is particularly liked by the women. Not only does it indicate a sheer gain in prestige which is applicable to both sexes, for water-dwelling has so long been despised, but for women it also spells far less drudgery, less discomfort in pregnancy, and much less actual physical danger for themselves and their young children (it is a remarkable fact that virtually no fisherwomen can swim). It also gives an opportunity for a woman to earn a small but independent income, either by working in a factory, where this is possible, or in petty trade, or, most frequently today, in some form of out-work, especially the making of plastic flowers which has become extremely popular since about 1960. But above all, the major attraction of living ashore is that the children can attend school regularly. This is the point that the water-people themselves mention first and most frequently, men and women alike.

In the long run, the cumulative effect of all these developments will be to integrate the one-time boat-people completely into the rest of the Chinese population. In fact Chinese in language, social structure, personality, and almost all aspects of culture, as I have demonstrated elsewhere, the water-people have continued to be regarded as but little removed from their supposed barbarian origins and they are well aware of their low status. The land-people have a number of myths about them, their believed-in physical peculiarities and immoral and un-Chinese activities. Among the myths is the belief that boat-people were traditionally 'always' forbidden to take the imperial examinations, to marry land-people, or even to live ashore. Whatever the truth of this vexed question in the past (see Ch'en Hsü-ching, n.d.; Ch'ü T'ung-tsu, 1961, pp. 130-32; Ho Ko-en, 1959-60), it is certain that there are no prohibitions at the present time. It is also highly probable that it has long been quite easy for an aspiring boatman to 'pass' into the land population, just as it has been relatively common for unsuccessful landsmen to become boat-people. The immediate future is likely to see a rapid speeding up of this process of assimilation in the landwards direction.

REFERENCES

Ch'en Hsü-ching. 1946. *Tanka Researches.* Canton (in Chinese).

Ch'ü T'ung-tsu. 1961. *Law and Society in Traditional China.* Paris.

Firth. R. 1946. *Malay Fishermen, Their Peasant Economy*. London (second ed. 1966).

Friedl, E. 1964. 'Lagging Emulation in Post-Peasant Society'. *American Anthropologist*, Vol. 66, No. 3, pt. 1.

Ho Ko-en. 1959-60. 'A Study of the Boat People'. *Journal of Oriental Studies*, Vol. 5,

Nos. 1 and 2. Hong Kong.
King, H.F.F. 1954. 'Duopoly in a Hong Kong Fishing Village'. *Journal of Oriental Studies*, Vol. 1, No. 1. Hong Kong.
McCoy, J. 1965. 'The Dialects of the Hong Kong Boat People: Kau Sai'. *Journal of the Hong Kong Branch of the Royal Asiatic Society*, Vol. 5.
Ward, B. E. 1954. 'A Hong Kong Fishing Village'. *Journal of Oriental Studies*, Vol. 1, No. 1. Hong Kong.
————. 1965. 'Varieties of the Conscious Model: The Fishermen of South China'. In M. Banton (ed.), *The Relevance of Models for Social Anthropology*. A.S.A. Monographs, No. 1. London.
————. 1966. 'Sociological Self-Awareness: Some Uses of the Conscious Model'. *Man*, N.S., Vol. 1, No. 2.

3. Varieties of the Conscious Model: The Fishermen of South China*

INTRODUCTION

In the article entitled 'Social Structure' in *Anthropology Today*, Lévi-Strauss (1953, pp. 526-27) draws attention to the distinction between culturally produced models and observers' models. The former, constructs of the people under study themselves, he calls conscious models; the latter, unconscious models. Conscious models, he points out, may or may not exist for any particular phenomenon, may or may not provide useful insight, but, being part of the facts (and probably among the most significant facts), are in any case worthy of study. At best, they can 'furnish an important contribution to the understanding of the structures either as factual documents or as theoretical contributions similar to those of the anthropologist himself'.

Lévi-Strauss insists, in this same article, that though it has often been differently named ('ideal pattern', 'norm', for example) the concept of the conscious, or 'home-made' model is by no means a new one. Nor, he might have added, is it in any way novel to find it being employed in arguments about social continuity and social change, as, for example and most strikingly, by Leach in *Political Systems of Highland Burma* (1954). The present paper attempts to extend its use to a discussion of some of the problems of uniformity and variation posed by the unique temporal and spatial span of Chinese society and culture. In the course of this discussion the concept itself comes under examination.

THE FIRST PROBLEM

Anyone who has ever asked unsophisticated Chinese informants why they follow such and such a custom knows the maddeningly reiterated answer: 'Because we are Chinese'. At first one assumes that this is simply a stock response to the uncultured foreigner or a way of fobbing off an impertinent outsider; after a time one realizes that most of one's informants do themselves

*Reprinted with permission from Michael Banton (ed.), *The Relevance of Models for Social Anthropology* (London: Tavistock Publications Ltd., 1965), pp. 113-37.

see it as the correct explanation of almost all their own cultural behaviour and social organization. The conscious model of their own social system which they carry in their minds and which they use to explain, predict and justify their actual behaviour is labelled 'Chinese'. It is perhaps unnecessary to add that this insistence upon 'Chinese-ness' is accompanied by an unshakable conviction that all things Chinese are inherently superior.

Yet we are faced with a problem. What the people of one locality or time in the vast territory and history of the Chinese people think of as 'Chinese' in this sense may not necessarily be recognized as such by Chinese people elsewhere. For example, Southern Chinese fishermen have frequently expressed polite surprise to the writer on hearing that widows should not remarry; saying: 'We think you are mistaken. Certainly we Chinese always permit widows to marry again, perhaps it is one of your foreign customs to forbid them?' Yet there are many references in the literature to the existence of a ban on widow remarriage in traditional China. It would be possible to mention very many other examples of differences between different Chinese 'homemade' models. Even within a single village there can be quite marked distinctions between the conscious models carried by different sections of the population; yet each section, though aware of the difference, calls its own conscious model 'Chinese'. In other words, there is not one Chinese conscious model but several.

If this is so, then to talk as we commonly do of '*the* Chinese family' or '*the* traditional social structure of China' is as misleading at the level of ideal patterns as it has long been known to be misleading at the level of actual patterns of behaviour. Instead, we have to postulate a number of different Chinese ideal patterns varying in time and space with varying historical development and the demands of particular occupations and environments. Nevertheless, although there are and have been variations (and probably many more than is commonly believed) they are undoubtedly all variations on one easily recognizable theme. Important though it is to correct the popular view of a changeless China, it still remains true that the most remarkable feature of Chinese civilization over its uniquely long history and wide geographical spread is its relative continuity and uniformity. The problem, then, is to provide such an explanation of continuity and uniformity as can at the same time accommodate an explanation of change and variation.

It is here that the concept of the conscious model may have some heuristic as well as descriptive value.

PRELIMINARY DISCUSSION

Historical reasons for this remarkable continuity and uniformity have often been stated. They are usually said to have been connected with the circumstances which made possible the long ascendency of a bureaucracy which, even in the most venal periods, remained open to talent. Entry into their ranks being through public, state-organized, written examinations in a narrow range of academic subjects, the bureaucrats were simply the most successful of a much larger category of the population, all of whom shared a similar education: the literati, or gentry. The facts that the bureaucrats controlled real power, that the needs of administration required that there could be no district without at least some bureaucrat in it, that the examinations were open to all, secured the China-wide prestige of the literati and their ideas. The fact that the examinations which they sat, and therefore the education which they underwent—often for more than twenty years of their lives—were almost exclusively concerned with the social ideas of Confucius on which they consciously modelled their own social norms, meant that in all parts of the country and at all times the literati held to what were essentially the same ideal patterns. In other words, it is likely that the conscious model of their own social system held by the Chinese literati (gentry) did in fact exhibit a very real continuity and uniformity, while at the same time its prestige was such that non-literati (whose ancestors and/or descendants might have been or might become literati) also aspired to follow it. Furthermore, all the actual sanctions of social order over literati and non-literati alike were in the last resort administered by bureaucrats, themselves literati, whose decisions and actions, inevitably guided by the Confucian norms of their own conscious model, necessarily had a wide influence.

Recent historical scholarship (cp. Wright, 1960) has stressed not only that the interpretation of Confucian norms varied from time to time but also that there were always minorities even among the literati who rebelled against them; nevertheless, the statement that the long period of bureaucratic Imperial government was one in which the ideal patterns of the literati were remarkably uniform and stable is probably broadly true. There is equally little doubt that literati norms were widely approved by the non-literati, regarded as 'best' even by those who could neither follow them in practice nor even fully know them in detail, and used consciously as a measure of progress and a target to aim at by those who were engaged in social climbing or as an index of failure by those who were on the way down. In such circumstances as these it would be reasonable to postulate the development of a degree of agreement between the several Chinese traditional conscious models which could be ascribed, at least in part, to the overriding prestige of one particular conscious model (the literati one) and the authority in society at large of those who held it. One of the objects of the present paper is to examine the validity of this argument.

Assuming it to be valid, one would expect there to have developed most uniformity in those areas of social life which the literati model mapped in most detail and/or those over which they exercised most successful control. Conversely, the areas of greatest variety, whether in time or space, would be likely to be those for which literati norms were irrelevant. A simple example is the role of women. Non-literati China showed a fair variety of actual patterns and, no doubt, of conscious models too (we have already noted the question of the remarriage of widows); by comparison the literati scene was much simpler, for literati women were expected to play purely domestic roles in the narrow sense, and there was therefore little scope for variety. The ideal patterns appropriate to literati women were simply irrelevant to most of the women of different socio-economic levels, over whose daily lives the literati had in any case no control. This is not to say that the literati were not aware of these social differences. Of course they were, as their novels give ample evidence. Their conscious models of Chinese society did not exclude the non-literati, but neither did they do anything to give them prestige, nor, usually, did they describe non-literati matters in any detail. And as very large areas of social living in fact fell outside the range of the literati's own practice, so, despite the very great influence of the relatively unchanging literati model, one can expect to find also considerable variety.

Now, in terms of groupings, the structures which the literati models mapped in most detail were those of family, lineage, and bureaucracy. But the bureaucracy exclusively and lineages essentially were literati structures. In China, non-literati, especially peasants, had no part in the one, and usually only a minor part in the other; overseas, neither existed. Thus one would expect local non-literati and overseas conscious models to show most agreement with their common (literati) model, and with each other, in matters of family structure. Where lineages exist, the conscious models of them are also likely to be fairly uniform, but other structures, being those less carefully or not at all described in the literati model, are likely to show much more variety.

A fairly wide reading of the literature, especially that on the overseas Chinese, has led me to think that a use of the concept of the conscious model somewhat on these lines can give quite valuable insight into the problem of variety-in-uniformity which the study of Chinese social systems inevitably poses, but only if the concept itself is fairly drastically reinterpreted. In what follows I attempt to illustrate this with reference to my own field material.

ILLUSTRATION: THE SOUTH CHINA FISHERMEN

The majority of the sea fishermen of Kwangtung (certainly the very large majority of the sea fishermen of Hong Kong) fall into the category Tanka, which is the Cantonese term for Cantonese-speaking boat-dwellers. The name, though used among themselves sometimes, is rightly regarded by the boat-people as a term of derision and disrepute. Until very recently, and to some extent still today, the boat-people have been despised, placed at the bottom of local systems of social stratification, and often referred to as exemplars of loose sexual morality and other undesirable characteristics. They are frequently explained away as being not really Chinese, and I have heard well-educated Cantonese describing their non-Han descent, their non-Chinese language, and the special biological distinction which gives them six toes on each foot. Eyes and ears alone are enough to inform anyone who cares to notice that the boat-people, who very often go barefoot, have the normal complement of toes, and speak Cantonese—albeit usually with a 'broad' accent and always with the specialized vocabulary necessary to their specialized way of life. The non-Han descent question receives fuller treatment below, but briefly it can be argued here (1) that the boat-people's descent is probably neither more nor less 'non-Han' than that of most other Cantonese-speaking inhabitants of Kwangtung; (2) that there have been continuous additions to and departures from the boat population, which is therefore in no way 'racially' distinct; and (3) that such apparently physiological diacritica as can be discerned (for example, browner complexion, rolling gait, small leg muscles, and heavy shoulder development), together with nearly all the Tanka's social and cultural peculiarities, can be readily and much more economically ascribed to their aquatic mode of life. All boat-people I have ever met emphatically maintain that they are as 'Chinese' as any other Cantonese speakers, and habitually refer to themselves in the usual Cantonese phrase which can be translated: 'We people of China'. In Kwangtung Province they probably number between two and three million; in Hong Kong about 150,000, of whom about 100,000 live aboard fishing boats.

At first sight, the Tanka, particularly the fishing-boat-dwellers, seem to present such an extreme case of adaptation to environment, so entirely outside the range of literati experience, that, following the above argument, their socio-economic arrangements and their conscious models of them might be expected to depart quite radically from any of the usual Chinese patterns. Indeed, it would not be surprising if local land-lubberly opinion were right and the Tanka were to prove in the socio-cultural, if not in the 'racial' sense, 'un-Chinese'. The fact that until the last few decades very few Tanka received any education and that there were periods of Chinese history during which they were forbidden to sit for the Imperial examinations lends plausibility to this suggestion. But observation does not bear it out. The fact is that, although their highly specialized waterborne way of life does pose certain problems which most Chinese do not have to face, there is precious little in Tanka social structure which cannot be paralleled elsewhere in China or in Chinese communities overseas.

Kau Sai, the community to which most of my most detailed observations apply, is a coastal village on one of the small islands which lie in the Port Shelter area on the eastern side of the British Crown Colony of Hong Kong. The present (1963) population comprises about 600 Tanka and three visiting non-Tanka schoolteachers. Nine Tanka households live ashore, the rest occupy some forty odd fishing boats, each with its permanent anchorage at the village. Except for the schoolteachers, all consider themselves Kau Sai people, and set a high valuation upon this claim. Most can, and do, quote genealogical information to show that they have been resident for at least four generations. The village contains a well-kept and well-patronized temple to a popular local sea deity, a newly built school, four or five small shops (selling mostly sweets, cigarettes, cakes, and soft drinks) and a new latrine, the hygienic nature of which is rightly a matter of immense local pride. There is a never-failing piped water supply, and ample space for net-drying and dyeing, fish-drying, etc. The village is most conveniently placed for each access to both fishing grounds and markets. Inshore purse-seining and inshore longlining are the two main types of fishing practised. The average-sized boat measures about 30-35 feet overall and about 11 feet in the beam, and is mechanized with a small marine diesel engine. The numbers of people on board vary between three and fifteen, and include women and children.

Actual Kau Sai families are nuclear, patrilocal stem, or patrilocal extended (or in one or other stage of development towards or away from one of these climax states). Inshore longlining of the small-scale kind practised from Kau Sai requires fewer able-bodied workers than purse-seining and can support fewer. There is no extended family among the longliners. Inshore purse-seining, on the other hand, could not be carried on by a nuclear family alone. The additional complement may be made up with hired men, but this is unusual; Kau Sai purse-seiners all house families of the patrilocal extended type or parts of such families. Until very recently purse-seining always required the joint participation of two boats, which could quite easily provide living quarters for even a climax state extended family. Nowadays, with experience in mechanization, the actual fishing operations are usually performed by single vessels, the 'surplus' family members living still on the second junk which has thus become simply a house-boat. (There is a strong movement at present throughout all the boat communities of Hong Kong towards housing non-productive older people and children of school age and under ashore.) There are no female household heads in Kau Sai. All existing marriages have been patrilocal.

The most striking thing about this picture of the actual composition of families among these Kau Sai Tanka is the way in which, while agreeing remarkably closely with certain basic points in the descriptions of actual family composition elsewhere in China and among overseas Chinese, it shows an even nearer approach than many of them towards what is usually regarded as the Chinese ideal (i.e. the literati conscious model). As elsewhere there is a clear correlation between family size and family income; the larger the income the larger the family. As elsewhere, too, the mean size of families is around six. As elsewhere there is a strong emphasis upon patrilocality, patriliny, and the advantages of having many sons. But in Kau Sai this emphasis seems particularly strong. To take two examples only; there is no case of 'matrilocal' marriage, described for so many areas as existing though frowned upon, and there are no women heads of households.

It would of course be naïve to argue from these two facts that so far from being 'un-Chinese', as popular opinion so often believes, Tanka family structure is on the contrary rather closer in practice to the literati ideal than are the family structures of most other non-literati communities. It is true that the Tanka in Hong Kong at present are in general more conservative than most other local Chinese, but 'conservatism' is a descriptive term which by itself never explained anything. In any case, both 'matrilocal' marriages and female household heads are to be found among other Tanka in Hong Kong. Small passenger craft in all the larger floating settlements of the Colony, including the main harbour, are very often owned and managed by females whose husbands are employed elsewhere. Among fishermen, even inshore fishermen as in Kau Sai, however, a female 'captain' is very rare. Whereas small-scale passenger transport in sheltered waters can be organized quite easily by a woman alone or with her unmarried daughters and younger sons, fishing on any scale above that of small hand-lining demands skills in handling men and boats at sea, in marketing procedures, including the organization of credit relationships, and in sheer physical strength which make it unsuitable for all but the most exceptional women. As for 'matrilocal' marriages, since it is known that in most Chinese communities only a relatively poor man will enter into such an alliance, their absence from Kau Sai is probably to be explained by the comparative prosperity of the village as a whole.

So one cannot explain the relative closeness of the actual patterns of Kau Sai family structure to the Chinese traditional ideal patterns as being simply a closer conscious following of the literati model. The sociological explanation is rather that the circumstances of a waterborne fishermen's life in Kau Sai seem to foster at least some of the same patterns as appear in that model. But this cannot be the whole story, for if technical and economic circumstances alone could account for Kau Sai's actual family structures we should be unable to explain their strong patrilineal and patrilocal bias. Male dominance can, and usually does, exist perfectly well in non-unilineal kinship systems or with matriliny. In Kau Sai, as we shall see, lineages can hardly be said to exist, yet patriliny is strongly entrenched. Why? It seems that after all the people's own explanation is right: 'because they are Chinese'. In other words, we are forced back to consider the conscious model again, for it is obvious that actual family structures in Kau Sai only make complete sense when they are seen as existing and developing within the framework of a strong patrilineal, patrilocal ideology. Kau Sai people do in fact hold a conscious model of family structure which is in essentials closely similar to that usually attributed to the traditional literati. They set a high value upon this model, and constantly invoke it as a yardstick for behaviour. Nearly all local gossip and discussion centre upon it, and the very large majority of personal decisions are referred to it. It is a model for social action, which not only provides criteria for justification or criticism after an event, but also influences choice and decision beforehand. Conscious models which are less highly valued and less frequently used may well be of less significance, but in Kau Sai the conscious model of family structure is one of the crucial social facts.

THE SECOND PROBLEM: WHAT IS A 'CONSCIOUS MODEL'?

I have earlier argued that one of the areas in which the prestige of the literati conscious model might be expected to have had most influence would be that of family structure because this was the one area which was common to both literati and non-literati, in the sense that all lived in families. Although it demonstrates that the conscious model alone does not explain the structure, Kau Sai material does suggest that in so far as the conscious model is significant this argument is likely to be borne out by the facts. Literati family norms, or some of them, do apply in Kau Sai, partly because they are appropriate to the technico-economic situation and partly because the people themselves give them high value and appeal to them every day. Does this then mean that it is useful, after all, to speak of a single China-wide conscious model of family structure? I think not; and for at least two reasons.

In the first place, by no means all the literati norms are to be found in either the observer's or the conscious models of Kau Sai family structure, nor are all aspects of the Kau Sai models in agreement with literati norms. We have already noted the remarriage of widows, occurring normally (and, one should add, appropriately) and believed to be normative too in Kau Sai, but banned in theory and very frequently in practice by the literati. We have drawn attention also to the differing roles of women, and it is obvious that there must have been a whole host of details of literati family etiquette, etc., which would be quite outside the ken of Tanka boat-people. Then, secondly, the Tanka themselves are well aware that there are differences, and would not dare to claim the literati model for themselves. One of the difficulties of the early stages of fieldwork amongst them is always the need to overcome their conviction that they do not know the 'true' Chinese ways. 'We are not educated people, why do you come and ask us these things?' they say. Thus clarity is probably more nearly attained and the Kau Sai people's own ideas more nearly reflected by postulating two conscious models with a degree of consensus: a Kau Sai model and a literati model.

The question then arises: of whose consciousness are we speaking? So far as the Kau Sai model is concerned, there is no particular difficulty. The community is small, its members show a marked awareness of themselves as a local unit with common values. Although there are inevitably differences of opinion and differing degrees of knowledge, the general agreement on matters of, say, family structure is easily observable. It is otherwise with the literati model. Up till now we have simply assumed its existence, mentioning as evidence a shared educational system, common examinations, access to the same literature, literati control of the administration (which included the administration of justice), and so on. But this is evidence of a different order from that from which we can deduce the Kau Sai conscious model. Moreover, the traditional literati are long since dead, and we can hardly observe their collective consciousness now. All we can observe at the present time is the set of norms which are believed by present-day Chinese to have been the conscious models of the literati. We can assume that rather similar believed-in models existed also in the past, when they were presumably liable to 'correction' by existing local literati, in the light of their then existing conscious models, on the occasions in which they took the lead in village and clan affairs, acted as mediators in local disputes, and so on; and we may suppose that what we have earlier referred to as the 'overriding prestige' of the literati model may have exerted its influence in practice largely through such a process of 'correction'. In so far as Kau Sai today is concerned, what we have up till now called the literati conscious model is a postulate in the minds not of the literati but of the people in Kau Sai. It exists for them as an ideal, incompletely known, towards which they aspire but which they know they fall short of. For them it is, as it were, the 'real Chinese way' and therefore the best way of ordering social arrangements, and their own model, which is also 'Chinese' and better than anything non-Chinese, only approaches excellence in so far as it approximates the 'real Chinese-ness' of this believed-in literati model.

Thus the two conscious models we have postulated are brought into contact with each other simply because they both exist as ideas in the minds of the same (for us, Kau Sai) people. These people have other models in their minds, too. Tanka in Hong Kong know a good deal about the social arrangements of other local Chinese: Hakka, Cantonese of varying occupations and economic strata, Hoklo, and nowadays even Shanghainese. But the constructs they make about them are like observer's models, constructs about other social systems as the Tanka see them. They are not used as models for their own action, and they are rather the objects than the standards of criticism. On the other hand, when a Tanka has to deal with non-Tanka or gives up water-living and takes to paid employment ashore, he has ready to hand a fairly useful working model of non-Tanka Chinese structures by which to order his behaviour. Moreover, and this is the significant matter, he knows that non-Tanka Chinese also carry in their minds versions of the believed-in literati model which are essentially similar to his own, and that all regard it as the true Chinese way.

We are now in a position to restate the first naïve version of our argument. Whereas originally we postulated the existence of as many conscious models as there have been different groups in China, one of which, the literati model, had overriding influence over the others, we now suggest that every Chinese carries several conscious models in his mind. Some of these are like observer's models; they could be called internal observer's models, that is models of the socio-cultural arrangements of Chinese subgroups other than his own. He does not normally use them as models for action or standards of judgement, though he may do so if he has to change his own group membership and they may assist him in intergroup contacts. In addition he holds two other kinds of model: the one, which we may call the homemade or immediate model, is his own subgroup's model of its own socio-cultural system as they believe it to be, the other his subgroup's version of what they believe the 'true Chinese' literati model to have been. This may be called the believed-in traditional model, or the ideological model. Being based, however remotely, upon once existing relatively uniform literati practice, the ideological models held by different Chinese subgroups vary comparatively little. Their various immediate models, on the other hand, may well be expected to show wide differences between each other, especially in those areas which the believed-in traditions do not cover—for just as there are always large areas of a subgroup's ideological model which are irrelevant to its actual pattern of living and hence to its home-made (immediate) model, so there are likely to be more or less numerous parts of its immediate model which, like the actualities to which they refer, lie outside the range of its ideological model.

Strictly speaking, the only people who can observe differences between immediate models are outsiders (or social scientists); what a Chinese layman compares is his own immediate model of his own social arrangements with his own 'observer's' model of the other fellow's. As we have pointed out, such comparisons usually serve merely to confirm his belief in the superiority of his own group, but this conclusion is not reached in quite the same way as, say, the apparently similar conclusion that European social patterns are inferior. Foreign patterns are judged by criteria which the foreigners themselves do not and are not expected to share; the patterns of other Chinese groups are criticized according to criteria set by what are believed to be, and very largely are, agreed standards—the standards of the believed-in traditional (ideological) models. Therein, indeed, in the eyes of a Chinese lies the degree of 'Chinese-ness' of any other groups (or individuals)—how far do they or do they not conform to the ideological model which he not only believes in himself but believes them also to share? Only patterns of living which are so aberrant as to imply that this traditional ideology has never been accepted are dubbed 'non-Chinese'.

Thus it is plausible for a Cantonese landsman who criticizes Hakka, on the one hand, and Shanghainese, on the other, for not being 'really Chinese' to dismiss the water-people who speak his own language as completely non-Chinese because all that he ever sees of their way of life is obviously very far indeed from any literati derived ideological model. What he sees *is*, in this sense, 'un-Chinese': people living on boats, making a livelihood by fishing or carrying cargo or, worse still, by carrying passengers—the last, being the most commonly seen by ordinary landsmen and therefore in their eyes the most 'typical', happens to be the one Tanka occupation with a high proportion of women managers, a grave departure from tradition. All in all, it would be surprising if the Tanka were not thought to practise all sorts of other non-Chinese traits (even matriliny has not infrequently been alleged), especially since the myth of non-Han descent is ready to hand and all landsmen are convinced that Tanka were never permitted to sit the Imperial examinations and so had no chance ever to have imbibed any education in literati norms. In their turn, the Tanka, measuring themselves and others by their own notion of the traditional, feel themselves entirely beyond criticism at sea, where literati-derived norms can have no place and they set their own standards, but, since they share the landsmen's views of their own ignorance, at a sad loss on land. 'Veritable dragons afloat', so runs one of their own sayings, 'but miserable worms ashore.'

FURTHER ILLUSTRATION

But let us return to Kau Sai.

The development of our original argument stated that what we are now calling the ideological model (the believed-in traditional model) would have most influence on those parts of any Chinese group's home-made model which dealt with family structures. We later claimed that the material from Kau Sai tended to confirm this view. The following brief consideration of non-family structures in Kau Sai may make this part of the discussion clearer.

We have suggested that Kau Sai family structure can only be understood if it is seen as existing in the framework of a strongly patrilineal ideology. In most parts of South China this traditionally found expression also in the actual existence of more or less strongly organized patrilineages together with highly developed conscious models of their structure, often written and usually ritualized. Leadership in these lineages was usually in the hands of their literati members, who were, of course, also responsible for their written rules. Thus for lineages there was usually quite a close fit between conscious models and believed-in traditional models. Kau Sai, however, a multi-surname village with no literati, has no lineages and, as far as I can ascertain, never has had any. In this, Kau Sai people are similar to other Tanka, to most Chinese in modern cities anywhere, and, indeed, to both rural and urban Chinese in many other parts of China and overseas. The lack of permanent landed estates, the potential physical mobility afforded by boat-dwelling, the absence of literati from among them, and their economic dependence upon people who usually were not kinsmen in any sense—these were probably the factors which prevented the emergence of lineages among the Tanka. Kau Sai contains no ancestral halls, no genealogy books, and no corporate ancestor worship. Each family remembers its own dead on the usual formal occasions, but this ritual has (following Freedman, 1957) to be classed as memorialism rather than ancestor worship proper. There is no grouping intermediate between the family and the village, and the village is in no sense a kinship unit.

Paradoxically enough, the very fact that the Tanka have no lineages may be used to point up the strength of the influence of the believed-in traditional model of the family. The actual existence of a highly organized system of patrilineages necessarily affects family structure. Such a system may be said almost to dictate a patrilineal, patrilocal form of family, with biases towards polygyny and against both divorce and free widow remarriage; it goes with the careful control of women's reproductive powers and the treatment of women in general as jural minors. Thus it is arguable that where patrilineages exist family structures need not owe anything to any ideological model. Conversely, if in the absence of patrilineages family structures exhibit these, or many of these, characteristics, then it is reasonable to look for other influences—of which the existence of a prestigeful believed-in model may well be one. Our discussion of Kau Sai family structure, above, followed this line.

Beyond the field of family and lineage groupings we come to village structure. Our original argument predicts that where literati models are inapplicable, there wide variety is likely to be found. It is obvious that a settlement such as Kau Sai—without even a history of literati connexions, and with a highly specialized occupational basis which is linked with an unusual physical environment and gives the potentiality of almost unlimited physical mobility—is well outside the range of any literati-derived model. The kind of local grouping recorded as typical of Kwangtung and Fukien provinces (Freedman, 1958) is a single-surname village, its members comprising a single lineage (with the wives of the adult men and without their married sisters) under the leadership of its educated 'elders', the focus of village solidarity being an ancestral cult centred upon the lineage ancestral hall, to which there is usually attached a greater or lesser amount of lineage land. Kau Sai is not at all like that. It is, as we have just said, a multi-surname village, with no educated members. There is a tacit agreement that all heads of families are equal and a marked disinclination to assert any kind of personal leadership at the village level. A local deity ('*shen*') provides the focus of village solidarity, which is centred upon his temple. There is no corporate ancestor worship, no ancestral hall, and no landed property of any kind. Certainly, these are very considerable differences, and to that extent our argument is borne out; such studies as there are of villages in other parts of China and overseas show a number of other variations too.

Beyond the village we are no longer dealing with group structures. Each Kau Sai person has a series of dyadic relationships with other non-Kau Sai persons: market relationships, kinship and affinal relationships, and relationships connected with ritual and recreation. An anthropologist can observe a general congruence between the spatial areas in which these different relationships are concentrated. Borrowing an image from zoology, I propose to call the space so demarcated a 'territory'. Those who live within it do not form a social group in the sense that they ever act corporately, and though they are aware that they have much in common they do not think of themselves as a unit. The territory is simply a mappable area whose boundaries form the limits of most intense socio-economic interaction. Only a few social or economic relationships lead outside it, but its population is in effect merely the pool from which individual Kau Sai people draw their contacts.

This, of course, is my own observer's model. As an anthropologist I see Kau Sai as one of a number of very similar local groups situated within an area definable only in terms of the degree of intensity of the (dyadic) socio-economic relationships existing within it. The Hong Kong Government, on the other hand, sets Kau Sai, along with some of these other villages and many more not included in the territory, within the boundaries of an administrative District which in turn is encapsulated, along with other similar Districts, within a larger administrative area, the New Territories. The governmental structure includes the positions of District Commissioner (for the New Territories), and District Officers (for the Districts), and a fairly regular system of Village Representatives and Rural Committees. Kau Sai people, though aware of these governmental notions, do not really share them.

Looking outwards from his own village, a Kau Sai man sees other fairly similar villages (the inferiorities of which he frequently remarks), the local market town, and the three major urban fish-market centres near the city of Victoria (Hong Kong island). There is also the District Office, which is situated in Kowloon. He does not see Kau Sai as in any way subordinate to any of these places, all relationships with which (including relationships with Government) he thinks of entirely in personal dyadic terms. In other words, like the anthropologist, he sees beyond the village level only sets and networks of dyadic relationships. His view differs from mine, however, in that he does not normally conceptualize what I have termed the territory—though if pressed he may be induced to recognize its existence. In so far as his own model sets Kau Sai within any embracing larger units, it selects only two or three rather vague entities, both thought of in cultural rather than in social structural terms: 'the water-people' (sometimes, also 'we water-people on the eastern side (of Hong Kong)') and 'the Chinese'.

Now, it is arguable that since the literati were so closely connected with the bureaucracy in traditional China their view of the place of village groups in the wider society was probably not far different from that of the Government of Hong Kong today. The boundaries of administrative districts, their nomenclature, and the titles of the officials of different ranks were of course different, but the model was of the same general bureaucratic type. But neither the Kau Sai home-made model nor the actuality have been influenced by it. How is this to be explained?

The difficulty is more apparent than real. The traditional Chinese bureaucratic apparatus stopped short of the village level at the town with the lowest magistrate's court ('*yamen*'). Non-literati villagers would have little contact with officialdom, and would do everything possible to make that little less. By no stretch of the imagination could the literati's bureaucratic patterns be regarded as models for peasant emulation as their family patterns could. We have stated that Kau Sai's relationships with the wider society today are not (from the point of view of Kau Sai people) conducted in group terms but as a series of dyadic relationships—and this was no doubt as true of its relationships with the bureaucracy in, say, the Ch'ing dynasty as it is with the British administration today. There was thus no clash between theory and practice to force a change of view, and Kau Sai's own conscious (home-made) model of its position in the wider society could co-exist quite easily with what little its people knew of the literati model. They just did not meet.

If this part of the evidence for Kau Sai may be generalized for China as a whole, then it would seem to follow that here (in the relationships between villages and the wider society) is another area of social life in which relatively wide variety is to be expected. Few studies of Chinese villages to date have been concerned with extra-village relationships, but I should be surprised if in fact there was not much more uniformity at this level than at the level of internal village organization. At least three factors make this likely. In the first place, there were similarities in such economic and technological matters as means of transport, kinds of market, types of produce and so on all over China which must have set certain rather similar limitations to the possibilities of variation; second, and probably more significant, where relationships with the bureaucracy were concerned, one party to the relationship was everywhere very much the same; and, third, there was, of course, the strong influence of the believed-in traditional models of the proper way for conducting dyadic relationships, which being based on the pattern of family and kin relationships were relevant to everyone. That they were also largely effective and largely uniform—as from our argument we would expect—is well attested by the literature which over and over again describes the 'personalization' of all kinds of non-kinship relationship among the Chinese.

A word must be said about religion. Because formally the literati despised the popular cults we should expect perhaps the greatest variety of all to appear in this sphere. There is a good deal of evidence in support of this contention. In other words, there being no literati-derived model for religious behaviour outside the state and ancestral cults (which were uniform), the popular cults could develop to suit local fancy—and did.

THE PROCESS OF ASSIMILATION

Finally, because our data refer to people usually believed to be marginal, if not foreign, to Chinese society proper, it is necessary to turn to history. I have already mentioned the 'myth' of non-Han descent, and stated that in my opinion the present-day Tanka are neither more nor less 'non-Han' than most of the other Cantonese-speaking inhabitants of South China. It is interesting to note that the People's Government appears to agree with this view, for in the Census of 1953 the Tanka are not listed among the fifty separate ethnic groups of China. Nevertheless, as we have seen, popular opinion and most of the very scanty literature about the Tanka still explain their supposedly un-Chinese social structure and customs in terms of their ethnic distinctness. In this sense the story of non-Han descent is a myth—

that is, it is a statement which, whether true or not, is used to explain or justify behaviour. (In this sense, too—the sense propounded by Leach (op. cit.)—the models we have so far been discussing are also myths.)

My views of the actual history of the Tanka follow fairly closely those of Wiens (1954) and Ch'en (1946). Wiens, basing his work on Eberhard, argues that the early Yüeh culture of South China was not in reality a separate culture at all, but that the term, 'Yüeh' hid the product of a mixture of different cultures blended into a new individuality. The mixture, which comprised at least Yao and Tan (from which the compound word Tanka is derived) and T'ai or Chuang elements, had already occurred with the appearance of Yüeh as a political concept, that is at the latest by the seventh century B.C.

Now, if Yüeh culture already contained elements of Tan culture as early as the seventh century B.C., then there are three possibilities: either the Tan were already as much 'part of' the common culture and society of South China as anybody else, or at least some of the Tan were so, or, at the very least, Tan and Yüeh culture cannot have been entirely foreign to each other. Even if only some of the Tan people had been absorbed by then—or none—it does not follow that a process of assimilation did not continue long after the seventh century B.C. We have, of course, ample evidence of continued assimilation in this part of China, particularly for the later centuries as Han culture, pushing steadily outwards, not only drew in what had been Yüeh but also pressed upon the border peoples hitherto unassimilated to Yüeh. There can be no reasonable doubt that the two and a half thousand years or so since Yüeh first appeared as a political concept have given full opportunity for the Tan, less remote than the hill tribes and more mobile, to be assimilated to the surrounding people.

But the upholders of the traditional view claim that the opportunity was never taken; that though not remote physically the water-people have always remained so remote socially that they have been able to retain their original culture and social structure virtually unchanged for all this length of time. Quite apart from the fact that if this were so then the original Tanka socio-cultural system must have been quite presciently 'Chinese', I remain sceptical about the alleged segregation. The points usually mentioned are that the Tanka were not permitted to sit for the Imperial examinations, to live ashore, or to marry with landsmen. The implication is that these were official prohibitions, but although Imperial decrees did from time to time (by no means always) include 'boatmen' in the list of those ineligible for the examinations, it is certain that for at least the last two hundred years there have been no official disabilities. Intensive literary research has led one of the Tanka's recent students, Professor Ch'en Hsü Ching, to the conclusion that it was probably always local prejudice rather than official policy that kept the Tanka out. A boatman who remained on his boat would necessarily find it almost impossible to become educated and certainly useless to marry a landsman's daughter, but a boatman who moved ashore could 'pass' without difficulty. Professor Ch'en asserts that there have always been many who did so, but that this has tended to go unnoticed because Tanka who have moved ashore successfully are no longer visibly Tanka at all and are careful to conceal their origins. Data from my own fieldwork in Hong Kong entirely support this view.

A point consistently overlooked in the traditional notion of Tanka separateness is that whatever their respective ethnic origins land- and water-people are and have long been inextricably closely interrelated through the facts of economics. The fishermen of Kau Sai, for example, are all involved in long-standing credit relationships with fish-dealers who are landsmen, and buy their boats, gear, and provisions from other landsmen—often also on credit. These are personalized relationships based as a rule upon long acquaintance (Ward, 1960) and requiring almost daily meetings, frequent mutual entertainment at the tea houses, and so on. In the face of so much daily intercourse with people whose ways of life they know to be of a kind they themselves must adopt if they are to gain any prestige in the wider society, the Tanka could only have maintained a markedly different system if they had resolutely rejected assimilation. There is considerable evidence of Southern hill tribes having done just that; there is no similar evidence (at least for several centuries) for any of the Tanka. And there is no doubt that today the contrary is true.

Moreover their system is not different.

And yet some non-Han, or at least non-literati, items have been retained, and even valued for their own sake. Such, for example, are the Tanka's ear-rings and bracelets, their using wooden figures rather than 'soul tablets' to represent their dead, and certain peculiarities fo their marriage customs. Items of this general kind show much variation locally in other parts of China too: in Hong Kong alone one can see daily the unmistakably typical Hakka hats or Hoklo silver hair ornaments. Why is this? I can only suggest that these are all things which are capable of being used as 'badges' of identification by the groups concerned, self-conscious marks of differentiation and local pride—which can undoubtedly co-exist with a firm belief in the ultimate superiority of a 'real' Chinese tradition which is known to reject such 'barbarisms'. Many of the literati's own customs in such matters as these were in any case out of reach of the peasantry, because of sumptuary laws or expense. It is worth noticing, too, that such items as these can easily be changed if a family decides to give up its old way of life and start the upward climb; they are more and more being discarded by go-ahead, urbanized water-people in Hong Kong at the present time.

We earlier referred to the remarriage of widows. This is far too widespread as a social fact in China to be a badge of differentiation nor is it on all fours with such purely cultural items as the wearing of jade bracelets. The 'rule' that a widow should not remarry was part of the literati ideal of the continuing patrilineal, patrilocal extended family. A continuing family household, with a secure economic background, can afford to support its widows; smaller households, breaking up every (or every other) generation, cannot. Since the actual numbers of continuing extended families were probably always few, so widow remarriage, even for members of the literati class, must have always been common. So it is not particularly surprising to find that Kau Sai people believe it to have been part of the traditional model.

We are arguing, then, that the very long history of assimilation affected the 'Tan' people no less than anyone else in South China, with the result that their social structure and culture have long been essentially 'Chinese'. And we would argue further that one of the main weapons by which Han civilization asserted its supremacy was its successful use of what we have called 'the believed-in traditional model'. We must add, too, that this was not due solely to the direct influence of the bureaucrats, though this played its part, or to their direct teaching, though that was important, but also to the more subtle influences of proverbs and legends, story-tellers, the drama and so on, and above all to the demands of social ambition—for since entry into the ranks of the literati was at all periods the major legitimate road to power and prestige, so almost all Chinese who were at all ambitious necessarily strove to acquire literati norms for themselves or their children. The gap was constantly, if irregularly, being narrowed—and always in the same direction.

SUMMARY AND CONCLUSION

The task set at the beginning of this paper was to discover a sociological formula which, while accounting for the uniquely widespread, uniformity and long continuity of traditional Chinese society and culture, would at the same time explain the continued existence of quite considerable variation within it. Historically it seems fairly clear that one of the most significant influences for conformity was the relatively uniform and largely written conscious (normative) model of social life held by the literati classes from whom the administration was recruited. But this statement does nothing to explain the variations, and begs most of the sociological questions about how this influence actually worked. Illustrative material drawn from the writer's own fieldwork in what can fairly be considered a still largely 'traditional', though unusual, village in Hong Kong suggests that the concept 'conscious model' (more often referred to as 'ideal pattern' or 'norm': cp. Lévi-Strauss, 1953) requires rethinking.

The people of Kau Sai appear to have three different kinds of model of Chinese social arrangements in their consciousness. First there is their own notion of their own social and cultural system; this, again following Lévi-Strauss, we called the 'home-made' model; possibly for scientific use the term 'immediate model' might be more acceptable. Second, there is their version of what they believe to have been the traditional literati system; this we named the 'believed-in traditional model', or, better because of wider applicability, the 'ideological model'. It acts for them as their measure of what is truly Chinese, and wherever it is relevant it is, and has been, used as a corrective for their immediate model and so for their actual structure. Then, third, there are the various models they have constructed of the socio-cultural arrangements of other Chinese groups. These we called 'internal observers' models'. As a type they differ from observers' models proper (i.e. the models constructed by outsiders, including social scientists) only in that they are held by people who consider themselves members of the same wider society with those whom they are observing.

This breakdown into three kinds of conscious model then allows us to see the process towards uniformity in China developing out of innumerable and continued shifts in the various immediate models of different local, occupational, and ethnic groups in the direction of their ideological models, which, being based on the relatively uniform actual literati structure, and often in the past subjected to correction by living literati (in the light of their own essentially similar ideological models), were in fact very much alike. Inevitably, however, ideological models derived from literati practice could not be entirely relevant to non-literati social life, which therefore had still a good deal of freedom to develop local idiosyncrasies in such fields as, for example, the sexual division of labour, village organization, and popular religion.

It is a striking fact that the one kind of structure which was lived in by all groups in China, and therefore the one to which the literati-derived ideological models gave the most value, namely: the family. Besides the patterns for family structures, the ideological models probably contained little that was of relevance to all actual group structures, though much (e.g. lineage patterns) which was relevant to many. However, since in setting the highest value upon family relationships they stressed also the rightness of 'familializing' all extra-family relationships, almost everything they contained about dyadic relationships of all kinds was relevant—and was given practical expression in the markedly similar cast of actual dyadic relationships throughout China.

Thus in speaking of the uniformity and continuity of the traditional

Chinese social system it seems that what we are primarily referring to is the China-wide existence of essentially similar family structures and similar ('family-like') methods of organizing dyadic relationships outside the family. Less wide-spread, but probably more uniform where existing, were patrilineal lineage structures, and over all, of course, was the bureaucratic structure which, though it was lived in by and formed a detailed part of the immediate model of only some Chinese, nevertheless affected all because it was the administrative framework of the state. Outside these areas of social structure there was much variety, but because these were the areas which were most highly valued public opinion—scholarly as well as lay, and Chinese as well as foreign—has usually tended to overestimate the uniformities and underemphasize the variations.

Lévi-Strauss' substitution of the term 'conscious model' for 'ideal pattern' or 'norm' has the merit of getting away from the philosophical and verbal difficulties inherent in these two terms, but if it implies that there is ever one single version of their own social system constructed in the minds of all the individuals of any society it is misleading. We can and must contrast conscious models, existing as constructs in the minds of the people under study themselves, with observers' models constructed by outsiders, including social scientists, but it is probably always useful to think also in terms of at least the three different kinds of conscious model we have here distinguished as immediate models, ideological models, and internal observers' models. The degree to which any society exhibits widespread or lasting uniformities is likely to be connected with, among other things, the degree of similarity between the ideological models held by different subgroups and the narrowness of the gaps between ideological and immediate models on the one hand and between both these models and the actual structures on the other.

REFERENCES

Ch'en Hsü-ching. 1946. *Tanka Researches*. Canton: Lingnan University Press (in Chinese).

Freedman, Maurice. 1957. *Chinese Family and Marriage in Singapore*. London: H.M.S.O.

————. 1958. *Lineage Organization in Southeastern China*. London: Athlone Press.

Leach, E. R. 1954. *Political Systems of Highland Burma*. London: Bell.

Lévi-Strauss, Claude. 1953. 'Social Structure'. In A. L. Kroeber (ed.), *Anthropology Today*. Chicago: University of Chicago Press.

Ward, Barbara E. 1960. 'Cash or Credit Crops?' *Economic Developments and Cultural Change* 8:148-63.

Wiens, Herold Jacob. 1954. *China's March toward the Tropics*. Hamden, Conn.: Shoe String Press.

Wright, Arthur F. (ed.). 1960. *The Confucian Persuasion*. Stanford, California: Stanford University Press.

4. Sociological Self-awareness: Some Uses of the Conscious Models*

A recent paper of mine (Ward, 1965) drew attention to Lévi-Strauss' distinction between the models any people make of their own social system and the models produced by observers from outside. The former, constructs of the people under study themselves, he calls conscious or 'home-made' models; the latter, unconscious or observers' models (Lévi-Strauss, 1953). Later in the same article I suggested that it is likely that any people possesses more than one kind of home-made model. With reference to a community of Chinese fishermen in the British Colony of Hong Kong, I distinguished at least three kinds of models of Chinese social systems which I believed most of them to subscribe to as part of their collective representations. In the first place there was the ordinary working-model, a kind of blueprint, of their immediate community, which I called the 'immediate model'. Secondly, there was their model of what they believe to have been the social system of China as the traditional literati saw it: this, which they regard as the proper Chinese model (to which they know their own community does not completely conform), I called the 'ideological model'. Thirdly, there was a varying number of other models representing the social arrangements of groups of other Chinese, neither literati nor fishermen, with whom they were more or less familiar: members of other dialect groups, farmers, traders, and so forth. These I called 'internal observers' models'.

I then argued the value of Lévi-Strauss' substitution of the term 'conscious model' for the more usual 'ideal pattern' or 'norm' because it enables us to escape from the philosophical and terminological difficulties inherent in the use of these two terms, and suggested that a further breakdown of the concept of conscious models, such as the one I have just put forward, would have the further merit of enabling us to avoid some of the methodological difficulties inherent in the assumption (commonly though not always explicitly held) that there is always *one* 'ideal pattern'. I attempted to illustrate the usefulness of my own suggested distinction by employing it to

*Reproduced by permission of the Royal Anthropological Institute of Great Britain and Ireland from *Man* (N.S.), Vol. 1, No. 2 (1966), pp. 201-215.

throw light upon a major problem of Chinese sociological history. This topic necessarily led me to concentrate in that paper mainly upon the ideological model—in other words, upon the model that I think the villagers I was discussing believe to have been a model of the proper Chinese social system. In the present paper I wish to examine in more detail the other two kinds of home-made model I postulated—namely, those I labelled 'immediate' and 'internal observers' ' respectively—and their interconnexions with each other and with the ideological model.

First, however, it may be useful to clarify the notion of model itself. Some recent arguments have given the impression that there is in some quarters an almost mystical belief that for any given social system there is, or should be, something which could be called '*the* model'. Students have been known to object that certain schemes of analysis *could* not be *accurate* because *the* model *must* have such and such additional characteristics. The italicised words betray the frame of mind. It may be that this misleading notion that there is a 'true model' somewhere is a result of confusing two of the several quite distinct concepts that the English language refers to by the word: 'model'. One common usage of this word refers to something after the nature of what the toy-shops call 'a realistic scale model'—a toy racing-car or aeroplane, for example, in which all the features of the real thing, or as nearly all of them as possible, are carefully included but on a small scale. In such toys the greater the detail the better the model, and the better pleased the customers. But if models of this kind are labelled scientific (and they often are), this is in the colloquial use of the word which equates 'science' with 'detailed accuracy'. In this usage there is a real sense in which '*the* model', the one which reproduces its original as nearly as possible, can be said to exist—even if only as an ideal.

In professional scientific usage, however, there is no such thing as '*the* model' of anything; instead there can be a host of different models of the same thing, depending only upon what kind of analysis is being made and for what purposes. Moreover, none of these scientific models is necessarily any more 'realistic' or even 'accurate' than any other, for neither realism nor accuracy, in any absolute sense, is the objective of model making. The old example of the use of geometrical models explains the situation well: there are many problems for which the models provided by the theorems of Euclid are useful, being relatively simple to handle and adequate for both explanation and practical application; there are also many other problems for which Euclidian models are no use at all, and those who work on these problems turn to other models. So with the models of social science: one constructs them in order to try to make sense of the phenomena; if they do not seem to help make sense, one alters them, or discards them and tries something else.

Similarly, if a particular model turns out to be less useful, or even not at all useful for a particular purpose, and is therefore rejected, it is not thereby disproved but merely disapproved; for it had, or should have had, no claim to 'accuracy' in the first place, but only to more or less usefulness for the task in hand.

Furthermore, and this must be stressed for the purpose of the analysis which follows, there is no rule about what sort of things ought to be included in any model. One can—must—decide deliberately to leave out certain matters in order to concentrate upon others. In other words, one decides to hold certain things constant or to proceed 'as if'; *as if*, for example, human beings always acted rationally for the maximisation of their economic assets; or *as if* they were motivated solely by the desire for power or prestige; or *as if* social groupings existed independently of cultural behaviour; or, again, *as if* social structure and social process were independent of each other.

There is nothing new in this method of thinking, nor even is it a method of thinking peculiar to science. It is, after all, what any kind of abstraction necessarily entails to some degree, and abstraction at some level or another is an essential tool of thinking, not only in science but also in everyday life. In other words, we all use models all the time, models of our own social relationships and groupings, of cultural behaviour, of the structure of the universe, and so on. Some appropriate in some contexts and some in others, they are all among the necessary intellectual tools of human living and, being part of our collective heritage, they are social facts and as such appropriate for anthropological study. In attempting to isolate and analyse the various home-made models of their own society used by certain Chinese fishermen in Hong Kong, then, this paper does no more than attempt an investigation into a small part of the culturally standardized intellectual tool-kit with which they confront their world.

The model which I describe first below, and which I am calling their 'immediate home-made model' (or immediate conscious model), is rather like a map, or perhaps a better analogy, a blueprint. On it are plotted the social groupings which these Chinese fishermen recognize. In themselves maps and blueprints are simply diagrams. Any instructions as to their use in getting from place to place or putting the parts together are additional. So with this model. It includes no references to rules of behaviour. It is simply an abstract plan of a number of interlinked groupings. It is, moreover, a plan of the general kind which readers of Evans-Pritchard's classic study of the Nuer will recognize at once, for it is a radially reckoned Ego-centred plan, much like the one drawn by him to explain one aspect of the view of their world as it is seen by his Nuer informants (Evans-Pritchard, 1940:114).

My informant was Mr. Chung Fuk-Shun, aged about forty-three, a fisherman turned shopkeeper, who lived in the village of Kau Sai, which is situated on a small island of the same name in the Port Shelter area of the eastern waters of Hong Kong. Barely literate, like most of his fellow villagers, Fuk-Shun has a rather wider outlook than they have, although most of his views are shared by them. Thus, though in detail any Ego-centred, radially reckoned system must be unique, my field data make it certain that in general terms the abstraction which is Fuk-Shun's immediate home-made model is closely similar to the other abstractions which are the immediate home-made models used by all his fellow villagers (and, what is more, by many, if not most, of the other Chinese fishermen in Hong Kong). In other words, models made from the points of view of the other fishermen in the same village very nearly coincide with this one, even in detail, and are certainly congruent in their broad outlines.

Looking outwards radially, with himself at the centre point, Fuk-Shun sees a number of groupings of which he is a member, some encapsulating others, some separate, and a number of other groupings of which he is not a member. First (the ethnographic present refers to the year 1953) there is his own family of procreation, a residential unit comprising himself, his wife, unmarried son and unmarried daughter. Second there is his 'brother group', siblings of the same sex as himself, together with their respective families of procreation. There are seven brothers altogether, all descended from one father and mother now deceased; the brothers are still living formally undivided.[1] These are the only two significant kinship units he sees: one residential, one not, but both including some shared economic basis (in the former a completely shared budget, in the latter only certain shared capital). Both groups are proclaimed by Fuk-Shun to be strongly solidary, but the second is ruefully admitted to be in fact on the verge of division. The residential group has a clear focus of authority (in himself); the brother group has no such clear focus (the eldest brother's primacy being only nominal).

Fuk-Shun does not see himself as belonging to a lineage.[2] Even the son of his father's full brother, living in the same village, is described simply as having the same surname; the relationship is described as being 'very distant' and there certainly is no common kin group membership recognized on any

[1] On the death of a father, each of his male issue is entitled to an equal share of his estate, but the actual division may not take place for several years, especially if there is felt to be any economic advantage in keeping the estate together. To remain 'undivided' is to gain considerable prestige, and to approach the fishermen's own ideoloical model of what is truly 'Chinese' behaviour.

[2] For the lack of lineage development among the fishermen of South China see *supra* pp. 29-30 and pp. 51-55.

occasion. Thus Fuk-Shun recognizes only two groups which are defined in kinship terms.

The non-kin groups to which he sees himself belonging are also few. First there is the village as a whole: Kau Sai. He may describe himself as a Kau Sai man, or refer, as he does very frequently, to 'our bay' as a membership unit. This includes all people for whom Kau Sai bay is a permanent anchorage, or who have houses ashore there. Clearly demarcated territorially, at a distance of at least 35 minutes by motorized junk from any other settlement, Kau Sai is certainly a community in the usual sociological sense of the word—an area of common life. The group of villagers has no shared economic basis, but the anchorage itself, the water supply (which is excellent), the flat places for drying nets and fish and so forth—these provide a common material base. Village solidarity, which is strong, finds ritual expression in the temple of the local fishermen's god. This temple, prettily sited and with good geomantic influences, is well cared for, and is a matter of explicit local pride. Once a year it is the scene of a five-day festival, the magnitude of which (it is popular well beyond the bounds of Kau Sai) is also a source of pride. The festival requires a good deal of organization, including the control of perhaps up to 10,000 visitors and the collection and disbursement of ten to fifteen thousand Hong Kong dollars.[3] All this is organized entirely by the fishermen, except that the Colony's water police sometimes look in during the excitement. There is no doubt at all that Fuk-Shun and the other Kau Sai people recognize the existence of their village as a group.

But it is equally certain that they do not see other wider, more embracing groups beyond it. Instead, looking beyond 'our bay', Fuk-Shun sees simply 'other places'. There are other villages fairly similar to his own, but of course inferior. There are agricultural villages too, both Hakka- and Cantonese-speaking.[4] There is the local market town and the three major fish market centres on or near Hong Kong island itself. There is also the district office which is situated in Kowloon. There are further Hong Kong islands, of course, and those which belong to China and the Chinese mainland. Indeed Fuk-Shun has seen and heard quite a lot about the great world. He does not see Kau Sai as in any way subordinate to any of these places; they are simply different. They are not 'our bay'; they are 'un-Kau Sai'. It is not that he has no relationships with people in other places—he certainly does. These include affinal relationships, market relationships, friendships, loan association relationships, and so on; but they are all (even including most relationships with the administration) conceived of purely in person-to-person terms. In other words,

[3] £1 sterling is equivalent to $H.K.16.

[4] These are the two most widely spoken Chinese languages in the Colony. Cantonese is dominant.

beyond the village level Fuk-Shun sees only sets and networks of dyadic relationships. (The Hong Kong government, of course, has quite a different view; but more of that later.)

So far I have been describing the very simple immediate home-made model of his own social system which a Kau Sai person constructs. Obviously, I too, as an anthropologist, constructed my own model of the same system, mine being what Lévi-Strauss would call an 'observer's model'. Up to this stage my observer's model and Fuk-Shun's home-made model are almost identical. As an observer, however, I detected a quite definite pattern in the extra-village dyadic relationships. In other words, I can draw on a map an outline of the area within which nearly all of the relationships fall. So demarcated the outline defines an unmistakable 'territory'[5] within which there is intensity of relationships and beyond which very few strands go. Basically, this territory is a market area. Fuk-Shun does not normally conceptualize this territory. I say not normally because if pressed, and I have questioned him and others quite carefully on this matter, he will agree that such a territory can be discerned. But it does not form part of the home-made model with which he normally operates. It is in any case not a social group; it is only a mappable area, the boundaries of which form the limits of most intense socio-economic interaction. Its population is in no sense a membership unit, but simply a kind of pool, from which the individuals within the territory draw most of their extra-village contacts. (It is relevant to add that it is not recognized in the administration's model which is described below, but in fact overlaps two different administrative districts and a small part of the Chinese coast line too.)

The question then arises: if Fuk-Shun's home-made model does not include this wider 'territory' which an observer can record, does he see himself as belonging to any groupings beyond the boundaries of Kau Sai, the village itself? If the question means: 'does he see himself by virtue of being a Kau Sai man in specific relationships with other people either in other or more embracing units?' the answer is that he does not. In other words he does not see Kau Sai encapsulated within another larger unit, nor does he see himself as a representative of Kau Sai *vis-à-vis* other similar or higher levels of organization. On the other hand, if the question means: 'does he see himself as belonging to any units which either lie outside or spread across the boundaries of Kau Sai?' the answer is that he does. Some of these units are the simple dyads mentioned earlier—official, friendship, economic relations—these including both fairly permanent and relatively shortlived relationships.

[5] *Supra* p. 53.

Some are groups. For example, he belongs to one or two loan associations comprising ten or a dozen members, some Kau Sai people and some not; these are usually fairly short-lived groupings, forming and reforming with different membership. There is also his particular friendship group, a trio formed by himself and two shopkeepers, one Hakka and one Cantonese, land-men who live in different towns outside Kau Sai (but within Kau Sai's 'territory'). The three meet quite frequently, used to travel together when younger, and now provide each other with hospitality, financial aid, business contacts, and so on; they always speak of each other with great warmth. In these various ways Chung Fuk-Shun perceives relationships involving him in rights and obligations outside his village, but involving him in each case as an individual and not as a representative in any sense of either a kinship or local grouping.[6]

This, then, is the total extent of his home-made model of his own social groupings and relationships. It is obviously the model of a very simple system, with few types of grouping and little differentiation of roles. Not a few so-called primitive societies could show a good deal more complexity.

There are, however, two things to be added. The first concerns the administration. However much the villagers may see their village as a separate unit, and their relationships outside as purely personal, the bureaucracy certainly does not agree with them. For it, Kau Sai is just one of a number of villages lying in one of the districts of the Leased (New) Territories. At the time to which this account refers (1953) there were four such districts. Each district is under the control of a District Officer who, in turn, is responsible to the District Commissioner, the administrative officer in charge of the New Territories as a whole, *ex officio* a member of the Legislative and Executive Councils of the Colony and directly responsible to the Governor. Looking downwards, so to speak, from the top, the bureaucracy sees Kau Sai as just

[6]It should be noted that this paper refers to the situation as I believe it to have been in 1953. Ten years later it had changed a good deal. By then, recent patterns of emigration as well as the now very obvious political demarcation between Chinese and British territory and waters had made meaningful the wider territorial unit known as Hong Kong, in which Kau Sai was situated. In other words, a diagram of Chung Fuk-Shun's immediate model as it existed in 1963 would have to include an extra solid line circle surrounding the circle labelled Kau Sai bay. The broken line circle labelled Kau Sai's 'territory' should then be drawn eccentrically, to allow for the fact that a part of this 'territory' lapped over into the Chinese areas. The difference between 1953 and 1963 is best illustrated by the fact that whereas in 1953 few parents had bothered to register their children's births, in 1963 all parents made a point of doing so: the object being to secure the right to a British passport and thus the chance of emigration to join the stream of Chinese restaurant workers which has flowed out from Hong Kong during the past decade.

one unit alongside other similar units, within a district, and this district within a larger unit, the New Territories, which in its turn is comprised within the Crown Colony of Hong Kong and ultimately within the total framework of the British Commonwealth. The two models are very different.

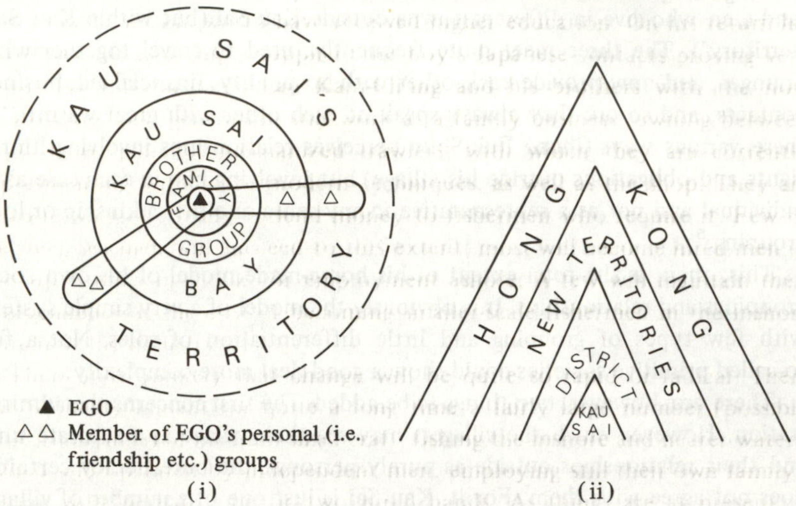

Figure 1. Immediate conscious models: (i) Kau Sai version, (ii) administrative version.

Most of the time, in fact, administration and village do not come into contact, and Kau Sai people can and do carry on *as if* their immediate home-made models were true statements about the actual structure. But occasionally relationships with the bureaucracy have to be entered into on behalf of the village as a whole: once a year at the festival various licences are required, occasionally public works have to be undertaken, and so on. In other words, action in terms of social groupings which the villagers' ordinary immediate model does not envisage is sometimes required. For the duration of such crisis situations Fuk-Shun and his friends are obliged to recognize the existence of the bureaucrats' model, and to act in respect of it. This is an important point to which I return below.

The second matter to add here concerns not the administrative framework but the cultural one. It has just been stated that Fuk-Shun does not normally see himself as a member of any groupings which encapsulate Kau Sai. Nevertheless, in discussing, say, wedding customs or manners, or religious beliefs, or ways of dressing, eating and so on, he may mention two or three other *categories* of people to whose practices those of Kau Sai are seen by him to conform. 'We water-people', he may say, or 'we Cantonese', or, probably most frequently when talking to a western enquirer, 'we Chinese'. Which of these designations he uses depends entirely upon the context and the matter under discussion. Indeed, in matters of wedding customs, for example, he might contrast 'our water-people on the east side of Hong Kong' who act thus and thus, with 'those people on the west side of Hong Kong' who do so and so.

The question then arises, what kind of units do these more embracing terms refer to? For Fuk-Shun and his friends, normally speaking, 'the water-people', 'the Cantonese', and 'the Chinese' are not groups to which they belong in the sense that membership gives them certain rights and obligations; they are not membership units at all. Instead they are simply categories of people with whom the people of Kau Sai class themselves because they share certain cultural attributes with them. Similarly, Fuk-Shun's notion of the Hakka, say, or the foreigners (westerners) is not a notion of other structural groups over against which his own structural group stands in relationships of opposition or apposition, but of other culturally distinctive categories of people with whom he does not class himself because he does not share their distinctive attributes.

So Fuk-Shun's home-made model may be said to have a cultural dimension which stretches much further than its structural dimension. This is, after all, a common situation—there are many tribal societies, too, with local units which are entirely autonomous, politically and structurally, whose members are yet conscious of their cultural uniformity, or at least similarity, with the members of other local groups. The difference is, of course, that, whereas in most tribal societies the wide cultural similarity is, in fact, only a wide cultural similarity, in China, the cultural category 'we Chinese' does in fact, though not in Fuk-Shun's immediate home-made model, coincide with an actual political unit with administrative machinery and all that this implies. Moreover, even the poorest and least educated Chinese fisherman does have in his mind another conscious model, the one I have previously called his ideological model, which does include these wider more embracing Chinese groups. Just as he knows there is a British bureaucrats' model, so also he knows that there is (or rather was) a (traditional) Chinese bureaucrats' model too.

However, before discussing the significance of the two different bureaucratic models (present-day British and traditional Chinese) that the fishermen know about but do not normally operate with, it is necessary to consider the third kind of home-made model whose existence was postulated at the outset of this paper: namely, what were there called 'internal observers' models'. The fishermen of Kau Sai are well aware that the water-people, among whom they class themselves, are only a small minority of the total population of even that small portion of the geographical area of China which is the Crown

Colony of Hong Kong. They know that there are many other kinds of Chinese, speaking different dialects, following different occupations, often with different customs and social arrangements. Indeed, they come into contact with representatives of a number of them almost every day; they observe them, gossip about them and interact with them. Because the Kau Sai people see other Chinese from the outside, so to speak, the models they have of their customs and social arrangements can appropriately be called *observers'* models; but because these people are also 'Chinese', and are known by the Kau Sai people to be members of the same overall cultural category as themselves, it is appropriate to call these models *internal* observers' models. As 'Chinese', both a Cantonese-speaking fishermen and a Hakka-speaking farmer, for instance, are 'insiders'—hence the adjective 'internal'—but *vis-à-vis* the other, each is respectively an 'outsider'—hence the term 'observer'.

Now all observers' models are alike in one respect; that is, by definition they are made by outsiders. Thus, as observers' models, the fishermen's models of the farmers' social arrangements (or the farmers' of the fishermen's) are in one fundamental sense the same kind of general constructs as the observers' models made by any other outsiders—such as social anthropologists, for example—however much they may differ in presentation and (perhaps) in analytical insight. Similarly, as observers' models they are fundamentally of the same kind as the other observers' models they themselves make: say, for example, their models of British or Japanese social arrangements, which they also see from the outside.

The reader will remember that the models described here so far do no more than plot groupings and their interconnexions. Kau Sai people are aware that some of the groupings they can perceive among other Chinese do not exist in their own immediate social system; corporate lineages, for example, common among both Cantonese- and Hakka-speaking landsmen in this area, they do not have. Certain associational groupings, and business relationships, and certain somewhat more formal village governmental organisations they also lack. Their internal observers' models of, say, a Cantonese farming village's social arrangements does not resemble in all points their immediate working model of their own system. Though not informed in all matters of detail, they are aware that there are differences.

(And if, for the sake of illustration, we shift our ground for a moment and, instead of a model plotting social groupings and their interconnections only, describe a different kind of model, a more 'realistic' one perhaps, which includes stereotypes about behaviour, even more striking differences appear—differences which often in fact provide the basis for a good deal of fairly innocent merriment, when Kau Sai's best mimic puts on his impersonations of this, that or the other landlubber, or British civil servant or foreign missionary.)

There are still two more points to be made about these home-made internal observers' models before the main argument is picked up again. The first concerns, once more, the sense in which they are 'internal'; the second their practical use.

It has just been stated that, for example, Hakka-speaking land-people and Cantonese-speaking boat-people both know themselves to be insiders in a single overall cultural entity which can be summed up in the phrase 'both are Chinese'. So they do, and so they are. Yet they speak mutually unintelligible languages, have many different customs and, as has just been shown, have only broadly similar types of social structure. In what sense, then, are they both 'Chinese'? Or, rather what is to be understood by their mutual 'Chinese-ness'? It cannot be in the political sense at the present time, for the individuals of both the groups we are discussing here all live in a British colony, and most of them carry British passports. We cannot even postulate that the immediate home-made models of both sets of people, admittedly different in detail, yet plot the same overarching corporate unit which they call 'China', because we have seen that the fisherman's immediate model contains no such embracing figure, and it is at least highly doubtful that the immediate home-made models of their own social system made by most Hakka land-people in the New Territories of Hong Kong contain such a figure either.

Nevertheless, both Hakka and fishermen's models would show in the cultural dimension a single overall cultural category—of the kind described above—to which both would subscribe. They both say 'we Chinese', not in the sense of 'we fellow members of an organized group', not referring at all to shared rights and obligations, but simply to shared attributes: 'we Chinese do thus and thus: you foreigners do so and so'. And in cultural terms, despite the differences there are, of course, in actuality many more similarities between the Hakka farmers and the Cantonese boat-people, or indeed any other Chinese-speaking people, than there are between, say, the boat-people and the British or any other foreigners.

These similarities, and the fact that they are fitted into more or less well-known internal observers' models, mean that it is often quite easily possible for a Chinese of one category to move into another. Kau Sai people do sometimes leave home and take up residence and a job ashore, as, for example, Cantonese shop assistants or wives of salaried workers. And when they do this, their erstwhile observers' models of Cantonese land society become the framework, so to speak, of their new immediate models as they *become* Cantonese landspeople. This process, which I have observed more than once, is closely similar to the phenomenon of 'passing' in certain multi-racial situations. It has never been rare and is becoming fairly frequent at the present time. As a Cantonese landsman, then, an ex-Kau Sai boat-man develops his new, land-dwelling Cantonese immediate model of his new social position, and, provided he is allowed to do so by other Cantonese landspeople, he can become a Cantonese landsman. Meanwhile his old Kau Sai model, though obviously it is not entirely forgotten, becomes inoperative for the time being, and unless or until he returns to his old life it takes on the status of an internal observers' (i.e. outsiders') model—rather especially detailed, it is true, but no more than that.

This is only one of the various practical uses of home-made observers' models. A Kau Sai man does not have to go to the length of adopting a Cantonese landsman's way of life in order to make use of his model of the Cantonese system. Almost every day he is in contact with Cantonese (and with Hakka) over business—selling fish, buying goods, raising loans and so on. A good deal of this business is conducted in tea houses and similar places. Partly because both parties have a number of 'Chinese' attitudes and values in common, but partly also because each is aware of the other's social position—each carries an observers' model of the other's system in his mind—they are quite easily able to interact. One can hear different parties gossiping at times: 'of course with the boat-people . . .' or 'of course these land-people . . .'.

Now when it comes to inter-relationships with the administration a somewhat similar situation prevails. The Kau Sai people, whose normal immediate model of their own social system is different from the British administration's model, know enough about the administration's model to be able to act in respect of it when necessary. In other words, they also have an observers' model of the present administrative system, they know its broad outlines and, when they have to, they can fit their actions to it. When they do so, however, it is their *ad hoc* action, not their own immediate model, which is fitted to the administration's view. They apply for licences, pay taxes, even elect so-called village representatives, but they continue in their own immediate model to regard the relationships so set up between them and various individuals in the government's service in the purely dyadic terms described earlier. The importance of knowing and getting on well with individual government servants is well understood; the significance of the administration's attempts to build local self-government in an articulated series of local groupings at different levels hardly at all.

Despite the fact that Kau Sai lies clearly within the political boundaries of a British colony, the conscious observers' model which its people have of the British administration and its view of the local socio-political structure would be more aptly termed an external than an internal observers' model. We noted earlier the way in which their immediate model of their own corporate groups stopped short at the boundaries of Kau Sai itself. It does not normally include any of the administratively defined districts or the Colony as a whole.

Moreover, the administration remains usually in conversation with a Westerner: 'your administration', or often in conversation among themselves: 'the foreign [lit: "devil"] administration'. For both these reasons it seems appropriate to regard Kau Sai's model of the British administrative structure as an outsider's model, or rather in the terminology employed here a (conscious) external observers' model. The significance of this designation will become clear in the discussion which follows.

We can now return to our consideration of the two different bureaucratic systems, traditional Chinese and present-day British, which the Kau Sai people know about. It is my belief that the actual relationship between the villagers and the traditional bureaucracy was very similar to their actual relationship with its present-day successor. It is obvious that the boundaries of administrative districts and their names, the titles of officials and their ranks, and the degree and quality of administration before and after 1898 were different; but the immediate models of their own administrative systems used by present-day British and traditional literati are both of the same general bureaucratic order. Furthermore, the bureaucratic apparatuses of both stop short of the village level—at the district office for the one and at the *yamen* for the other. In traditional times, as now, non-literati villagers would have had little contact with officialdom, and would have done, as they now do, everything possible to make that little even less. Most of the time they did not, as they do not, have to see any contact between their own immediate models of the social structure and the bureaucrats'. But on the rare occasions when contact was necessary, they too had another model ready to hand, one which told them enough about the bureaucrats' system for them to be able to act within its context. In this, as in other ways, it is arguable that the actual structural situation of Kau Sai has altered remarkably little since the British took over control in 1898.

But whether or not their actual structural situation is different, and whatever the similarities between the immediate models used by the people of Kau Sai then and now, there is no doubt that their models of the two bureaucracies would show important differences in kind if not in content. We have just explained how they see the present-day British bureaucracy from right outside; their model of it is a home-made (i.e. conscious) external observers' model. But the traditional system must have been known to be 'Chinese', and their home-made (i.e. conscious) observers' model of it has therefore to be classed with other internal observers' models. This is another way of saying that the British are known to be foreigners and the literati were known to be Chinese, but it is possible to add something more. It should be noted here that the term 'observers' model' refers not to the extent to which a model so classified is derived from actual observation, but to the fact that it is a model made from an observer's point of view, i.e., from 'outside'. It is the point of view that is essential to understanding this concept; observation, as such, is not necessarily involved. Part—probably the greater part—or any conscious observers' model is embedded in the people's cultural heritage, accepted from the say-so of others rather than observed afresh by each generation. There is no reason to suppose that this was not true of the internal observers' models used by Kau Sai people in the nineteenth century. But it has to be remembered that the Kau Sai people, like other Chinese, also had another model of their bureaucracy, one which was part of what I have earlier called their ideological model. Although conceptually quite distinct, the fact that these two models referred to the same actual structure and were learned about in much the same way must have meant that in practice they were often confused—at least by the unsophisticated. Thus it is possible to suggest that before 1898 the home-made observers' model the Kau Sai people had of the bureaucratic system under which they lived differed from the model their present-day descendants have of the British system, not only in content and in being an internal, not an external, model, but also in being, at least to some extent, merged with a part of their ideological model.

This, the second of the three types of conscious model listed at the outset of this article, was described fairly fully in my previous article.* The description is not repeated here, but in the light of what has now been put forward about the other two types of conscious model it seems necessary to add a few words about the relationships between all the three types.

Lévi-Strauss' original distinction was between 'conscious' or home-made models and 'observers' ' models. My hypothesis is that Kau Sai fishermen (and I assume many other Chinese too) hold in their minds at least three conceptually distinguishable kinds of conscious (home-made) model of the social structural situation in which they live. These I term respectively:

1. their immediate model
2. their ideological model
3. their observers' models, which can be sub-divided into
    a internal observers' models
    b external observers' models.

The distinction between the immediate model and the observers' models has been made clear above; the distinction between the immediate model and the ideological model formed part of the subject matter of the article just mentioned. It remains to consider the distinction between the ideological model and the observers' models.

*'Varieties of the Conscious Model: The Fishermen of South China', *supra* pp. 41-60.

It has been suggested to me that it would be more logical to classify type 2 and type *3a* together since they share the important attribute of 'Chinese-ness' and are therefore both to be thought of as what one might call inside observers' models. This would still leave three types of conscious model, but they would be differently sub-divided. Although this is obviously a possible cross-classification which might be useful in certain contexts, I consider that in most kinds of analysis it would be more likely to lead to confusion than add to clarity; for the significance of this similarity is to my mind altogether outweighed by the fundamental difference which exists between any construct that is endowed with the power of ideology and any other that is merely noted. In other words, the conscious ideological model is the model which stands as the 'ideal' in the usual anthropological sense; that is, it represents what 'ought' to be, what is proper in the eyes of the people under study. And because of this it must differ in status from a mere observers' model, for it is in fact used as the yardstick to measure the moral rightness or otherwise of the systems which are merely seen from the outside. It is surely not illogical to insist that the model which is the measure of value for other models must by that very fact of its nature be placed in a different category from them—even though there may be some contexts in which other criteria for classification may be more appropriate and useful.

I shall now consider some of the ways in which the proposition that several different kinds of conscious model can be conceptually distinguished may be useful in further analysis.

Some of its possible uses in helping to elucidate processes in a particular social system have been demonstrated here. The earlier brief mention of the ways in which people of one Chinese sub-culture can make use of their own observers' models of other Chinese sub-cultures, and of foreign cultures too, was one example. This idea, which is obviously applicable to the study of any social system, has something in common with the well-known notion of stereotype. I should like to suggest, however, that the notion of conscious (home-made) observers' models is more flexible and potentially more useful. The concept of stereotype is usually employed to explain uniformity in attitudes and behaviour between the members of two social units whose contact is limited—with consequent limitations upon their mutual knowledge. The concept of conscious observers' model is not so limited either in scope or in content. People in all kinds of social unit make observers' models (of some kind) of all the other social units of which they are aware, no matter how frequent or infrequent the contact with them. Thus this concept allows for the inclusion of greater or lesser degrees of knowledge about, as well as differences in affect towards, the 'other fellow's' social situation, and at the same time it admits a more positive approach to the study of inter-unit relationships in the manner illustrated above.

It would, I think, also be possible to claim that the device of distinguishing between an immediate and an ideological model has enabled us to see the nature of Chinese society more clearly by showing that members of Chinese sub-cultural groups have in their ideological models (however rudimentary and even disjointed these may be) a yardstick by which to evaluate not only other Chinese sub-cultures but also their own (as well as, of course, foreign cultures). And we can understand—although it has not been demonstrated here—that Chinese in the position of Kau Sai fishermen, for instance, can enjoy a high degree of tolerance, for they know that in any case the 'proper' system (the ideological model) is different from their own (the immediate model as well as the actuality). One might expect that at the upper levels of Chinese society the literati, whose immediate and ideological models more nearly coincided, might well have shown more rigidity. It is a hypothesis that could be tested. Its implications might also prove of value in the study of other social systems besides those of China.

The main theme of my previous paper was the hypothesis that throughout China and throughout most of China's history ideological models were essentially similar, and that this is one of the facts that help to explain the uniquely long continuity and wide similarity of the Chinese socio-cultural system. This hypothesis is implicitly comparative. One is bound to ask: what, then, was the situation in other such systems? How were they different? Why? With what concomitants?

There is, of course, another set of concepts which has been widely used in the study of India and other peasant societies. This is Redfield's notion of Great and Little Traditions (Redfield, 1962).[7] It was Redfield's thesis that it is the existence of a Great Tradition which all recognize and respect (however different from it the Little Traditions of their local sub-cultures may be) that distinguishes a peasant from a tribal culture. It has been suggested to me that Redfield's Great Tradition and my ideological model are similar concepts. Certainly they are reminiscent of one another, but they are not, I think, identical. A Great Tradition belongs with at least some degree of literacy, learning, metropolitan culture—in short with all the phenomena that are usually summed up in the word 'civilization'—but ideological models are produced in all kinds of human societies. One can safely assume that the members of even the most isolated, small, and technologically limited human

[7] Redfield 1962 is a reprint of an article published in 1950 (*Measure* 1,60-74), one of the earliest of his many references to the concept of the Great and Little Traditions, which appears worked out in more detail in several other papers in the same volume: see especially the paper entitled 'Community Studies in Japan and China: A Symposium', first published in *Far east. Q.* 14:1 and reprinted in Redfield (1962), 302-10.

groups have ideas about the 'proper' way of ordering their social arrangements; this conscious ideological model may or may not be closely similar to the way in which their society is actually structured (as the anthropologist sees it . . .) or to the everyday immediate model with which they themselves commonly work, but if the community is an isolated one it will certainly have no connection with any Great Tradition. On the other hand, the members of a community living within the boundaries (culturally or politically defined) of a Great Tradition—a community such as Kau Sai, for example—may, as Kau Sai has, have an ideological model that corresponds to *some parts of* that Great Tradition. The significant words here are 'some parts of', for, as I understand it, the Great Traditions are not conceived of as models of social systems but as repositories of knowledge, religion, history, cosmology, literature, morals and so on. Such storehouses of wisdom may include ideological models of the social systems to which they appertain in much the same way as a library may contain maps of the district on which it is situated, but just as it does not make sense to equate maps with libraries so we cannot argue that ideological models and Great Traditions are the same things.

Nor can the two concepts be used in the same way. The concept of the Great Tradition is useful for description, and for comparing different types of cultural situation, degrees of conformity to the Great Tradition, and, of course, the content and compatibility of Great and Little Traditions both within and between societies; but as we have seen, its analytical usefulness is limited to the study of 'civilizations' and their influence, and it can contribute nothing, as it stands, to the comparative study of social structures. But that part of a Great Tradition which corresponds to the ideological model is not so limited. This latter concept may, therefore, prove rather more useful in certain types of analysis.

It remains, finally, to consider the place of the study of conscious models in general social anthropology. Although there have been many honourable exceptions, it is still true to say that too many writers have too often failed to distinguish clearly enough between the home-made and the anthropologist's models. To describe this simply as a failure to distinguish the ideal from the actual seems to me to oversimplify the issues and miss a good deal that is significant. This is not the place to argue what is meant by 'the actual' or discuss the ambiguity in the word 'ideal'. It is better to avoid both expressions and talk instead of anthropologists' models and home-made or conscious models, to recognize the possibility that there may well be a variety of both sorts, and that more subtle analyses may require their separate consideration.

Much recent discussion turns on problems of cognition and, in particular, following Lévi-Strauss, on questions of native cosmology, myth, symbolism and so on. The study of conscious models is a poor relation in such company, but it does have something to say about people's own ideas about their own social situation and what they themselves consider to be directly relevant to it.[8]

REFERENCES

Evans-Pritchard, E. E. 1940. *The Nuer.* Oxford: Clarendon Press.

Lévi-Strauss, C. 1953. 'Social Structure'. In A. L. Kroeber (ed.), *Anthropology to-day.* Chicago: Chicago U. P.

Nadel, S. F. 1951. *The Foundations of Social Anthropology.* London: Cohen & West.

Redfield, R. 1962. 'Social Science Among the Humanities'. In Margaret Park Redfield (ed.), *Human Nature and the Study of Society: The Papers of Robert Redfield*, 1. Chicago: Chicago U. P.

Ward, B. E. 1965. 'Varieties of the Conscious Model: The Fishermen of South China'. In M. Banton (ed.), *The Relevance of Models for Social Anthropology* (Ass. Soc. Anthrop. Monogr. 1). London: Tavistock Publications.

[8] Field work in Hong Kong was carried out in the years 1950-53, 1969-60 and 1963, thanks to generous grants from H. M. Treasury (under the Scarborough Committee), U.N.E.S.C.O., the Hayter Committee and the London-Cornell Project for Chinese and South East Asian Studies.

5. Folk Models, Decision, and Change

By the early nineteen sixties the fishing industry of Hong Kong stood on the threshold of a second stage of development.[1] Mechanization of the existing types of vessel had been the first stage. Official policy was now to push ahead into the next. Technologically this was possible; politically, administratively, and economically it seemed highly desirable. Because for both ideological and pragmatic reasons compulsion was out of the question, and because approximately 95% of Hong Kong's fishing vessels remained owner operated, the answer to the question whether or not the policy would succeed depended upon the separate, private decisions of almost 5,000 individual master-fishermen.[2]

This paper arose out of an attempt to understand why the initial response to the new innovations was slow. The emphasis in an earlier version (written in 1970-71 and submitted to the Department of Agriculture, Forestry, and Fisheries for discussion but not published) was on development and decision making, and the argument relied heavily upon the notion of the definition of the situation, first developed by W. I. Thomas (Thomas and Znanieki, 1918; Thomas and Thomas, 1928; Merton, 1968). Although the case-studies below are exactly the same as those that were discussed in the earlier version, this present paper is less narrowly focussed. Taking my bearings partly from two previous articles of my own (1966 and 1967), but much were importantly from Garfinkel (1974) and Berger and Luckman (1966), I wish to discuss the

[1] The fieldwork on which this study was based was carried out during the summer of 1967 while I was employed as a Leverhulme Exchange Professor at The Chinese University of Hong Kong. My thanks are due to the Chinese University, to the Trustees of the Leverhulme Trust and to the authorities at the School of Oriental and African Studies, University of London who arranged the details of this exchange. I also wish to express my gratitude to the Department of Agriculture, Forestry, and Fisheries in Hong Kong without whose patient assistance and encouragement none of my studies of Chinese fishing communities would have been possible.

[2] The records of the Department of Agriculture, Forestry, and Fisheries of the Government of Hong Kong show nearly 10,000 fishing vessels in Hong Kong waters in the early sixties. Of these nearly 50% were mechanized. The almost 5,000 of the text refers to the masters of mechanized vessels only.

relationship of decision-making to what I shall refer to hereafter as 'folk models'. Further than that, I shall also discuss some of the reasons why it is possible for people to take decisions which appear to imply that they have accepted and internalized radical alterations to their folk-models without their having done anything of the sort in fact.

For the purposes of the present paper I began by working with two concepts which I am labelling Folk Model (upper case initials) and personal model (lower case initials) respectively. The difference between them is rather like the difference between 'langue' and 'parole'. A people's Folk Model is, in effect, their whole culture seen from the 'emic' point of view. Thus it includes 'values' and 'beliefs' as well as folk taxonomies, cosmologies, etc. and all the native knowledge of the practice and theory of the objects and patterns of everyday living, economic, political, kinship, and religious behaviour and so on and so forth. A Folk Model in this sense is, of course, a construct, but it is not simply an invention made by outside observers; natives also assume that something of the sort exists, and refer to it by some such phrase as 'our customs', 'our way', etc. It is, however, unlikely that any one native carries his/her Folk Model 'in his/her head'; rather, he/she posits it as existing 'out there' and then refers his/her actual behaviour, statements etc. to it. ('We do this/that in this/that way because our customs are thus/so.')

The individual natives' own 'models', 'carried in their heads' are here called their 'personal models'. These are the operative *models of* and *models for* used in everyday living for explanation and justification to oneself and others, by means of which one understands the world, and by references to which one makes decisions. Asked, a native may well be unable to describe the relationship between his personal model(s) and his peoples' Folk Model, in much the same way as a native speaker who constantly uses 'parole' may well be unable to describe the grammar of his peoples' 'langue'.

One or two further points of conceptual clarification may help to make the steps of the argument about decision-making that follows plain. First, people take decisions about specific matters in specific situations. The distinction between 'matters' and 'situations' is significant. 'Matter' refers to the topic about which the decision is to be made; 'situation' to the perceived position (social, economic, political, personal etc.) of the decision-maker and the perceived constraints within which and pressures under which he is making his decision. Second, assuming that decision-makers are reasonable men and women within the limitations of what Garfinkel calls the 'rationalities of everyday life', I assume further not only that they are capable of deciding but also that they normally do decide upon courses of action which are in accordance with the rationalities of their everyday lives as they see them. In other words, given freedom to choose, a person's decision on a given matter and in a given situation depends on (*a*) how he himself interprets (defines) the matter and his situation and (*b*) his evaluation of his own balance of advantages and disadvantages in the situation so defined. Normally (that is, for most decision-makers most of the time) both (*a*) and (*b*) must derive from the decision-makers' own personal models.

BACKGROUND TO DECISION: THE HONG KONG FISHING INDUSTRY IN THE MID-SIXTIES

For purposes of analysis the Hong Kong fishing fleets can be divided into two major sectors: deep-sea and inshore. Very roughly the division runs between those who fish inside and outisde territorial waters, Chinese as well as British. Quite considerable differences in degree of capitalization and size of income, as well as in size of vessels and types of technique employed, exist within each category.[3] By the early sixties both sectors were almost completely mechanized, but it was already becoming clear that there was a limit to the increase in productivity that could be brought about by mechanization of the local fishing junks alone.

The spectacular success of mechanization in the first ten or so years after World War II (Ward, 1967) both accounted for and masked a number of individual failures in both sectors. No records of failures are kept, but the annual returns for the overall numbers of fishing craft show a clear reduction in the sixties (Department of Agriculture and Fisheries, 1967). Too much should not be read into these figures, but some part of the decline was undoubtedly due to over-capitalization and subsequent withdrawal from fishing.[4] Brought up to be shrewd in all matters concerning money, most fishermen were, nevertheless, still ill-educated and inexperienced in handling

[3] The division into two sections is, adequate for most sociological purposes, though from a strictly technical point of view a threefold classification into inshore, middle-distance, and deep-sea fishermen would be more appropriate. The really wealthy master-fishermen are only to be found working deep-sea and sometimes middle-distance vessels; successful inshore men can make a more comfortable living than many of the poorer deep-sea trawlers.

[4] Other factors included: (*i*) the acceleration of a general move towards living on land, which for less successful fishermen often involved exchanging the uncertainties and dangers of fishing for the relative security of regular wage employment ashore; (*ii*) changes in certain techniques, consequent upon mechanization, such as that (for example) the same operation was now performed with a single boat instead of a pair, and in some cases specialization has decreased; (*iii*) labour difficulties for some of the deep-sea fishing masters (longliners), who, for lack of the necessary large, skilled crews, had to go out of the business altogether (cp. Ward, 1967). In the seventies, modern so-called multi-purposed vessels, using different methods of baiting and mechanized sampans and requiring fewer workers, returned to long-lining in fair numbers.

accounts. It is not surprising that in the first fine enthusiasm for mechanization some of them failed to understand the principle of diminishing returns.[5]

Failures apart, by the early sixties the limitations of even the most successful mechanization of existing types of craft were becoming obvious. In the early years of mechanization incomes had risen sharply, later the curves began to flatten out or even to fall. This was a general trend, which in the opinion of some officers of the Department of Agriculture, Forestry, and Fisheries at the time was exacerbated in the case of the inshore fishermen by the depletion of stocks.

For the inshore men mechanization had initially brought much bigger catches, largely because more operations could be carried out in a given period of time. It seemed obvious to the Department that this must also mean that the local inshore waters, already threatened with over-fishing in the later days of sail, were beginning to show serious signs of depletion. This threat was not eased by the contemporary local political situation which resulted both in a considerable influx of fishing craft from the neighbouring coastal districts of China,[6] and in the stricter administration of conditions imposed upon those who fished in Chinese territorial waters.[7] Fishermen who for one reason or another did not care to visit Chinese ports dared not fish in Chinese waters. Such men, being inshore fishermen with boats and gear unsuited to deep-sea work, had no alternative but to increase the over-fishing.

So far the matter has been presented as it appears to a Western outside investigator. Substantially the same view was taken by the officers of the Department of Agriculture and Fisheries in Hong Kong both British and Chinese, but by no means all the fishermen saw it in the same light. Their own or others' experience had made most of them aware of the more glaring dangers of over-capitalization, but almost as many remained too unsophisticated to understand the threat of gradually diminishing returns and very few agreed that there was any possibility of depletion of resources. Approaching the same matters, departmental officers and fishermen were operating with different conceptual frames of reference, in other words, with different folk models. As it is obvious that they were also in very different situations (both objectively and subjectively), it is necessary to consider them separately.

[5] For an example see Ward 1967, 285-86.

[6] This influx was particularly noticed in the middle and late fifties. Its effect on the statistics of the fishing population partially obscures the tendency to reduction noted in the text.

[7] Almost every local fishing vessel carries a license issued in China as well as one issued in Hong Kong. Many carry a Portuguese license from Macao, as well. Vessels which fish in Chinese waters have to sell a certain quota of their fish in the appropriate fishing communes.

DEPARTMENTAL DECISIONS

The departmental view of the state of the fishing industry as mechanization approached completion was quite similar to that outlined above. It derived ultimately from a twentieth century Western Folk Model, some relevant parts of which were based upon the biological sciences and systematic research and on recent developments in the technology of fishing (mainly as practised in Great Britain). It entailed two major decisions: to direct interest to deep-sea fishing, in order to offset the depletion of the inshore waters,[8] and to develop new equipment, in order to transcend the technological limitations inherent in the continued use of traditional hulls and methods of fishing.

By the early sixties both decisions had begun to bear fruit. Unfortunately the first breakthrough in deep-sea work following the explorations made by the department's own experimental vessel into the Gulf of Tong King, proved only temporary because of the Viet Nam war but it was fairly soon taken up again and was rapidly developed both to the north (near Taiwan) and to the south as soon as the fighting in Viet Nam came to an end. Meanwhile in the early sixties the technical experts produced their own trump card: a design for a wooden stern otter-trawler with an overall length of sixty-six feet. Intended for deep-sea work, it had a balanced steel rudder, thermally insulated storage facilities, and a modern trawl winch, and was to be powered by a 200 B.H.P. marine diesel engine.[9] A working model of this revolutionary vessel was put on display at the annual fisheries exhibition at Chinese New Year in 1962. The little boat chugged round and round a plastic pond, obligingly catching and releasing a small shoal of goldfish in a most engaging manner.

Thus far the decisions have been presented in terms of the department's understanding of the matters at stake in the fishing industry as such. In fact, however, these were not the only matters that had to be taken into consideration, for the department had a kind of dual mandate under which it was committed to serving the interests of the Colony at large as well as raising the standard of living of the fishermen. Recent and contemporary developments in the overall political and economic situation of Hong Kong had resulted in a governmental decision to press ahead still more vigorously with all programmes of social-economic betterment and also with attempts to make Hong Kong if not self-sufficient in foodstuffs (an impossible goal) at least somewhat

[8]Official thinking about over-fishing the inshore waters has varied from time to time with varying evidence. The opinion expressed here was often heard in the fifties, but in 1968 I was told that the department's views were much less definite. In the seventies the depletion of the inshore waters and pollution were frequent topics of discussion.

[9]The scale of the first prototype otter-trawlers was dictated largely by economic considerations. Later officially sponsored vessels have been larger, and the overall designs are subject to continual modification in the light of experience and research.

less dependent upon imports. At about the same time, the policies of the Peoples' Government in China and the activities of its local agents on the coasts and in the waters of Kwangtung were making it more and more desirable to try to divert fishermen from inshore to deep-sea fishing in order to avoid political incidents.

Here attention should be drawn to the situation in which members of the department took their decisions, and the fundamental differences between their situation and that of the fishermen. For the fishermen, even the idea that there was such a thing as government policy as a whole was vague or, much more probably, non-existent. Members of the department, however, not only knew about general policy but they were also directly subject to it. Although, unlike the fishermen's, their situation was not one in which their livelihood and their families' modes of living were at stake, it was inevitably a situation which involved their self-image (and, possibly, as they may have seen it, their hopes for future commendation and promotion). Consciously or non-consciously, an officer's view of his role as a responsible civil servant is an inescapable situational aspect of the process of decision-making in any government bureaucracy. As in this case, it is likely that virtually all the members of the Fisheries Department also gave full intellectual acceptance to the general policy, one can argue that the department's earlier decisions to concentrate upon the development of deep-sea fishing and radical technological change, which had been based on consideration of the matter of the fishing industry as such, were simply reinforced by their appreciation both of their own situation and of the demands of government policy as a whole.

In October 1960 a Fisheries Development Loan Fund was set up with a sum of $HK5,000,000. Much the largest of the loan funds issued to date, this money was specifically intended for the development of deep-sea fishing.[10] Moreover the rubric indicating the uses to which it could be put stated categorically that it was not only for the mechanization of existing vessels, installation of modern gear and aids etc. but also 'in special cases for the purchase of new vessels either of existing type or *of a prototype to be designed by the . . . department*' (Department of Agriculture and Fisheries 1966, my italics).

Nevertheless, up to December 31, 1964 although loans to the value of $HK3,928,216 had been made from this fund and thirty new vessels were in operation, no fisherman had agreed to order a stern otter-trawler.

[10] A previous loan fund with a total of $HK3,000,000 which had been set up in 1948 had been the major instrument of mechanization to date; other funds have since been added, until at the time of which I am writing more than $HK8.3 million were available for loans to fishermen. The exchange rate in March 1968 was approximately $HK6.12 per $US1.00.

THE FISHERMEN'S VIEW

It goes without saying that the situation of the local Hong Kong fishermen was both objectively and subjectively entirely different from that of the members of a government department, but, of course, the significant point here is that not only do the differences between the perceived situations of each party help to explain the differences between their decisions but that (because the decisions of one party, the department, were intended to affect the decisions of the other party, the fishermen) the subjective views of each about the fishermen's situation were also very different. In other words, basing their opinions each upon their own personal models (which, it must be remembered, include values) officials and fishermen produced contrasting evaluations of the latter's situation.

Whereas departmental officials continued to regard the fishermen's situation as precarious and predicted a decline in productivity, most fishermen in the mid-sixties were likely still to be rejoicing in the relative affluence which mechanization had brought rather than worrying over the possibility that the upward curve in their incomes might be flattening out. All could remember the toil and danger of the days of sail, the much greater poverty and all that it entailed. Many could recall the real hardships of the war years. Thus the successful ones tended to be content to stay as they were; the unsuccessful ones were seldom in a position to invest in new equipment anyway.

Mechanization, a fairly rapid process begun (with a few earlier examples) in the early fifties and more or less completed by about 1965, had been the result of relatively easy decision-making during which the major topics discussed among the fishermen had been income, initial finance, and safety. In that decision the fishermen had seen themselves as choosing to alter no more than the method of propulsion of their familiar vessels. They had not realized that in the long term fishing grounds and techniques, boat building methods, family living patterns, and economic relations in general would also be involved. The stern otter-trawler was different. The fact that its adoption must entail quite drastic changes in social and economic relationships was sufficiently obvious from the beginning. Unlike traditional junks, these new vessels could not double satisfactorily as family dwelling-places. Despite the increasing move towards shore dwelling which had characterized the last twenty years, it is possible that in 1967 well over half the fisher families still lived on their boats, which meant that for most people the change to stern otter-trawling would necessitate a change in family living patterns. Welcome though this might be, it would entail major domestic upheaval and add more expense for rent, furniture (boat families have almost none), and perhaps key-money to the already big outlay required for the new boat.

Equally drastic, and obvious from the beginning, were the concomitant changes in economic relationships. The new boats had to be built from plans, which had been drawn in the department. Only a few of the existing junk builders were competent to follow such plans, and the department (which put up the money) quite reasonably insisted on selecting the boat yards and supervising the construction. Traditionally fishermen have always chosen their own boat builders, and usually taken an active part in planning and construction. Frequently, too, the relationship between boat builder and boat-owner was of longstanding, and though primarily economic carried overtones of personal 'friendship (*kam-ch'ing* 感情). In the eyes of many fishermen in the sixties, departmental officers who warned prospective owners of stern otter-trawlers not to 'interfere' with the building plans for their own boats were themselves guilty of gross interference.

The problem that dominated the fishermen's debates, however, was the question of the magnitude and management of finance. In the late sixties a new stern otter-trawler, complete with gear and navigational equipment, cost around $HK250,000. Such a sum, though available from the department's loan funds, was beyond the normal range of even the most successful of the semi-traditional (i.e. mechanized) inshore fishermen, and its repayment would be likely to spread over many years, even granted good catches throughout that period. It was a widely expressed opinion that anyone who was willing to take such a risk was likely to be either a knave or a fool. Moreover, he would inevitably also give himself still more 'bother' (*ma faan* 麻煩) because (for almost the first time in Hong Kong's fishing history) such big loans as these had to be secured by mortgages on the boats, and covered by insurance.

Taken together all these changes and their repercussions add up to that alteration in the structure of the industry that I referred to above as the change from Stage I to Stage II. Fishermen did not think in terms of 'stages', but they were well aware that the adoption of stern-trawling would require, in addition to the technological changes, more radical transformations in their situation than many of them were prepared to risk.

For reasons which it is not necessary to detail here, the fishermen have the reputation of being the most 'traditional' part of the population of Hong Kong. Highly skilled in their specialized craft and brilliant sailors, most of them were totally without book learning until about 1920-30, and even then such schooling as a small minority among them obtained was confined to learning to read a few hundred characters, write a little, and do simple calculations. From 1947 onwards a number of schools for fishermen's children were opened, but in spite of these (and in spite of some missionary effort and the influence of the cinema, radio, and early T. V.), it is certain that by the mid-sixties very few fishermen—and they only among the younger generations—can have had any inkling of a 'scientific' model of the natural environment.

The traditional Folk Model of the universe to which most fishermen still subscribe has been well delineated by Anderson (1972). For present purposes it is enough to mention some of these parts of the Model which explain success and failure and the presence or absence of fish in the sea. Briefly, success and failure in fishing, as in other enterprises in human life, are attributed both to inherent individual skill and intelligence and to what in the common twentieth century Western Folk Model is called 'the supernatural'. It is highly doubtful whether traditional-minded fishermen think of the powers of the spirits (good ones: *shan* 神, and bad ones; *kwai* 鬼) and the ancestors (*tzo sin* 祖先) and the forces of Feng Shui 風水, to which they link also calendrical observances of several kinds and the recognition of certain taboos (connected, for example, with pollution and particular kinds of 'sacred' fish) etc. as *super*-natural, on the contrary I have argued elsewhere that for them there is but one single cosmological system that includes both the 'natural' and the 'supernatural' of the post-Cartesian West (Ward, 1979). Be that as it may, it is certain that the fishermen's Folk Model had virtually nothing in common with the department's.

Although success is seen as the proper reward of skill and intelligence, it cannot be expected to follow from these qualities alone but depends also on paying proper respect to the gods and ancestors, observing the taboos, taking part (however vicariously) in exorcisms and other rituals, and behaving in a proper manner towards parents, kinsmen, neighbours, and others. Annual and other calendrical rites, both comunally and privately observed, ensure that these precepts are not forgotten; and stories of the disasters that have befallen people whom everybody knows drive them home.

As for the theory about over-fishing, most Hong Kong fishermen in the sixties rejected it altogether. In the traditional Folk Model fish were 'just there', as a free good.[11] Thus the fishermen lacked a conceptual apparatus with which to grasp the idea of scarcity in this respect, and nothing in their daily experience helped them to do so. After all, fish were always being

[11] There was no traditional parcelling out of fishing grounds. Anyone was free to fish anywhere. Disputes were over such matters as stealing nets or lines or traps, fouling nets or lines, stealing fish that had already been caught, interfering during an actual fishing operation, dangerous navigation and so on; they were not phrased in terms of the violation of exclusive rights over particular resources. It is possible that a good deal of the irritation expressed against the Chinese fishing communes and against attempts to control fishing areas in Hong Kong arises from the fact that under them claims to such rights are being made for the first time. The fishermen of Hong Kong today probably feel much as the cottagers of England felt when the commons were enclosed and the rabbits which had hitherto been seen as free goods were denied them.

caught. It was true that sometimes one had good catches and sometimes bad, but this had always been so. It was explicable in terms of Feng Shui and proper conduct towards spirits and humans and so forth. As long as these traditional views remained intact, fishermen could not share the department's and the outside experts' anxieties about absolute depletion of stocks.

Their understanding both of their own situation and of matters relevant to their resources being so different, it should come as no surprise that for some considerable time the majority of the fishermen appeared to be unimpressed by the department's suggested remedy for their problems. For most of the successful men there were no problems that could not be dealt with as they had been dealt with before; for the unsuccessful the only problem was to find any kind of employment at all. Until the middle sixties at least, most fishermen, deep-sea and inshore alike, looked at the proposed stern otter-trawler with curiosity, but thought no more of building one for themselves than of buying an aeroplane or a tractor.

However, the years 1965-70 saw also three quite other kinds of response. First, some fishermen (it is not possible to estimate how many) gave careful consideration to the proposed new vessel, only to reject it in favour of continued use of the semi-traditional mechanized methods which had served them well since the end of World War II. For them the first ('pre take-off') stage of development was enough. Unlike the idle curiosity of the majority, their interest had been serious, and their response deliberate, though negative. Second, there were those (perhaps a few dozen in all) who also weighed the department's proposals and rejected them, but who then went on to produce counter-proposals which when implemented (as with the department's full and generous assistence they have been implemented) put them squarely in the second stage of development though by a route different from the one the department was primarily advocating. Finally, at first very slowly and then with a rush some master-fishermen actually chose the stern otter-trawler and so broke into the same stage by following the department's lead. The following three case histories illustrate the first and third of these responses.[12]

FIRST HISTORY: NEGATIVE DECISION

In 1967 'Ma Shing-Tsui', an inshore fisherman, owned two mechanized junks, each about forty feet overall length, and two sampans. Now fifty-five years old, and a boatmaster for about eleven years, he had four sons, all married, two married brothers, and enough nephews to make it unnecessary to hire

[12] All data were obtained by observation and discussion with fishermen. Names are fictitious.

extra hands. He was a careful man, who decided to mechanize his original sailing vessels only in 1960 after long assessment of the experience of others less cautious than himself. Illiterate himself, he had seen to it that his own and his brothers' children had all had at least four years' primary schooling; everyone of the grandchild generation of the right age (male and female) was still at school, one even starting secondary education.[13] The entire family wholly rejected the theory of over-fishing, giving as evidence their own admittedly excellent catch records ever since they had mechanized, on the proceeds of which they were thinking about building a small house ashore.[14] They agreed that some people seemed to have had rather poor luck recently, but that was just how things were and maybe they deserved it anyway. For themselves they were always careful to placate the gods and perform the right rituals at the right times. And they never fished outside Hong Kong's territorial waters.

There is a sense in which Ma Shing-Tsui was too successful to be seriously interested in further technological change. He recognized but saw no harm in the fact that his income had now settled to a fairly steady level after the sharp rise which occurred during the first three or four years after mechanization. (It doubled in three years, and then rose by nearly a quarter again.) As he said, he was a great deal better off than he had ever been before, and he had 'enough'. Nevertheless, he had at one time seriously considered the possibilities of stern otter-trawling and rejected them.

Asked why, he replied that the change would be 'too much bother' (*ma faan*). Invited to explain further, he began by pointing out that neither he nor any one in his extended family had the know-how for trawling let alone deep-sea trawling (this although he knew that the Agriculture and Fisheries Department provides free training in stern otter-trawling and navigation on board). He then drew attention to the problems of building the boat; it needed special plans, and the department insisted upon having a free hand in choosing the shipyard and supervising the construction from start to finish. How, he said rhetorically, could be possibly allow that? He had always taken a personal part in designing the boats he ordered in the past, and anyway how could he face his old ship builder friend, Wong Foo-Tak, if he was made to take his custom elsewhere? He agreed that as he was already considering building a house on shore, the change to a more-or-less Western type of vessel with no place for the children would not cause much additional domestic

[13]They will be the first fishermen's children from their village to go beyond primary school.

[14]Hong Kong fishermen, like most of the others in South China, are traditionally boat-dwellers. The move to living ashore has been gathering momentum since about 1955; for further discussion see Ward (1967) and Kani (1967).

disruption, but then how could he possibly contemplate shouldering the enormous financial responsibility that building the new-fangled vessel would involve? Borrowing so much money would be extremely unwise; it would be a burden for the rest of one's life and for one's children and grandchildren later on. Why, look at Chan Luk for example, he had tried it and was a sick man as a result, worn out with work and anxiety.

SECOND HISTORY: ACCEPTANCE

In 1967 'Chan Luk' was thirty-nine years old. An inshore fisherman, he had lost his father early and so found himself in charge of his own vessel just at the time when mechanization was beginning. In 1952 he obtained a private loan from a fish dealer (middleman) with which he installed a small marine diesel engine in his junk. He was one of the first inshore fishermen to do this.

He took some time to repay this loan, and in the course of his struggle to do so became one of the first to discover that the fruits of mechanization included increased flexibility in types of fishing techniques. In 1964, having tried a number of different methods and several boat builders, he was running a successful long-lining business fishing the middle-distance waters with his third mechanized boat, a 54-footer, manned by himself, his wife, his eldest son, then fourteen years old, and his three brothers. His own younger children and the wives and children of his brothers were living ashore with his mother.

During the years of success since 1951, he had paid off his private debts and developed an excellent relationship with the department from which he had received two loans of about $HK20,000 each (for his second two mechanized boats) and several smaller ones. All had been repaid promptly.[15] Earlier, he had married a wife who like himself had had five years' mission schooling, and had seen to it that she, as well as his three brothers and himself, had studied for and passed the examinations necessary to obtain the coxswain-engineer's certificate which the Hong Kong authorities require of any person in charge of a mechanized vessel. His enterprising nature had been further demonstrated by his pioneering the then wholly new idea of mechanizing not just the mother-ship but also the sampans used in long-lining. In 1962 he was elected to office in one of the largest fishermen's cooperatives in Hong Kong. Early in 1965 Chan applied for, and received, a loan of $HK192,310 (about £12,000 at the time) for building a stern otter-trawler.

In 1968, when he had already been running the new boat successfully for

[15] Prompt repayment has been a consistent feature of all the official loan schemes organized for the benefit of Hong Kong fishermen. Since the late forties, the number of bad debts has averaged less than 1% per annum. This paper does not discuss the numerous unofficial loan relationships that also exist.

nearly eighteen months, I asked him why he had chosen to build it. He gave two major reasons. First he referred to his own conviction, based on having tried several different kinds of inshore fishing and on discussions with officers from the department, that the nearer waters were being over-fished. He drew my attention to the fact that he had already moved into the middle-distance waters before 1965, and he touched upon the present political situation and the reorganization in China which had brought difficulties for the inshore men who wanted to fish outside territorial limits. Second, he mentioned his trust in the department's opinions and know-how, and described the excellence of the advice and assistance he had received from its officers in connection with the new boat. Finally, for justification, he quoted the undoubted success of the venture so far.

The reader will remember that the cautious and successful 'Ma Shing-Tsui' denied the very possibility of over-fishing. Now 'Chan Luk' put it forward as one of his major reasons for wanting to adopt the new kind of vessel.

THIRD HISTORY: ACCEPTANCE

By the Spring of 1968, eight new stern otter-trawlers were in operation. A number of the masters of the other new vessels shared outlooks and circumstances similar to Chan's. There was, however, a second type of accepter among them, a much more 'traditional' type, whose decisions were made in different circumstances. The point of view of these men can be summarized briefly in the history of 'Shek Yau-Tak'.

A man of about fifty, Shek Yau-Tak had been running a deep-sea pair trawling business with his younger brother, Yau-Foon, since the death of their father ten years before. Neither brother was educated, and both were deeply traditional in outlook, and careful in religious observances; they normally consulted the local temple god before taking any serious decision. In 1960 the Sheks had had a labour force which included three daughters-in-law and four of their unmarried daughters. By 1968 they had lost all the daughters in marriage and all three daughters-in-law, now much preoccupied with their numerous small children, were longing to move ashore. As a result, whereas ten years before Shek had needed to hire only about thirteen extra workers, by 1968 he needed about twenty. (Yau-Foon's second son, who in the old days would have joined the work force by now, was still at school.) By 1968, too, good fishermen workers became increasingly hard to find and expensive to keep, since factory work was often more attractive and rewarding, and the Shek brothers faced the very real risk of going out of business altogether if they stayed in pair trawling. By 1967, indeed, they had seen this happen to a number of their acquaintances, and this fact was probably the most important single feature of the situation as they saw it.

But they saw a number of other things too, notably the experience of 'Chan Luk' with his successful stern-trawler and his strong departmental support. They therefore decided, after long debate and with the local god's agreement,[16] to sell their two trawling junks, which were in fair condition, and so raise enough money both to acquire shore accomodation of a sort (with the prospect of resettlement in a government housing scheme in the fairly near future) and contribute towards a new stern otter-trawler. They applied for and were awarded a departmental loan of over $HK200,000 to cover the rest of the cost, and were offered all the same technical supervision and help that they now knew Chan Luk had enjoyed. And they knew too (and this was crucial) that for this vessel they would not need to employ more than one or two extra hands at the most. By the end of 1968 they were in business as stern-trawlers, and, their previous deep-sea experience serving them in good stead, doing quite well.

ANALYSIS

It is easy to draw up a conventional table cross-listing some of the observable attributes of the persons described above and their decisions, in the manner of inductive objective social science. For example:

Table 1. Selected observed attributes of boat masters, 1967

		1	2	3
	Name	MA	CHAN	SHEK
A	(a) Decision	reject	accept	accept
	(b) Date of decision	1967	1967	1968
B	Age:			
	(a) in 1967	55	39	50
	(b) at time of taking command of boat	44	21	40
	(number of years in command)	(11)	(18)	(10)
C	School education:			
	(a) self	nil	5 yrs.	nil
	(b) wife	nil	5 yrs.	nil
	(c) highest level attained by son(s)	primary	secondary	secondary
D	Office holder	no	yes	no
E	Number of family members in crew	13	7	5
F	Owns/rents family accomodation on land	not yet	yes	not yet
G	Current degree of economic success*	very good	good	fair

*relative to past performance as measured by official Fish Marketing Organization records.

[16] By divination in the local temple.

Inspection of this table immediately suggests the possibility of significant correlations between willingness to accept the new stern-trawlers and (*i*) a relatively small number of family members ready and able to serve as crew (row E), (*ii*) a degree of current economic success rather below the highest (relative to past performance or the current performance of others of previously similar economic standing) (row G), and/or (*iii*) being a late decider (row A(b)). These common sense hypotheses are similar to those used by the department in an informal way in the late sixties as a basis for forward planning. The events of the next decade, when, following the demonstrated success of the very few true innovators (like Chan) scores and then hundreds of other fishermen hurried to acquire the new vessels, showed that they had high predictive value.

But, although, of course, it does test the regularity of a correlation, prediction contributes nothing to understanding the relationship itself (cp. Bateson, 1973:26). In this case it seems obvious that the most important elsement in the later flood of positive decisions was the demonstrated success of the new boats (which was greatly enhanced when one of them returned to port after successfully riding out a full-scale typhoon). The more interesting question is what was it that induced Chan and one or two others to decide to risk accepting the new technology before it had been put to the test of commercial operation under local conditions?

Column 2 in Table 1 suggests some possible correlations between willingness to innovate in this sense and (*i*) age of taking over command of a boat and number of years in command (row B(b)), (*ii*) own education and wife's education (row C(a) (b)), (*iii*) experience in holding office (row D), and (*iv*) possession of family accomodation on land (row F). Again, these are largely common sense hypotheses that seem to throw some light on the question at issue, but the innovators were very few, and there were many other fishermen with the same, or very similar, attributes who held back. To understand more about the innovators it is likely to be more useful to shift the focus from the (objective) attributes of decision-makers to the (subjective) process of decision-making, and consider the fishermen's perceptions of the matters about which they had to decide and of their own situations as they saw them in the light of their personal models.

The reader may recall that I began this study using two concepts which I labelled Folk Model and personal model respectively. I now find it necessary to discuss these concepts a little more and introduce a third which I shall call 'personal version of the Folk Model' or 'personal folk model' for short. It should, of course, be borne in mind that all three concepts are introduced solely for heuristic purposes.

The concept 'personal model(s)' as I am using it here includes all an individual's personal stock of knowledge (cp. Schutz, 1967). It therefore includes his knowledge about the objectified Folk Model that the members of his group (society) postulate as being 'out there' (cp. Berger and Luckmann, 1966 *passim*), but probably in all cases and certainly in any highly differentiated society a personal model is likely to include also a number of matters which are unique to the particular individual. Thus at any given time a given individual may be thought of as having a personal model (his whole stock of knowledge about how things are and ought to be) a larger or smaller part of which is his personal (idiosyncratic) version of the objectified Folk Model of his group.

This is because human knowledge is always acquired by learning. For my present purposes that which is learned may be regarded as a kind of 'deposit' comprised of what one has remembered from having been 'told' by others (including *telling about* and *telling to* [*do*]) and what has been 'borne in' from one's own experience. These are colloquial ways of putting the matter which neatly express the 'other originated' and 'self acquired' dichotomy I have in mind. 'Telling', as I am using it here, includes all forms of communication of subject matter and precept; 'experience' can be broadly categorized as direct or indirect.[17]

It is possible to imagine that as a member of a very small, simple, stable, undifferentiated, and isolated society one could be told all there is to tell quite early in life, and that thereafter the content of repeated 'tellings' would vary very little over time. In such a society, too, it is likely that one's own experiences and those of one's fellows would be relatively similar and repetitive. In such a society, most people (at least, most people of the same sex) would have very similar personal models each of which would probably approximate quite closely to their society's Folk Model as it might be constructed by an outside observer. (Presumably some such assumption as this lies behind many anthropological accounts of simple societies.)

Hong Kong society is not like that. Although as children Ma Shing-Tsui, Chan Luk, and Shek Yau-Tak were almost certainly 'told' much the same information about the Boat People's Folk Model (according to the stock of knowledge in their parents' personal models), and although many parts of that Model must have been reinforced for them by their repeated exposure to other communications relevant to it (including amongst other things ritual performances and the traditional theatre) they had also, to varying degrees, been exposed to still other communications (from school, cinema, radio, T. V., conversation with people of different 'backgrounds' etc.) which had

[17]It should go without saying that this paragraph is intended to do no more than point to the everyday observation that human individuals obtain their knowledge from different (and different kinds of) sources.

'told' them about other kinds of Chinese Folk Model (cp. Ward, 1965 and 1966) and also about parts of the quite different Folk Model(s) which were developed originally in the West. Inevitably in such a highly differentiated situation (which is, after all, typical of any modernizing plural society today) each individual's selected remembrance of what he has been 'told' is likely to be almost unique, the more so because in a complex, heterogeneous society each individual's complex of experiences is also likely to be unique. As a result, in such a society the separate personal models 'in the heads' of the separate individuals are likely to differ more or less widely both from the traditionally postulated Folk Model and from one another.

Furthermore, because in a traditionally complex society the traditional Folk Model is usually highly complex too, it is unlikely that any one individual's personal model will include more than a possibly quite idiosyncratic version of it or of certain parts of it only, existing alongside (so to speak) all the bits and pieces of information about other Folk Models which he has been 'told' about and the rest of the 'deposit' acquired through his own particular complex of experiences. Thus it may be useful for certain purposes to think in terms of three concepts: (*i*) *Folk Model* (postulated, objectified, thought of as being 'out there'), and (*ii*) *personal model* (total stock of a particular individual's knowledge about how things are and ought to be) of which one section, so to speak, is, (*iii*) the personal version of his people's Folk Model or *personal folk model* for short. It is also necessary to add that, because all human knowledge is learned, both personal models and personal folk models are always subject to change. Strictly speaking there can be no such thing as x's personal model, but only x's personal model (and x's personal folk model) at time y.

Thinking like this makes it possible to see that in 1967 and 1968, despite their similar 'backgrounds', Ma, Chan, and Shek were likely to bring different personal models and different personal folk models to the appraisal of the same decision. The questions are: how did these differences affect the decisions they actually made, and, more particularly, were there any peculiarities about Chan's personal model(s) that help to explain why he became a pioneer?

Table 2 suggests that in 1967-68 Chan's personal model differed in every respect from Ma's, and in respect of what can be assumed to be certain relevant aspects of adherence to the Folk Model (rows A and B) from Shek's. It is likely that the 'tellings' each man received in childhood were rather similar, but the fact that Chan was born more than ten years later than either Ma or Shek and that his father had been modern enough to send him to school for five years (Table 1) argue that there may have been significant differences. It may also be relevant that Chan was brought up and still lives

Table 2. Personal models 1967-68: Some indicators

		1	2	3
	Name	MA	CHAN	SHEK
	Decision	reject	accept	accept
	Date of decision	1967	1967	1968
A	Observes traditional religious practices	yes	sometimes	yes
B	Stated views about traditional beliefs	believer	agnostic	believer
C	Stresses particularistic relationships	yes	no	?
D	Denies possibility of over-fishing inshore waters	yes	no	?
E	Directly experienced results of inshore fishing	very good	poor	no direct experience
F	Direct experience of deep-sea fishing	no	some	yes
G	Direct experience of variety of fishing methods	no	yes	yes
H	Direct experience of handling fairly large loans	no	yes	yes
J	Direct experience of close relationship with departmental officers	no	yes	no
(K	Indirect experience of success of new vessel		—	yes)

in Hong Kong's major fishing port,[18] whereas both Ma and Shek have spent most of their lives in much smaller, more remote centres.

To this can be added, as no doubt they can be partly ascribed, Chan's own later experiences (rows E, F, G, H. J). Failure in inshore fishing (row E) led him to try the middle-distance waters (row F). Probably, together with the potentially liberalizing effects of his relatively prolonged educational experience (Table 1 C(a)), it also prompted him to accept the department's view about the depletion of inshore stocks (row D) which he had been told about many times while studying for his coxswain/engineer's certificate (an experience shared by neither Ma nor Shek). It was during this period, too, that he had struck up personal relationships with the departmental officers (row J) who were teaching him and with whom he had already been in quite close contact about negotiating loans (row H).

[18] Aberdeen, on Hong Kong island, contains the largest concentration of fishing vessels and boat building yards, the main wholesale fish market, and the best educational, welfare etc. services for fishermen. It is also a centre for missionary activity, tourism, and (today) industrial development.

It is not difficult to see in all this some of the ways in which Chan's unique complex of experiences may have influenced the formation of his (overall) personal model and affected his thinking over the years in such a way as to lead him (probably unknown to himself) to modify his personal folk model, with the result that by 1967 it deviated in at least some significant respects from the postulated Folk Model of his people's tradition. In Ma's case, on the other hand, the personal folk model acquired in childhood and unmodified by school education seems to have been supported, in the main, by experience (and thus by most other aspects of his [overall] personal model). As a result, Ma's personal folk model and the postulated Folk Model of his people were unlikely to be far apart. In other words, Ma's conservative behaviour was in consonance with his traditionalist stock of knowledge. As for Shek, he seems to have been one of the many with appropriate experience whose judgement was affected not by any change in personal folk model but simply by the example of Chan and consideration of his own situation.

At the beginning of this paper I discussed the role of personal models in the evaluation of 'situation' and 'matter' in the making of any decision. As far as the matter of the new stern-trawler was concerned, Table 2 implies most of the relevant points as the three men themselves probably saw them. The new boat was adapted to deep-sea work (row F), and a variety of fishing methods (row G), could only be built with the aid of a very large loan of money (row H) and (at that time) in a certain boat-yard (row C). The personal model of a man who, like Ma, lacked appropriate technical and financial experience was scarcely likely to lead him to evaluate the new boat positively, especially as his personal folk model remained essentially traditional. It is likely that such a man could only have decided to accept the new boat if his situation had appeared to him to be on the verge of disaster and he saw no alternative. In fact, however, Ma considered his situation to be good. In 1967 he had a large, and largely male, family; for years his fishing had been successful; his income was showing a steady annual increase. It was thus not on the cards that he would choose the new boat even if he had foreseen the forthcoming demonstration of Chan's success.

Chan's personal model, on the other hand, was likely to predispose him to a positive evaluation of the matter, and, given the situation in which he felt that he was being less economically successful than he might be, knew he could not expand his labour force cheaply, and believed that he could rely on the department, his decision to go ahead was almost predictable. Members of the department, who had previous experience of his enterprising personality, were well aware of this. They talked with him and prevailed. Chan became their first (and very successful) convert, but his own perception of the matter and his situation were almost certainly crucial. Table 3 lists the perceived situations of the three men:

Table 3. Perceived elements in the "situation" 1967-68

	1	2	3
Name	MA	CHAN	SHEK
Decision	reject	accept	accept
Date of decision	1967	1967	1968
A Perceived degree of own current economic success	good	fair only	declining
B Perceived current labour problems, own case	none	none yet	serious
C Number of family members in crew (cp. Table 1 row E)	13	7	5
D Perceived relationship with department (cp. Table 2 row J)	good but distant	good close	good
E Family living on land	no	yes	not yet

Shek's case was different from both Ma's and Chan's. As regards the matter of the decision, his personal model (stock of knowledge), which already included almost all the technological know-how needed for the new boat (Table 2 rows E and F), probably led him to evaluate it positively, but at the same time the seriousness of his economic situation (Table 3 rows A and B), though it prompted him to look for alternatives, forbade him to take risks. Once someone else had proved that the gamble paid off, Shek was willing to follow suit. There is no evidence of any change in his personal folk model. He was, and has remained, a strong believer in and fervent practitioner of traditional rituals. It is virtually certain that the great majority of the several hundred other fishermen who also followed Chan's lead during the next decade were like Shek. They too assessed the matter of the decision mainly in the light of their indirect experience of the demonstration effect and evaluated their own situations in terms of calculations about income and labour. Their personal folk models were not normally involved, or, in Weberian terms, instrumental rationality did not entail value rationality.

Often such a situation as this is described as a case of 'cultural lag', it being claimed that change in one part of 'the system' has occurred first, but changes throughout *will come*. In the absence of either coercion or a strong fashion set by a dominating elite, one wonders if this is necessarily so. At the very least, the 'lag' may be almost indefinitely prolonged. Given circumstances similar to those existing in Hong Kong at present, I see no reason to expect changes in the fishermen's Folk Model in the near future: the British government is remarkably tender towards what many people regard as 'local superstitions', the kind of 'supernatural insurance' they afford is highly plausible to believers, and it is a fact that expenditure on and attendence at local temple festivals in Hong Kong today (1980) are much larger than they have ever been before. There seems to be no validity at present in the theory of cultural lag; on the contrary, it could be argued that modernization seems to have entailed enhanced traditionalism in certain respects.

This paper is being written in 1980. There are now nearly 500 stern otter-trawlers operating out of Hong Kong fishing centres, and a very large number of other vessels whose construction and gear and the know-how that goes with them are essentially 'modern'. Yet the boats remain owner-operated. In other words, it is only the techniques not the relations of production that have changed. It is, however, possible that inflation and other causes may soon bring about changes in the relations of production too. It remains to be seen whether such changes, if they occur, will be accompanied by changes in the personal folk models. It has to be remembered that it has long been the practice for fishing crews to include wage workers as well as members of the owner-operators' families. Indeed, in deep-sea fishing the number of employees on a boat quite often used to surpass the number of family members. I have no evidence that the employees today or in the past subscribe to a Folk Model essentially different from the one their employers recognize, but this situation could change rapidly if fishermen became absorbed into a general occupationally (and ethnically) undifferentiated proletariat outside the fishing industry. At present, however, fishermen and ex-fishermen still remain in many respects a distinct ethnic category (cp. Anderson, 1972; Ward, 1965), and it is possible that their traditionalistic personal folk models, which apparently do not obstruct instrumental rationality, are a significant aspect of their ethnic-occupational identity. They also provide opportunities for invoking traditional beliefs and staging elaborate festivals both of which may have important latent functions.

It is also a fact of the present time that after thirty years of socialist reconstruction in China, and nearly fifteen years of suppression, religious activity—now permitted again its more respectable forms, such as Buddhism, Islam, and Christianity—appears, at least in some areas, to be attracting followers from among the generations born since 1949 as well as from among the older people who may have practised it before. It is interesting to speculate about the possible response if the temple festivals and other not-so-respectable practices which have immense popular support in Hong Kong, Taiwan, and Chinese communities overseas were also permitted to return.

Finally, let me repeat that the concepts used here and in my two previous papers on 'conscious models' were developed solely for heuristic purposes. If the words in which they have been expressed seem to my readers to be unappropriate or clumsy, I can only say I tend to agree. Perhaps while retaining 'Folk Model' for the objectified construct 'out there' and 'personal folk model' for the mental representation of it 'in here', it might be less confusing to use 'personal stock of knowledge', or some other phrase, for what I have here called the (overall) personal model (which includes the 'personal folk model') 'in here'. But these are not very important matters. What may be important is that I have found these concepts useful tools for thinking with in trying to understand the micro-processes of change in this one instance. But the phenomenon of modernization is world wide, and the concepts used here may possibly be of use not only in understanding the decision-making connected with it but also, and more importantly, in showing how it is that, contrary to many people's expectations, the adoption of instrumental changes may not (indeed is probably not even likely to) entail the internalization of new sets of values or the development of new Folk Models.

REFERENCES

Anderson, Eugene N. 1972. *Essays on South China's Boat People*. Asian Folklore and Social Life Monographs Vol. XXIX. Taipei: The Orient Cultural Service.

Bateson, Gregory. 1973. *Steps to an Ecology of Mind*. St. Albans: Paladin.

Berger, Peter L. and Thomas Luckmann. 1966. *The Social Construction of Reality: A Treatise in the Sociology Knowledge*. U.S.A.

Garfinkel, Harold. 1974. 'The Rational Properties of Scientific and Common-sense Activities'. In Anthony Giddens (ed.), *Positivism and Sociology*. London: Heinemann.

Government of Hong Kong, Department of Agriculture, Forestry and Fisheries. 1966. *Statement of Fisheries Development Loan Fund* (Mimeographed).

———. 1967. *Annual Report*. Hong Kong: Government Printer.

———. 1968. *Annual Report*. Hong Kong: Government Printer.

Kani, Hiroaki. 1967. *A General Survey of the Boat People of Hong Kong*. Hong Kong: New Asia Research Institute.

Merton, R. 1968. *Social Theory and Social Structure*. Enl. ed. New York: Free Press.

Schutz, Alfred. 1967. *The Phenomenology of the Social World*. Ill.: Northwestern University Press.

Thomas, W. I. and Dorothy S. Thomas. 1928. *The Child in America*. New York: Knopf.

Thomas, W. I. and Florian Znanieki. 1918. *The Polish Peasant in Europe and America*. Boston: Richard G. Badger.

Ward, Barbara E. 1965. 'Varieties of the Conscious Model: The Fishermen of South China'. In M. Banton (ed.), *The Relevance of Models for Social Anthropology*. London: Tavistock Publications Ltd.

———. 1966. 'Sociological Self-awareness: Some Uses of the Conscious Models'. *Man* (N. S.) Vol. 1, No. 2.

———. 1967. 'Chinese Fishermen in Hong Kong: Their Post-Peasant Economy'. In M. Freedman (ed.), *Social Organization: Essays Presented to Raymond Firth*.

London: Frank Cass & Co. Ltd.
————. 1979. 'Not Merely Players: Drama, Art and Ritual in Traditional China'. *Man* (N. S.) Vol. 14, No. 1.

Section II

Socio-economic Papers

6. A Hakka Kongsi in Borneo[1]*

THE HAKKAS

In China the Hakka people form a distinct linguistic group, speaking a dialect which may be described as about mid-way between Cantonese and Mandarin.[2] It is generally held that they originated in Central China and gradually travelled southwards in a series of movements as a result of pressure from the north. Between the T'ang and Sung dynasties (907-959) Hakka-speaking groups had reached Fukien, and during the Southern Sung dynasty (1127-1279) they moved into Kwangtung. Two more big movements during the Ch'ing dynasty (1644-1911) took Hakkas as far afield as Szechwan, Hainan, and Formosa.[3]

At the present time the total number of Hakka-speaking Chinese is estimated at something over sixteen million[4] concentrated mainly on the borders of Kiangsi, Fukien, and Kwangtung. Actually ten *hsiens* 縣 in Kiangsi, eight in Fukien, and fifteen in Kwangtung are purely Hakka-speaking. In addition to this, Hakkas are to be found living side by side with speakers of

*Reprinted from *Journal of Oriental Studies*, Vol. 1, No. 2 (July 1954) with permission.

[1] This article was originally planned as Appendix II to Dr. J. K. T'ien's 田汝康 book *The Chinese of Sarawak* (London: London School of Economics Monographs on Social Anthropology No. 12, 1953). In the event, that book was published without appendices. The present writer, who had the privilege of collaborating with Dr. T'ien in the writing of that book, and was herself responsible for the appendices, wishes to make full acknowledgement to Dr. T'ien.

[2] R. D. Forrest, *The Chinese Language* (London, 1949), p. 220.

[3] The details of Hakka history have been discussed in numerous publications, both Chinese and English, of which the following is a selection: Lo Hsiang-lin 羅香林, *An Introduction to the Study of the Hakkas, in Its Ethnic, Historical, and Cultural Aspects* 客家研究導論 (Canton, 1938) (in Chinese, English summary attached); Charles Piton 'On the Origin and History of the Hakkas', *China Review*, II (1973-74), pp. 222-26; E. J. Eitel, 'An Outline History of the Hakka', *China Review*, II (1873-74), pp. 160-64; R. Lechler, 'The Hakka Chinese', *Chinese Recorder* (Shanghai, 1878); E. J. Eitel, 'Ethnographical Sketches of the Hakka Chinese', *China Review*, XX (1892-93), pp. 263-67; S. M. Shirokogoroff, *Anthropology of Eastern China and Kwangtung Province* (Shanghai: Commercial Press, 1925), Chapter VI, pp. 113-41; Li Chi 李濟, *The Formation of the Chinese People* (Harvard University Press, 1928).

[4] Lo Hsiang-lin, *op. cit.*, Chapter III.

different dialects in a hundred and five other *hsiens*, in Kiangsi, Fukien, Kwangtung (including Hainan island), Kwangsi, Szechwan, Hunan, and Formosa.[5] In the past, the cultural and linguistic differences between the Hakkas and their neighbours, especially in the mixed areas, led to frequent strife. The years 1855-67, for example, saw a prolonged period of fighting between Hakkas and Cantonese in which about half a million people are said to have lost their lives.[6] Whatever the actual number of casualties, at least the troubles of these twelve years caused a revival of interest in Hakka culture, and it is from this period that most of the literature on these people dates.

THE HAKKAS IN MALAYSIA

Hakka-speaking people have migrated overseas in large numbers, particularly to the Nan Yang 南洋, which is the Chinese term for the Malay Archipelago. The overseas Hakka come almost exclusively from Fukien and Kwangtung, in which provinces they are to be found mainly in mountainous areas where there is a considerable shortage of land.[7]

It is estimated that there are more than two million Hakkas in the Nan Yang.[8] According to the Census Report of 1947 there are 437,407 Hakkas (out of a total of 2,614,667 Chinese) in the Federation of Malaya and the Colony of Singapore.[9] It is noteworthy that Hakkas from the same place of origin in China tend to congregate together also in the Nan Yang. For example, the majority of the Hakkas in Johore come from the Hopiu 河婆 district of Kityang *hsien* 揭陽縣 in Kwangtung,[10] the majority in Kuala Lumpur come from Hweichow (present Hweiyang *hsien* 惠陽縣), Canton, in Ipoh from Kwangsi, and in Malacca and Singapore from Tap'u 大埔縣. There is also a strongly marked tendency towards congregation in certain occupations: in Singapore twenty-five of the twenty-six pawnshops are run by Hakkas, twenty-four of them from Tap'u,[11] and a hundred and ninety of the three hundred-odd Chinese drug-stores are in Hakka hands, also mainly from Tap'u. Sarawak in British Borneo has been called the Hakkas' 'home from home'. Out of a total of 145,158 Chinese, Hakkas make up 45,409.

Many Hakkas originally moved into Sarawak from Dutch Borneo during

[5] As well, of course, as in Hong Kong.

[6] Lo Hsiang-lin, *op. cit.*

[7] *Ibid.*, Chapter III, p. 100.

[8] *Ten Years of Singapore* (Singapore, 1930) (in Chinese).

[9] In Singapore: 40,036.

[10] In Calcutta most of the Hakkas are from Kityang *hsien*, and the same is true of the urban Hakkas in Jakarta. In Dutch Borneo, as a general rule, urban-dwelling Hakkas are from Kityang, and rural dwellers from Mei *hsien* 梅縣.

[11] Twelve of these are owned by two individuals.

the troubled period in the mid-nineteenth century. There they had been agriculturalists and gold-miners, members of self-governing Kongsis. The Kongsi type of organization existed also in the districts around Bau in Sarawak, but was more elaborately developed on the Dutch side, for which also there exists fuller documentation. As an understanding of present-day social organization demands not only contemporary but also historical treatment, it has been considered useful to analyse here the Kongsi[12] organization as it is described for the gold districts in Dutch West Borneo.[13]

THE KONGSI SYSTEM

The Kongsi system had its roots in the village organization of China. Those who see it as something apart, without recognizing its connection with the basic Chinese social structure and with the historical and geographical environment in which it developed, tend to fall into one or other of two errors. Either they see the Kongsi as a secret society, conspiring to thwart all regular civil government, in which case they condemn it; or they see it as a prototype of modern republican democracy, in which case they eulogize it. Both views are misconceived. As de Groot was at such pains to prove, the Kongsi system was naturally developed out of the experience of Chinese

[12] The term *kongsi* 公司 is translated in Matthews' *Chinese-English Dictionary* as 'public company'. The character is further given as: 'an officer, to control, to manage, to preside; a subdivision of a district'. In the Nan Yang today a Kongsi may be any kind of association, from a club to a limited company. As used for the Chinese communities in West Borneo in the eighteenth and nineteenth centuries the term may refer to: (*i*) any group of any size banded together for any purpose, political, social or economic; or any sub-group of these; (*ii*) the officers who are at the head of such a group; (*iii*) more specifically the political groups described below, or sub-groups of these, or their officials.

In the text Kongsi is used to refer to the large political groups in the mining districts of West Borneo.

[13] The information in the following paragraphs is drawn from: (*i*) J.J.M. de Groot, *Het Kongsiwezen van Borneo* (The Hague, 1885). This contains a Chinese record of the Langfang Kongsi 蘭芳公司歷代年册 written by Yap Hsiang Yun 葉祥雲, with a translation and commentary in Dutch. (*ii*) Lo Hsiang-lin 羅香林 'The Establishment of the Langfang Presidential System by Lo Fang Pak in Borneo' 羅芳伯所建婆羅洲坤甸蘭芳大總制考, *Kwangchow Hsüeh-pao* 廣州學報 (Canton), I, No. 1 (1937), pp. 1-38 (in Chinese with an English abstract). This contains quotations from an unpublished MS on the history of Pontianak by Ling Fong Ch'iu 林鳳超. (*iii*) The accounts of European travellers, especially E. Doty and J. Pohlman, 'Tour in Borneo from Sambas, through Montrado to Pontianak and the Adjacent Settlements of Chinese and Dayaks during the Autumn of 1838', *Chinese Repository*, VIII, No. 6 (1839). G. W. Earl, *Eastern Seas* (London, 1837). (*iv*) Li Ch'ang-fu 李長傅, *History of Chinese Emigration* (Shanghai, 1937 (in Chinese). (*v*) Wen Hsiung-fei 溫雄飛, *General History of Nan Yang Chinese* 南洋華僑通史, (Shanghai, 1929) (in Chinese). (*vi*) The accounts of informants in Sarawak.

immigrants, coming in compact clan and village groups to a strange land in which they had to fend in all matters completely for themselves.

THE TAKONG KONGSI AT MONTRADO, WEST BORNEO

A description of the Kongsi in the early nineteenth century and an analysis of their organization will make this clearer. Their location was in the western part of what is now Dutch Borneo, where gold-mining was their major enterprise. They varied in number and strength according as movements towards consolidation by one or other strong group led to feuds and conquests from time to time. The three most important, at least for our present purposes, seem to have been the Takong Kongsi 大港公司, the San-Ti-Qu Kongsi 三條溝公司, and the Langfang Kongsi 蘭芳公司, all of which flourished at the beginning of the nineteenth century.

Earl, who visited West Borneo in 1834, with the object of opening trade relations with the Chinese, has left quite a detailed description of his visit to the first of these. At that time the Dutch had small settlements at Pontianak and Sambas, about ninety miles apart on the west coast. The Chinese colony to which Earl was bound lay inland between these two places, with its capital town at Montrado. Despite the, not disinterestedly expressed, misgivings of Malays and Dutch on the coast, Earl's party found nothing but honour and hospitality in Montrado, and but for Dutch interference his mission would undoubtedly have met with entire success. The description of the journey into the interior gives an impression of orderly government which permitted the erection of 'houses for the entertainment of travellers at intervals on the road side—at one of which the Englishmen had their first taste of noodle-soup, 'a preparation of rice, much resembling macaroni'. The town of Montrado itself consisted of a single street, three-quarters of a mile long, with the 'governor's house', a uniquely large building, standing slightly detached from the town at one end. Although it was raining hard the 'governor' and chief men of the town met the Englishmen at the gate of the courtyard, dressed in their best attire, and honoured them with a salute of three guns. On the following day Earl met the chief men, about fifty in all, of Montrado and the neighbouring districts, and discussed with them the prospects of opening up direct trade with Singapore. He seems to have been deeply impressed by the political acumen of the 'governor', and the organization of political authority struck him as being 'extremely well suited' to the situation of this Chinese community, though he was, of course, unaware of its derivation. He stresses the complete independence of this Kongsi which was subject neither to the Emperor of China, who acknowledged no colonies, nor to the Dutch, who had totally failed in the attempt to establish their authority there.

Deploring the Dutch trading monopoly which had virtually put an end to the once flourishing China trade of the whole of West Borneo, Earl foresaw the speedy approach of an economic crisis which would bring about the ruin of Montrado. Four years later two missionaries, Doty and Pohlman, visited the town. They reported it diminished in numbers, but stated that the diminution had been caused by feuds among the Chinese themselves, fomented, 'as the [Dutch] resident of Sambas informed us', by the Malay sultan. Even so, however, they estimated that probably ten thousand persons resided under the 'kongsi-ship' of Montrado. The Chinese themselves, they add, reckoned twenty thousand.

From Montrado they visited Sipang, which was the headquarters of the San-Ti-Qu Kongsi, and estimated about eight hundred to one thousand people there.

THE LANGFANG KONGSI AT MANDOR

They also visited Mandor, the capital of the Langfang Kongsi. There they found one principal street, about a quarter of a mile in length, with another running parallel, and some at right angles. The houses were in good order, and well built. Most of them were constructed of wood, and covered with shingles. The streets were unusually wide for a Chinese village, and remarkably neat and clean. They declared themselves 'somewhat surprised at the small number of inhabitants. Compared with Montrado, we were reminded of the deserted towns in America during the prevalence of the cholera. Instead of being literally crammed, as is generally the case, so that one can scarcely move without treading on his neighbour, the dwellings are larger than usual, and few, if any, inhabit each'. This was explained by the exhaustion of the local mines, but as we shall see later there was more probably a political explanation. Later on the Langfang Kongsi was to regain much of the position it had had before, and to outlast its rival, Takong, by about thirty years.

The Dutch scholar de Groot has published a Chinese document, written by Yap Hsiang Yun, the son-in-law of the last 'governor', which describes the structure and history of this Langfang Kongsi in fair detail. Earl's remarks on the organization of Takong, and de Groot's reiterated insistence on the similarity between Chinese village-structure and Borneo Kongsi-structure, make it clear that there was little difference between different Kongsi. In describing the structure of Langfang we are describing the structure of all.

The Langfang Kongsi, like nearly all the others, consisted almost entirely of Hakka people. De Groot suggests that the Hakkas, who in China live surrounded by members of other dialect-groups, have possibly developed a peculiarly strong tendency toward in-group cohesion. Be that as it may, it is perfectly clear that the basis of the Kongsi was the clan and village structure and sentiment which the immigrants brought with them from China. Lo Fong Pak 羅芳伯, the founder of Langfang, arrived in Pontianak in about 1772[14] with a hundred-odd Hakkas from his own department, Kiaying 嘉應,[15] in Kwangtung. Whether these men were all members of the same clan is not quite clear.[16] This group seems quickly to have formed a nucleus around which other Kiaying Hakkas in Pontianak soon gathered.[17] Pontianak, however, contained large numbers of Teochows 潮州 who were continually harassing the Hakkas. Lo Fong Pak decided to lead his group elsewhere, making first for Shan Hsin, an upstream settlement of Tap'u Hakkas which he attacked by surprise. The leader of the Tap'u settlers, Chiang Ah Ts'ai 張阿才, fled with his followers. Lo Fong Pak installed himself in his place, and by kind treatment won over those who had not fled to his side. This new mixed group of Tap'u and Kiaying 'brothers'[18] went on to open up the forest, dig wells, build houses, and develop mining further inland at Mandor. Far away from all external control the new settlers naturally set up their own political organization, building on the already existing group-structure under the able leadership of Lo Fong Pak. This was the beginning of the Langfang Kongsi.[19]

Several Chinese miners, mostly Hakkas from Kityang and Ch'aoyang 潮陽縣,[20] were already settled in Mandor.[21] These seem to have accepted Lo Fong Pak's leadership, and he later turned his attention to the Hakka communities at Mao-yien and in the neighbourhood of Minwong. Mao-yien[22] consisted of two separate bazaars; the old bazaar contained about two hundred shop-houses with emigrants from Kityang, Ch'aoyang, Haifong 海豐縣, and Lufong 陸豐縣 *hsiens*; the new bazaar was much smaller, with only twenty shops, but all their inhabitants came from the Mei *hsien* of Kiaying. Lo Fong

[14] In *Post-War Overseas Chinese* (Shanghai, 1947), p. 3, the editor, Hsü Yi-ch'uan, writing on the history of West Borneo, gives the probable date of Lo Fong Pak's first arrival as 1758.

[15] The department of Kiaying 嘉應州 in the Ch'ing dynasty contained five *hsiens*: Mei *hsien* 梅縣, Ch'ang-lo 長樂 (present Wu-hua 五華), Chen-p'ing 鎮平 (present Chiao-ling 蕉嶺), Hsing-ning 興寧, and P'ing-yüan 平遠. Lo Fong Pak himself came from Mei *hsien*.

[16] De Groot calls them *familieleden*.

[17] The Chinese text mentions a total of a hundred and eight, but this is a mystic number in Chinese.

[18] The Chinese text has 弟兄.

[19] Lo Fong Pak settled in Mandor in 1777. The name Langfang 蘭芳 means orchid fragrance: a symbol of brotherhood.

[20] Ch'aoyang being in a mixed Teochow-Hakka area, some of these men may have been Teochows.

[21] Otherwise known as Ke-Mondor.

[22] The exact location of this settlement was unknown in de Groot's time. The Chinese gives Mao-yien Shan (Mao-yien mountain).

Pak, himself from this same *hsien*, made a secret agreement with Kong Miu Pak 江戊伯, the headman of the new bazaar, who unexpectedly attacked Wong Kui-pei, headman of the old bazaar, leaving him no alternative but to surrender. In this way the whole of Mao-yien, together with its satellite settlements, Kunjit, Lungkong, Senamen, and others, was added to the Langfang Kongsi. This left Minwong, a settlement of about five hundred Tap'u Hakkas, with its dependents, as the sole Chinese rivals in the immediately neighbouring gold districts. Liu Kong Siong, headman of the Minwong Kongsi, kept up the struggle with Langfang for several years, even extending his own influence at times almost to the boundaries of Mandor itself. In the end, however, Minwong was defeated in what appears to have been a pitched battle, Liu Kong Siong drowned himself in the river and Lo Fong Pak's control was complete.

For some time he nursed the desire to annex the Montrado gold districts, which lay further to the north west. At that time there were seven large Kongsi and six smaller ones in that area: the most important being Takong and San-Ti-Qu. On examining the terrain, however, Lo Fong Pak decided that it would not be profitable to attack.[23] He therefore withdrew, leaving the potential rivalry between Langfang and Takong to flare up at a later date.

Withdrawal from Montrado was followed by a successful struggle with the Sultan of Landak, to the south east. Landak itself was besieged for nine months, and only taken on the attackers' digging a tunnel into the *kampong* and so forcing their way in.[24] Peace was made, and the boundaries demarcated by planting bamboos which were still visible in the eighties.[25]

The story of Lo Fong Pak is completed with references to his opening up a new silver-mine, his frustrated desire to attach his realm to the Chinese Empire and to pay regular tribute, and his magical powers of controlling crocodiles. He died in 1793.

The silver-mine, opened a year before his death, was the occasion of bitter feelings. A man from Chen-p'ing (Chiao-ling) was entrusted with certain valuables with which he was to raise money for provisions in Pontianak. He absconded to China. In an assembly of all the leading men of the Kongsi, Lo Fong Pak swore an oath that for the future only a Kiaying Hakka from Mei *hsien* should hold the highest office in the Kongsi. This became a convention,

[23] The Chinese text explains that Lo Fong Pak, having climbed above Montrado on reconnaissance, declared it to be 'like a sauce-pan'.

[24] Incidentally the leader of the tunnelling party is named Chiang Ah Ts'ai in the Chinese document. This was the name of the leader who once fled from Shan Hsin; apparently he was now reconciled to his old enemy.

[25] Yang Ping-nan 楊炳南, *Hae Luh* 海錄 (A General Record of Foreign Nations) (Shanghai, 1848), also mentions a successful attack under a Langfang commander, named Wu Yuan-shen, upon a Dyak settlement called Tajan.

followed until in 1823 the Dutch cut off direct communication with China.[26]

The history of Lo Fong Pak's successors is largely concerned with troubles with the Land Dyaks and relations with the Dutch.[27] Success against the Dyaks in the early nineteenth century was followed by further clashes in which the latter gained the upper hand in the thirties. By then, too, Dutch pressure, direct and indirect, was beginning to be felt. The American missionaries[28] described Mandor as a declining town in 1838. The decline continued into the forties. In 1849 the Dutch banished the headman and installed one Liu Ah Sin 劉亞生 in his place. At the price of recognizing their suzerainty and remaining consistently pro-Dutch, Liu Ah Sin rebuilt some of the prosperity of Langfang. But its days were numbered. In 1857 Dutch policy came to fruition with the abolition of all the other Kongsi in West Borneo. Langfang alone remained; stripped of most of its sub-districts it out-lasted the others by nearly thirty years, until the death of Liu Ah Sin's son in 1884.[29]

[26] J. Hunt, *Sketch of Borneo*, p. 25, mentions the mines of Mandor as he heard of them in 1812: 'Mandor is about one day's journey from Pontianak . . . it is reckoned a very rich mine though but recently wrought. There are as yet only twelve pallets of about two hundred men each, but it is capable of extension. Likewise are found in this district some very rich specimens of copper ore, not as yet wrought, gold being deemed a much more productive article. . . . Numbers of Chinese are settled in this district and the population is annually increasing.'

[27] The Dutch annexation of West Borneo was completed in 1823.

[28] Doty and Pohlman, *vide supra.*

[29] The following entry appears in the *Sarawak Gazette*, December 1st, 1884: 'Reports of serious outbreaks of Chinese miners at Mandor (about forty miles north of Pontianak) against the Dutch government are continuously being brought over the border, and have been confirmed from Singapore. The ideas prevalent among the Chinese in Upper Sarawak of the magnitude of this outbreak are conflicting, and undoubtedly exaggerated, as to what has already occurred, but are supported in some way by the fact that the Dutch government are despatching troops from Samarang, but this may be in case of the rising becoming general. At present it is confined to Mandor, the Montrado and other Chinese having refused to afford any assistance to the Mandor Kunsi [*sic*], though this on the other hand is denied. By the most reliable accounts it appears that after the funeral of the old Kap Tai, or headman of the Kunsi, which the Controlleur stationed at Mandor himself attended, the government notified many radical changes with regard to the conditions upon which the Kunsi would be allowed to continue to work for gold, imposing tax, doing away with their right of hearing and settling cases amongst themselves, and causing their flagstaff to be cut down. The next day the Controlleur went to the Kunsi house. When he expressed his determination to hear the case there, the Chinese there and then rose and killed him, afterwards burning the government quarters down, and sparing none of the government servants. The Mandor Kunsi are supposed to be able to muster one thousand strong, it is also stated that they are supported by the Malays and Dyaks in the vicinity, that they are well armed and have a large quantity of gunpowder, and rice sufficient to last them for over a year. Many refugees have arrived, principally women and children, who have come by sea, and a few men came overland.

THE CONSTITUTION OF THE LANGFANG KONGSI

De Groot's description of the constitution dates from this period, but harks back to the time before 1857.[30] At its widest extent the Langfang Kongsi comprised at least seven sub-districts—Mampawa and Poko-Klappa, Sungei, Purun, Kampong Baru, Landak, Sepata, and Tunang and Menjunkai, under the leadership of Mandor. After 1857 the structure of authority was carefully defined. At the head was the *Kapthai* 甲大 of Mandor, appointed by the Dutch authorities, to whom he was responsible. The Kapthai in his turn appointed the district heads (*kapitan*) and the village heads (*lo thai* 老大), each appointment being subject to Dutch approval. In this way authority was delegated from the top downwards, and, in theory at least, supreme power, under the Dutch, was lodged in the Kapthai.[31] In practice, however, the Kapthai still relied upon popular consent; he did not rule by force and therefore had to choose his various headmen according to the popular will.[32]

Before 1857, authority in the Kongsi had been delegated from below upwards. According to Yap Hsiang Yun[33] each district had a similar number of officials, who at Lo Fong Pak's death were four in number. These were: a headman, an assistant headman, and two other assistants known as *mi-ko*

Many more are expected, though, owing to the prohibitions imposed by the Dutch government against their crossing the border, they will probably experience some difficulty in effecting their purpose. These Chinese belong chiefly to the agricultural and petty trading classes, who are fearful, however the matter may eventually end, they will meet with trouble. On the one hand, should the Chinese win, they would certainly be squeezed of their small gains, and on the other hand the punishment that would follow a general rising might be extended to themselves.'

[30] De Groot (*op. cit.*, p. 134) stated that no material existed for a study of the constitution before 1850, though there might be important data in the archives of Pontianak and Batavia. He did not explain why these were not available to him.

[31] De Groot likened his position to that of any of any indigenous prince whose authority depended entirely upon Dutch support (*op. cit.*, p. 129).

[32] The Government report for the Netherlands Indies for the year 1857 stated: 'The Kapthai had to contend with the people of bad will who did not desire a better organized administration; but there was no open revolt' (de Groot, *op. cit.*, p. 130). On the other hand Dutch opinion of Liu Ah Sin was thus expressed in 1856 by the highest civil and military officer Lt.-Col. Andersen: 'I must draw your attention to the Kapthai. He is a man of much discipline, who rules in an excellent way and who has *complete power* over the Chinese. He uses his influence wisely and has proved that he understands and will pursue the betterment which the Dutch government must necessarily bring in. As long as he is at the head of this district you can leave the government of the Chinese in Chinese hands.'

[33] Son-in-law to Liu Ah Sin; writer of the document published by de Groot. See note 13.

尾哥 and *lo-t'ai* 老大.[34] Each district had the same grade of officials, those of Mandor being the head men of the Kongsi as a whole. Each settlement of any significance had an assistant headman, a *mi-ko*, and a *lo-t'ai*. The assistant headmen were paid, but the *mi-ko* and *lo-t'ai* held honorary posts. Earl states that the headman of the Takong Kongsi (Montrado) received an annual salary of a thousand dollars.[35] The adult men in each settlement elected their local officials. These in their turn were responsible for electing, from their own number, the district and Kongsi officials.

The method of election is nowhere described.[36] De Groot points out that it was always the richest and most influential men in the individual villages who were chosen. These influential men also provided the district heads, and one of them was at the head of the whole Kongsi.[37] From this writer's insistence upon the close resemblance between the Kongsi system and village organization in the Hakka-speaking districts of Kwangtung and Fukien, it is possible to infer that each settlement in West Borneo was probably a fairly close-knit group of immigrants most of whom were either clan relatives or at least from the same locality in China. In the new environment the criterion of mere seniority, said to be all important for clan and village leadership in the stable community life of China, would be of less importance than considerations of personal ability and prestige. The settlements were not merely groups of people who happened to live near one another; most of the men were fellow-workers in a gold-mine. Qualities of leadership would necessarily be recognized and utilized; the choice of leaders would not be difficult.

Earl, writing of Montrado (Takong Kongsi) in 1834, remarked: 'The territory [is] divided into districts, each of which is governed by several representatives, elected by the people, every male inhabitant having a vote.

[34]Headman: *thai-ko*, elder brother: 大哥 ; Assistant headman: *fu t'ou-jen*: 副頭人; Assistant (*i*) *mi-ko*, younger elder brother: 尾哥 , (*ii*) *lo-thai*, elder: 老大 .

These terms are given here in the Dutch romanization of the Hakka pronunciation. See de Groot, pp. 20-21. Actually it seems that only the Kongsi head himself (at Mandor) was called *thai-ko*. The district head of Mampawa, for example, was *ni-ko* 二哥 (second elder brother, *ibid.*, p. 139). *Kapitan* was the term applied by the Malays to the district heads, who in some places at least acquired this name as a title from the local sultans. The definite allocation of the terms *Kapthai* (Kongsi head), *Kapitan* (district head), and *mi-ko* (village or settlement head) was a late development.

The word *Kapthai* had a curious origin: the headman of the Kongsi was apparently referred to as *Kapitan tuan*. In the Fukien dialect this *tuan* was equated with *toa* 頭 meaning 'great'. In Hakka 'great' is *thai* (Mandarin *ta*). The well-known Chinese predilection for using only one syllable of a foreign name if possible thus accounts for the bastard word *Kapthai* (*ibid.*, p. 139).

[35]De Groot, *op. cit.*, p. 191.

[36]But see de Groot, *op. cit.*, p. 128, footnote.

[37]*Ibid.*, p. 127.

The representatives, or Kung Se,[38] elect the governor who has the direction of all the affairs of the territory, domestic and foreign, but he is expected to consult the Kung Se when transacting any business of importance.[39] The latter are entrusted with the administration of justice in their respective districts, but capital offences are always referred to the governor. They continue in office as long as it suits the pleasure of their constituents, who, on suspicion of misconduct, will depose the obnoxious members and elect others in their room.'[40]

Consultation with the district and settlement representatives was a feature of all the Kongsi. 'The president', wrote de Groot, 'had to discuss nearly all matters of importance with the leaders of lesser rank'.[41] This, together with their power to elect—and depose—the Kongsi and district heads,[42] obviously gave to the district and village officials the most influential position in the whole Kongsi. It was important, therefore, that these men should represent the various groups within the Kongsi satisfactorily. The majority of the Langfang population was of Hakka origin, but there were some members of other groups. Clearly a small settlement was likely to be made up of people from the same place of origin, often indeed members of the same clan. Where this was so, there would be no difficulty in electing as officials people from that same district or even clan.[43]

Larger settlements, districts, and, of course, the whole Kongsi itself would contain people of several different places of origin. There is evidence that in such cases officials might be specially chosen to represent minority groups.

[38] The term Kongsi (Kung Se) may be used to apply to the whole community or to the governing body of officials alone. See note 12.

[39] The reality of this convention was proved to Earl by the events of his visit. On reaching Montrado he was met by 'the governor and Kung Se' but it was not until the following day when all the officials of the sub-districts were present that the governor would discuss business: 'It not being his wish to make any arrangements before these officials had been consulted [p. 285]. . . . At the time appointed, the Kung Se of the neighbouring districts, to the number of about fifty, assembled in the great room of the governor's house, and after deliberating about half an hour, they all entered my apartment, and the governor informed me that they had agreed to open the port to me and they hoped that hereafter their communication with Singapore would be more frequent' (p. 288).

[40] *Ibid.*, pp. 290-91.

[41] *Op. cit.*, p. 127.

[42] Deposition is mentioned by Earl (above); de Groot (pp. 130-31) describes how, in Langfang and Takong, Kongsi heads who were too pro-Dutch were repudiated.

[43] De Groot, *op. cit.*, *passim*, e.g. 'The Kongsi was composed of a group of families sprung from the same clan, or of a collection of such groups . . . each with its own leader . . . the headman of the whole Kongsi was exactly like the "patriarch" in a Chinese village: no more than the leader of the foremost group, a "primus inter pares" ' (pp. 118-19).

In Mampawa district at one time, for instance, there were two headmen: one Hakka and one Teochow, and a similar double leadership existed in the settlements of Naala, Pak Wulu, Lumut, and Senamen which 'each had the honour to have an extra Tap'u headman'.[44] We have also seen how at his death Lo Fong Pak had laid it down that although the Kongsi head must always be a Kiaying Hakka from Mei *hsien*, the assistant head should be a man from Tap'u. Thus there seems to have been an attempt to balance the possibly contending interests of different groups within the Kongsi and its sub-districts.

Within their own areas the elected officials were responsible for the maintenance of law and order and for dealing with disputes and offences. Consultation in the settlements was with the family heads, and at the district and Kongsi levels with the other officials. Judgement on 'important matters' had to be discussed with the Kongsi head, and cases of robbery, murder, and political crime were brought before a court consisting of the Kongsi head and other officials sitting in the Kongsi house in Mandor.

This Kongsi house[45] had been built in Mandor as an assembly-hall and a dwelling-place for the Kongsi head. It filled the place of the ancestral hall in a Chinese village, being the centre for executive and judicial meetings, election assemblies, and community ritual. De Groot describes the hall of ustice as he saw it in the eighties:[46] 'Just opposite the main entrance stood a large, high table: the "bench". On it were arranged a number of outsize imitation brushes and other writing implements, boxes containing the seals of the Kongsi government and cases of bamboo sticks'.[47] In all this the Langfang Kongsi was following the customs of China. On both sides of the main door stood split bamboo sticks, with leather whips and red- and black-brimmed sugar-loaf hats—all part of the uniform of a Chinese police official. The split bamboos and whips were the chief instruments of punishment in China, used, as the fasces in Rome, to clear crowds before the mandarins. In Mandor in the eighties they were carried in procession before the Dutch resident. Outside the entrance stood a few ancient cannon, fired in salute on important occasions.

The Kongsi house had been built by Lo Fong Pak, and at his death a tablet had been erected for him in the assembly room. The founder of the Kongsi

[44] *Ibid.*, pp. 55, 58.

[45] *T'ang* 堂. The Kongsi house at Mandor as it was in the nineteenth century, has been described, with a plan, by P. J. Veth, *Borneos Westerafdeeling*. It is still standing today, and is now the local Chinese school. *Post-War Overseas Chinese*, 'West Borneo', p. 25; see note 14.

[46] *Op. cit.*, p. 123.

[47] Each case contained five sticks. These were thrown at a convicted man to indicate the number of times he had to be flogged.

thus became, in de Groot's phrase, its 'protecting deity'.[48] On feast-days, and on the anniversaries of his birth and death, his worship was performed with sacrifices by the Kapthai and other officials. The people of the Kongsi fully realized that their welfare depended upon the continued care of their founder. When a new mine was opened, when crops were in danger of flood, when any matter or high importance was afoot, sacrifice was offered to Lo Fong Pak.[49] This kind of pseudo-ancestor or culture-hero cult was complemented by the worship of Kwanti 關帝.[50] A picture of Kwanti hung in the inner hall of the Kongsi house, and every year, on the 13th of the First, Fifth, and Eighth Chinese month, food-offerings were placed before it. The rites were performed by the Kongsi head himself, but in the presence of all the district and settlement officials. Their presence being obligatory, the opportunity was usually taken to use these occasions for consultative, judicial, and electoral meetings—held under the eyes of both spiritual patrons.

OTHER KONGSI OF SARAWAK

There is no reason to suppose that the other Kongsi of West Borneo were essentially different from Langfang. The predominantly Hakka population, the gold-mining background, the settlements composed largely of people nearly related to each other or from the same locality in China, grouped in districts under the central authority of a Kongsi head at a capital town, the principle of two-stage election which left the reality of power in the hands of the representative officials of settlement and district but gave the highest ritual authority to the Kongsi head, the lively, classless spirit—these existed in all.[51] The political development of each Kongsi also followed a similar cycle: origin in a close-knit immigrant group under the charismatic leadership of an able individual, and expansion by accretion and conquest (or

[48] Mandarin: *Ta Pai Kung* 大伯公. The term was used by the Dutch for any Chinese deity or spiritual being.

[49] Outsiders were permitted to approach the tablet only if they were sufficiently exalted persons. Thus de Groot himself was excluded, but the Dutch resident, van Zutphen, was allowed in.

[50] Described by de Groot as God of War and of merchants (cf. J.J.M. de Groot, *Annual Festivals and Customs of the Amoy Chinese*). Kwanti is also famous as a guardian of sworn brotherhood groups.

[51] The writer of an article (in Chinese) published in *Post-War Overseas Chinese* (Singapore, 1948) tells how his grandfather described the original Kongsi organization as an almost ideal form of common weal. The members worked together in all matters. The gold they secured was buried and dug up at the end of each year for equal distribution. They planted vegetables and bred pigs, sharing the produce equally amongst themselves. Except for a very few imported goods, such as salt, they were completely self-supporting.

alternatively absorption into a larger group), was followed by clashes with the indigenous peoples and struggles with the Dutch. With these clashes and struggles inter-Kongsi rivalry was deeply confused.

In July 1850, the most powerful of the West Borneo Kongsi, Takong,[52] attacked members of its rival San-Ti-Qu Kongsi[53] in Seminis, and drove them out of the town. Some escaped northwards, others fled to Pamangat, from where they sent a messenger begging for help from the Dutch at Pontianak. Dutch rivalry with Takong was already acute, and Sambas, the Sultanate in which these events were occurring, was theoretically under Dutch control. Infantry were despatched, but arrived, just a day too late, to find that the San-Ti-Qu Kongsi house in Pamangat had been blown up by their enemies and that all who could had fled. Some escaped across the Sambas river, to the right bank, where they were succoured by the people of Langfang, themselves rivals of Takong and allies of the Dutch; others went north into Sarawak, where, with their 'brothers' from Seminis, they formed a group of three thousand-odd refugees in the Bau area.[54]

Chinese Kongsi had been in existence in the interior of Sarawak for some time. We know from Rajah Brooke's own account that he had had a brush with a San-Ti-Qu Kongsi in 1842[55] and it seems that this was a branch of the San-Ti-Qu of West Borneo. Certainly many of the new arrivals settled in the Bau area and swelled the San-Ti-Qu Kongsi there to what St. John called 'inconvenient' dimensions.[56]

There is evidence of at least two other, much smaller, waves of refugees from Dutch territory, in 1854 and 1856,[57] and it is tempting to suggest a fairly direct connection between the events in West Borneo in 1856 and in Sarawak in 1857.[58] Sufficient evidence is not available to the writer, however, and it is enough at present to connect the strong Hakka element in Sarawak today with the situation of a hundred years ago and before. Further immigration by land from Dutch territory and, especially, by sea from China has, of

[52] Capital at Montrado.

[53] Capital at Sipang.

[54] The head of the San-Ti-Qu Kongsi in Bau was Liu Shan-Pan. Even to this day it is believed that he opened up the Bau area and his tablet is revered and his name mentioned on all festival occasions. The dominant clan in the Bau area today is 'Liu', and the present Capitan China is one Liu Yüen-Fu who claims to be the third generation there.

[55] R. Mundy, *Narrative of Events in Borneo and Celebes down to the Occupation of Labuan, from the Journals of James Brooke Esq.* (London, 1848), pp. 285-94.

[56] Spenser St. John, *Life in the Forests of the Far East*, Vol. II, p. 345. There was a Kongsi house at Bau in 1850. Before the Japanese war the Kuching Museum held two copper coins of a type once minted and circulated by the San-Ti-Qu Kongsi.

[57] *Ibid.*, pp. 347-52.

[58] In 1857 there was a serious Chinese uprising in Sarawak.

course continued over the years. Many who would have gone to join their relatives and neighbours in West Borneo must have come to Sarawak instead. Hakkas certainly still constitute the greater part of the Chinese population in the First and Second Divisions of Sarawak.

7. Cash or Credit Crops?*

An Examination of Some Implications of Peasant Commercial Production with Special Reference to the Multiplicity of Traders and Middlemen

> When I first knew Sarawak practically every Chinese Bazaar was an exact copy of every other except in size. The days of plate glass windows, show cases and English speaking assistants had not arrived. The same goods were stocked in the same way—rather higgledy-piggledy to our lights—but according to a system of their own. Boxes of rice, carefully graded according to quality. Tubs of various pastes, all rather smelly but undoubtedly good—pickled eggs of some antiquity, strings of vermicelli, exotic looking Chinese dried fruits, layers and layers of salt fish, salt, sugar, bits of shark, birdsnests; all these foods which the people love. Behind were bales of calico, that unbleached cloth known as 'blachu', dark blue cotton, bright red cotton. Bundles of cheap flowered cloths, imitation 'batik' sarongs, and butter muslin. Straw hats, sock suspenders, purse belts, singlets, made-up bow ties, and hair ribbons. Tiger balm, camphor oil, Dr. Williams' Pink Pills, and vaseline. Tin plates, kettles, clogs, and pocket knives—what a collection! —but all desirable to the people. Candidly, I don't know how all these shops carried it all. Then of course the ways of Chinese commerce are a mystery to us. *In a small town you might get twenty or thirty of these shops, all the same and all receiving custom.*[1]

Many writers have remarked the multiplicity of apparently identical small shops and petty traders in many parts of the non-Western world. Many have taken the line that this reduplication is necessarily uneconomic, only to be explained by the 'irrationality' of the local people or, as here, the 'mysteries' of the Orient. In certain parts of the British Colonial Empire, notably Uganda, attempts were early made to limit the numbers of retail traders by insisting upon a system of licences which would, it was believed, protect the 'genuine' traders from such 'uneconomic' competition. The multiplicity of middlemen to be found in the export trade of many of the colonial territories was (and is) often under a similar fire of criticism both from the local administrations and from Whitehall.

Recently there has been a reversal of attitudes, if not on the part of

*Reprinted by permission of University of Chicago Press from *Economic Development and Cultural Change*, Vol. VIII, No. 2 (January 1960), pp. 148-163.

[1] J. B. Archer, 'Autobiography', unpublished MS. quoted in T'ien Ju-k'ang, *The Chinese of Sarawak*, London School of Economics Monographs on Social Anthropology No. 12 (London, 1953), p. 37.

governments, at least on the part of some economists and economic historians. P. T. Bauer[2] in particular has emphasized that there are certain essential economic services concerned with both the distribution of consumer goods and the collection of primary produce which can best be supplied for a largely peasant producing population by a great multiplicity of middlemen. In the following pages attention is drawn to the significance in this respect of one other essential service: namely, the provision of credit.

THE FIELD

The material on which the following observations are based has been drawn mainly from the British Crown Colony of Sarawak, with supporting evidence from Hong Kong, the Federation of Malaya, Uganda, and Ghana.

With the exception of Malaya and Hong Kong, the territories under consideration in this paper are overwhelmingly composed of peasant producers.[3] Even in Malaya at least 40% of the total production of rubber comes from smallholdings,[4] and in Hong Kong I am confining my attention solely to the 25,000 or so people who draw their livelihood from the family-based production of the inshore fishing grounds.

SMALL-SCALE COMMERCIAL PRIMARY PRODUCTION REQUIRES MIDDLEMEN

The common characteristic of those sections of these several societies which are concerned with commercial primary production by peasants is not the crop, nor the rhythms and methods of production—for these are all different—but the need to put the primary product on the market in order to obtain any reward at all. It is here in the marketing and especially the first level (produce-buying) marketing of the primary products that comparable features are to be looked for.

Rubber, sago, fish, coffee, cotton, cocoa differ fundamentally in production, but share one negative property in that none in itself provides subsistence for its producer: all have to be marketed. Most, also, have to be processed in some way, or ways, essential to their final acceptance on the world markets, to which they must in addition be 'communicated' through the often complex systems of overseas export. Both processing and communication may be

[2] P. T. Bauer, *West African Trade* (Cambridge, 1954), Ch. 2.

[3] R. W. Firth, *Malay Fishermen: Their Peasant Economy* (London, 1946), pp. 22-27 and *passim.*

[4] Figures refer to 1953 production. Federation of Malaya, *Annual Report for 1954* (London, 1955).

difficult, even impossible, for the peasant producer himself to perform. Sarawak's sago must be refined, bagged, and shipped to Singapore; Uganda's cotton must be ginned and exported to America, Britain, or India; much of Hong Kong's fish must be dried and salted or made into pungent red sauce, and although most of it is eaten in the colony itself, no fisherman has the time or skill to see to his own retailing. Thus, as has often been remarked, because peasant producers themselves do not usually have the requisite time or skill to do more than start their produce on the first rung of the market ladder, societies in which their type of commercial production predominates necessarily require middlemen to take over the primary products and handle them on their way to the wider markets.

There is an obverse to this situation: commercial primary producers require not only to sell but to buy. A society of this kind therefore necessarily also demands middlemen in the distributive trades, from the big importers in the ports down to the small shopkeepers, street hawkers, and so forth who go to the most minute villages and settlement up-country.

It is thus with the relatively small-scale trade with which peasant producers are involved that this paper is primarily concerned. Estate workers (wage laborers) have a place in this trade, but only as buyers of consumer goods (including foodstuffs), not as sellers of primary produce. Peasant producers, whether small landholders or fishermen, are involved in both buying and selling.

Despite the lack of exact enumeration, there is no doubt that except where they have been deliberately restricted by administrative action, the numbers of small-scale middlemen in the societies under consideration are large. So are those of retailers. How is this to be accounted for?

Obviously, one explanation lies in the difficulties of transport and communication in underdeveloped territories. Cocoa farmers in the depths of the Ghana rain forest, sago gardens up the Oya River in Sarawak cannot all be visited easily by one or two large-scale produce buyers, and cannot all be served easily by one or two large central stores. Though it carries force, however, this argument does not explain why—to let just one example stand for many—one small Hong Kong fishing village, with a total population (including women and small children) of just over 400, had (in 1953) room for two almost identical general shops and made use of the services of up to 13 fish buyers.[5]

My suggestion is that such a state of affairs is at least partly to be accounted for by the fact that in many of the small-scale kinds of situation we are

[5] All data for Hong Kong are drawn from my own field notes. I am deeply indebted to the Committee for Foreign Languages and Cultures set up by H. M. Treasury (the Scarborough Committee) for enabling me to spend the years 1950-53 in Hong Kong.

considering here, a large proportion of the everyday commercial transactions —produce-buying, retailing, paying for services of all kinds, including those of a predominantly 'social' nature such as funerals, weddings, etc.—is carried on by means of some form of credit arrangement. In the vast majority of cases the creditor parties to such arrangements themselves have very little capital, and the number of debtors they can serve is therefore closely restricted. Furthermore, these are nearly always arrangements of personal trust made between individuals who are well acquainted with each other, and there is a limit to the number of individuals any one creditor can know well enough to trust in this way, even if he has (as he usually has not) a relatively large stock of capital.

The rest of this paper is devoted to amplifying and defending this point of view.

THE DEPENDENCE UPON CREDIT

In a book entitled *The Chinese of Sarawak, A Study of Social Structure*, T'ien Ju-k'ang[6] describes in detail the relationship which exists between Chinese primary producers and Chinese middlemen in that country. This is based upon an elaborate system of credit.

In Sarawak the Chinese village shopkeepers are at the same time the lowest level middlemen in the rubber trade. This congruence of middlemen and retailer roles in one individual is not particularly common; it simplifies but does not essentially alter the general picture. T'ien claims that 'in effect these Chinese village shopkeepers in Sarawak who own some capital act as loan making capitalists and bankers, while the planters, who have none, constitute a labour force in their employ'.[7]

What happens in fact is that, although a Chinese rubber planter in Sarawak does his shopping in the street markets for cash, and also pays for larger items —such as furniture, a bicycle, a radio, a watch, school-fees, or a wedding for his son—with cash (very often borrowed), he gets most of his everyday supplies of rice, other groceries, kerosene, hardware, etc., from the village shop of his choice on credit. The middleman-retailer (i.e., the shopkeeper) keeps a small notebook for each planter family. In it he writes down a credit and debt account of rubber (or other produce) again 'groceries'. (The account is always kept in money values; there is no question of barter.)

Rubber planters who have a long-standing connexion with the shop simply send their rubber sheets in, almost every afternoon, often by the children,

[6] *Op. cit., passim.*
[7] *Ibid.*, p. 37.

trusting the shopkeeper to write down the correct current price. Others may spend a long time each day ascertaining the current price and making sure that it is correctly entered. In either case the next daily step is to order the daily grocery supplies—from the same shop. If all goes well, the value of the rubber brought in may be just enough to cover the cost of necessities, if not each day, then at least over a reasonably short period. . . . Through a long process of accumulation it has now become established that by paying off only a portion of his outstanding debt a regular client can always get further provisions on credit. As the average rubber holding is small and the price of rubber low, a client can almost never pay off the whole debt. . . ."[8] Moreover, be it noted, neither he nor his creditor expects him to do so.

The uglier word for 'credit', of course, is 'debt'. The Chinese planters in Sarawak are continuously in debt to their local Chinese middlemen-*cum*-retailers. It is a situation which may well give scope for unscrupulous exploitation. But to stress only this potential (albeit sometimes real) evil, without appreciating the indispensability of both the middleman's function and the provision of credit and without even noticing the safeguards which in fact exist, is to be unrealistic.

We earlier discussed the essential nature of the middleman's function in societies which depend largely upon peasant primary production. We have now shifted our interest to the apparently equally indispensable requirement for some system of credit. The small planters alone would not be able to get their produce out to the markets, nor would they be willing to produce at all without consumer goods to buy. At the same time they are extremely short of cash. In these circumstances the credit system acts as a kind of lubricant which keeps the machinery of production going. Thus the export of primary produce depends as much upon the rural retailers and middlemen as it does upon the peasant small holders.[9]

The sago-producing areas of another part of Sarawak further demonstrate the essential, lubricating nature of credit.[10] Northeast of Kuching, in the Third Division of Sarawak, an indigenous people—the Melanau—are engaged almost exclusively in the small-scale peasant production of sago flour. This they produce by rather arduous methods and then sell to the local middlemen in the sago trade for further processing and resale. These middlemen are all

[8] *Ibid.*, p. 43.

[9] Moreover, as T'ien points out, 'it is not only the primary producers who are in difficulties. The rural middlemen-*cum*-retailers, too, are faced by an apparently insoluble dilemma. They cannot afford to go on lending in this way, but they can do nothing else either, for only by allowing credit in return for part payment can they hope to get any return at all' (*ibid.*, p. 44).

[10] H. S. Morris, *A Melanau Sago Producing Community* (London, 1954).

Chinese. Like their counterparts in the rubber trade, they are also local retailers and manage their businesses in the same way. It is quite clear, from the published description, that they fully appreciate the economic significance of the credit system, for they deliberately use their position to compel the sago farmers to keep up a steady supply of flour.

The Melanau do not share the Chinese passion for work: rather than time being money to them, they take the line that money is time—money being valued only insofar as it can buy prestige and time for leisure and conversation. Thus a Melanau family which has produced a certain amount of sago flour will hope to sit back for a while. Knowing this, the Chinese middleman-retailers do their best to keep the Melanau in the red so that they can continually be reminded of their debts and urged to bring in more sago under threat of having their supplies of credit cut off. In this way two purposes are served: on the one hand, the retailers' clientele is bound ever more closely to him, thus making poaching by other traders (or, incidentally, the entry of new traders, including of course non-Chinese) difficult; on the other hand, and from the point of view of the economy as a whole more importantly, the flow of sago to the exporters is maintained and at a fairly steady rate.

A very similar state of affairs obtains in the fishing villages of Hong Kong. A small fisherman is likely to be in debt to his fish dealer (middleman) because he has had to borrow cash from him at some time or another in order to buy new gear, or repair his boat, or marry his son—for example. In return, he gives no security other than a lien on future catches. Boats and gear are not 'mortgaged', but in effect, future catches are. The middleman recoups his loan by installments (usually at Chinese New Year) and takes interest by deducting from the price of the fish which he can get in the official markets. It pays both producer and middleman that their relationship should be an everlasting one: the fisherman knows he can raise a loan without delay; the dealer has a steady source of income. Indeed, like their compatriots in Sarawak, these small-scale fish middlemen do not expect ever to call in all their loans, nor do the fishermen expect ever to pay up completely.

Unlike the Sarawak agriculturalists, however, the Hong Kong fishermen usually maintain at least two credit relationships, for the middlemen in the fish trade are not usually connected (at least not directly) with retail business. For his groceries and so forth a fisherman must go to separate local shops. He cannot usually pay fully in cash, not having enough, but if personally known to the shopkeeper can open a credit account on which to buy daily necessities. (Once again, as in Sarawak, large items are bought with cash—usually borrowed from the fish middlemen—and street marketing is also always done in cash.) When the Chinese New Year comes round the theory is that all debts should be paid. Sometimes they are. More often, the fisherman seeks out the shopkeeper, entertains him at some expense in the teahouse, and confers with him as to how much should be paid off. (He does exactly the same thing with his fish middleman.) An installment or a loan keeps credit open for the next year. Usually the prices entered in such credit accounts with the shops are not higher than those paid by cash buyers, but a percentage may be added to the total sum in the books (the actual rate often varying with the relationship of the debtor to the shopkeeper).

The successful continuance of Hong Kong's fishing industry, no less than that of Sarawak's cash crop economy, depends upon the existence of a working system of credit and/or of loans. For Malaya the works of Bauer[11] and Firth[12] tell a similar tale, and it seems that in the eastern parts at least of Uganda[13] and the cocoa areas of Ghana[14] something similar may be true: at least in all the peasant producing areas of three territories, locally organized systems of credit and/or loan-giving are well established. I am not trying to argue that all those who give cash loans or allow credit to peasant primary producers do so out of a sense of social obligation. Of course they do nothing of the sort, and of course they take whatever economic (or other) advantage of the position of relative power which the status of creditor implies that they can. On the other hand, they are performing an essential economic service, for which no other agency exists at present.[15] Moreover, as we shall have cause to mention again, most of them are small men, very frequently themselves indebted to others, and in the last resort, as dependent upon their own debtors as these latter are upon them. Finally, in the very multiplicity of creditors lies part, at least, of the debtors' safeguard.[16]

THE MULTIPLICITY OF CREDITORS

But it is this multiplicity with which we are here concerned. Others have argued the significance of credit, but rather less attention has been paid to the multiplicity of creditors.

Two essential features of the types of credit system under discussion are: (1) the creditors themselves are normally small men with very limited amounts of capital at their disposal; (2) credit is almost invariably given without

[11] P. T. Bauer, *The Rubber Industry, a Study in Competition and Monopoly* (London, 1948).

[12] *Op. cit.*, Ch. VI.

[13] Dr. J. la Fontaine, verbal communication.

[14] Polly Hill, *The Gold Coast Cocoa Farmer*, Chs. V, VI, VII.

[15] P. T. Bauer has on several occasions pointed to the safeguards provided by the existence of large numbers of middlemen competing among themselves. See, for example, his *Rubber Industry in Malaya*, pp. 361 ff., and *West African Trade*, Ch. 18.

[16] I.e., credit sales amounting to this sum.

security in the full sense, simply on the personal reputation of the debtor, or rather one should say on the personal knowledge of the creditor. These two facts between them account for the multiplicity of creditors and hence very largely for the multiplicity of small-scale middlemen and retailers.

Little appears to have been published about the amounts of liquid capital available for cash lending to primary producers. It is information which would, in any case, be not too easily obtained in the field. Nevertheless, some indications that it is often very small do exist. As regards the granting of credit by village shopkeepers, it is well known that in these two territories at least, and in Malaya, a small village shopkeeper is often himself dependent for stock buying upon a credit account with another businessman (sometimes another retailer) higher up the scale. In Sarawak, indeed, there appears to be a regular 'ladder' of credit accounts of this kind leading right up from the small rural bazaars to the importers in Kuching, who themselves may be in a somewhat similar relationship with bigger firms in Singapore.

As for the personalization of credit, that too is well authenticated. One small shopkeeper in a Hong Kong fishing village told me: 'I give credit to anyone who anchors regularly in our own bay; but if it is someone I don't know well, then I think twice about it unless I can find out all about him.' T'ien makes much the same point when he describes how small Chinese rubber planters in Sarawak tend always to patronize shopkeepers with the same surnames as themselves. The notion is that shared surname implies shared kinship, and kinsmen are by definition 'known' and trustworthy. It is, indeed, fairly obvious that small-scale peasant producers are not likely to be able to get credit on any other than personal terms such as these. Much of the work of the cooperative movement in underdeveloped territories is based precisely—and successfully—upon just this argument. In other words, the successful working of a system of commercial primary production by peasants requires the existence of a credit system that is not only extensive but also highly personalized. But if credit is to be advanced only to personal acquaintances, then there is a limit—and a fairly low limit—to the number of clients any one creditor can have.

Figures collected by T'ien in Sarawak and by myself in Hong Kong give ample evidence in support of this common sense observation. Writing of the scale of the rural credit system in Sarawak, T'ien reports: 'At one point along the Simanggang Road there are about 15 shops. Most of these are small, single-line establishments, but 7 are fairly large grocery-*cum*-rubber-dealer stores. Of these the 3 most recently opened have each about $2,000 out on loan, 4 others between $4,000 and $6,000, and one, the largest and oldest. . . . claims an outstanding loan of about $7,000. In a certain bazaar in the Bau area there are a dozen grocer-dealers. Six of them claim to have advanced goods to the value of between $4,000 and $5,000, five $5,000, and one, the largest . . . as much as $10,000. In one coastal bazaar the majority of the 20 grocer-dealers stated in 1949 that they had advanced between $1,000 and $2,000 worth of goods, but 2 claimed $8,000 and the largest . . . stated himself that he was owed as much as $15,000.'[17] T'ien points out that all these figures were collected by direct questioning shopkeepers, and it is possible that an element of boasting may have led to exaggeration, in which case the actual value of goods advanced on credit would be even less. It seems, for example, that other shopkeepers did not share the last man's estimate of his own position, but suggested that the true sum was probably about one-third or even one-half smaller.

The amounts owed to the shops by individual debtors range in value from about $50 to about $2,000.[18] For example, the distribution of debts owed to one shopkeeper in the Bau area is listed by T'ien as follows:[19]

Amount owed	Number of debtors
$ 40-50	9
51-100	15
101-200	21
201-300	24
301-400	9
401-500	2
501-600	1
601-800	2

Now these are not very large sums. Say a rural shopkeeper has outstanding credit accounts amounting to $2,000. This means that he has at the most 10 credit customers with a $200 debt each, or, if the average debt were as low as $50, which is unlikely, this still would give him only 50 credit customers. Yet nearly all custom is done on credit; it is no wonder that there is such an apparently disproportionate number of traders.

My own figures for the inshore fishermen of Hong Kong tell very much the same story. The two small centres of Tai Po and Sai Kung in 1951-52 were the main marketing bases for 327 and 322 fishing boats respectively. In Tai Po there were only three successful middlemen and a small, fluctuating,

[17] *Ibid.*, p. 43. The Straits dollar was at that time worth about 2/6d sterling. Thus the sums mentioned here range from about £125 to about £1,850. The term 'grocer-dealers' refers to shopkeepers described elsewhere in my text as 'middlemen-retailers'.
[18] I.e., about £6.5.0d. to about £250.
[19] *Ibid.*

number of less successful ones. But Tai Po itself housed a wholesale fish market, and it was easily possible for very many Tai Po fishermen to market their own catches direct. In other words, most Tai Po fishermen do not require the handling services of a middleman. The successful Tai Po middlemen were those three who had enough capital to be able to provide the service the fishermen could not perform for themselves: they could all make loans. But between them they did not have more than about $H.K.14,000,[20] at most, out on loan in 1952. At, say, $H.K.100 a client—and most loans would be larger—this gives an average of about 46 or 47 clients apiece. In Sai Kung where the nearest wholesale market is at Kowloon, fourteen miles away overland, there were 16 middlemen to the 322 fishing boats enumerated there in 1952. Some Sai Kung area fishermen take their own fish direct by sea to the market; some even accompany it overland; but even assuming that all dealt exclusively through these middlemen, there would be 20-21 fishermen only to each one. Actually, of course, the Sai Kung middlemen were not all equally successful. Once again the successful ones were those who were able to make loans (usually from funds supplied to themselves on loan from further up the market ladder in Kowloon), but again, the number of clients was quite small—between about a dozen and about two score.

Now it is my suggestion that the small size of these various clienteles is not to be wondered at, because the creditors themselves have little capital to invest (and much of that little is itself in the form of credit) and because no creditor can be expected to know more than, say, perhaps one hundred people well enough to extend personal credit to them. Indeed, the maximum number of such relationships of personal trust may well be considerably less.

The hypothesis to which we are led may be stated as follows: if, in a population which depends upon a wide distribution of credit, no creditor can be expected to have more than a limited number of debtors, then necessarily that population must include (or have access to) a large number of creditors.

It follows that if, as in Sarawak and Hong Kong, the most usual sources of rural credit are the local middlemen and retailers, there must, irrespective of transport and other factors, be expected to be a large number of these people. As indeed there are.

TESTING THE HYPOTHESIS

The most obvious and satisfactory test for this hypothesis would be an examination of its corollary. That is, to discover what, in the kind of economic

[20] I.e., about £850. The Hong Kong dollar is worth about one-half of the Straits dollar, and was at this time valued at about 1/3d or approximately 16 to the £ sterling.

situation we are considering, creditors with more liquid capital available for investment actually do with it. Do such men advance personal credit to more individuals than whatever the expected maximum for their particular community may be? Or do they simply make bigger loans but keep the number of debtors reasonably small? Or do they break out of the personalized system altogether, and go in for 'more businesslike' arrangements, demanding security and fixed terms, putting pressure upon defaulters, and so forth, and if so, at what point on the increasing scale of their activities does this change begin? Or is it more usual for increased capital to be used not for individual loans of this kind at all, but for other forms of investment—land, building, expanding business of various kinds?

These and similar problems lie outside the scope of this paper. They would appear to be crucial to understanding how societies largely dependent upon peasant commercial production may proceed to more differentiated forms of economy. All that I am in a position to do here, however, is to consider my hypothesis, which is already supported by data from Sarawak and Hong Kong, in the light of evidence from other underdeveloped territories in which certain of the conditions which obtain in these two territories do not apply. I shall refer very briefly to Malaya, Uganda, and Ghana.

But first it is necessary to take note of the significance of certain distinctions.

DIFFERENT TYPES OF PURCHASE

Examples of different types of purchase were quoted earlier. They fall into three simple categories, as follows: first, all extraordinary once-and-for-at-least-a-long-time types of expenditure (buying a bicycle, a boat, a sewing machine, clothing, paying for a son's wedding, or a funeral), as well, of course, as those for which official regulations demand payment in money (taxes, school or medical fees, etc.) are made in cash. The payments may be spread out a little, if agreement to do this can be made, but there is not usually a long delay in completion. Such payments which are usually fairly large are made either out of a man's own resources or from loans he has raised from a third party or parties. They are not made on credit accounts.

Second, all petty purchases in street markets or from hawkers, as well as payments for small services (such as bus or ferry fares, hair cuts, entertainment expenses, small religious offerings) are also usually paid in cash. Such small outgoings usually come from the purchaser's own pocket, or possibly an immediate loan of a purely friendly nature.

The third form of purchase is made on a credit account. Goods bought in this way are usually daily necessities (where these have to be obtained from retailers), for example: rice, sugar, tea, kerosene, perhaps cigarettes.

Thus the first type of expenditure (A) often leads to the creation or reinforcement of a loan relationship, the second (B) usually requires the use of ready money, and only the third (C) involves the steady use of a credit account. Some such threefold distinction seems to be widespread. The explanation appears simple. Few peasant (or wage-earning) primary producers are likely to have enough ready cash available to make one of the large-scale payments demanded by type A goods and services out of their own pockets. At the same time the sellers of type A goods and services are usually specialists and/or non-local residents in the bigger trading centres who, in a situation where only personal security is acceptable, cannot be expected to give credit. The purchaser therefore must resort to borrowing cash from someone who does trust him. Type B goods and services, requiring relatively very small if very frequent sums, are sold by individals who are also not in a position to give credit, whether because they have far too little capital themselves, or because they are (often) itinerant or (often) temporary petty traders with inadequate personal knowledge of their customers. It is only type C purchases which, because they are necessarily recurrent and localized and consist of goods which can be successfully stocked only in a permanent building and by at least a relatively full-time and experienced trader, are truly suitable for the type of personal credit account which we have described.

It is therefore necessary to consider in what circumstances daily necessities, particularly staple foodstuffs, do have to be purchased in this way.

DIFFERENT TYPES OF DAILY NECESSITIES, PARTICULARLY FOODSTUFFS

In the modern world it is no longer possible to find any commercial primary producers who are at the same time completely self-sufficient in their own subsistence. Nevertheless there are many who are self-sufficient in at least certain respects. These differences in degree of self-sufficiency are particularly significant insofar as they concern the people's daily necessities.

All the primary producers discussed here make regular purchases of such items as tea, sugar, kerosene. In Sarawak, Hong Kong, and Malaya they also depend upon regular purchases of something more fundamental, namely, rice, and imported rice at that. By strong contrast the staple food of Uganda's cotton and coffee growers and Ghana's cocoa farmers is home grown or purchased (often in already cooked form) from local markets to which they have been taken from the hands of local growers.

THE SIGNIFICANCE OF THESE DIFFERENCES: CREDIT ACCOUNTS

A population completely dependent upon the purchase of imported supplies of its staple food, as are the landless fishermen of Hong Kong upon rice, is necessarily closely tied to the retailers of that commodity who, by its very nature, must be at least relatively substantial men—unless, indeed, they are government agencies, as has happened in the past in Hong Kong, and seems to be the rule in China at present. Such men are likely to be in a position to allow at least some credit buying. Hong Kong's inshore fishermen are, as we have seen, usually involved in credit relationships with their rice suppliers, who are very often their tea, sugar, and kerosene suppliers too. Similarly in Sarawak the rubber and sago producers do not grow their own rice, but buy it from the local stores at which they have the credit accounts already described. Professor Bauer wrote of a similar thing in Malaya, and Dr. Benedict[21] has described it also for Mauritius.

But in Uganda and Ghana the basic condition for this situation does not exist to the same degree. Tea, sugar, kerosene, etc. may be purchased from shops, but they can also be acquired from petty traders, and the staple food-stuffs are either home grown or bought with cash in the street markets; they are not imported. There is therefore less need for a close dependence upon shopkeepers than in the rice-importing countries, and one would not then expect Uganda and Ghana to exhibit such a development of credit account purchasing or such a multiplicity of general stores in the rural areas. It seems likely that this expectation is in accordance with the facts.

Nevertheless, to say this is not to invalidate the hypothesis that where credit purchasing does exist each creditor shop necessarily has a restricted number of customers, and therefore a multiplicity of such shops is only to be expected. On the contrary, such evidence as I have appears to support this hypothesis on two counts. First, there is some evidence of credit purchasing in Uganda which we shall examine. Second, there is clear evidence that in Ghana the number of rural lenders of money is markedly high for the size of the rural population, a fact which gives *prima facie* support for the basic assumption on which this hypothesis rests.

Let us consider these two counts in turn.

CREDIT RETAILING: UGANDA

We may consider the case of the Bagishu coffee growers of eastern Uganda. All coffee has, by law, to be sold exclusively to local cooperative societies,

[21] Personal communicaton. See also Burton Benedict, 'Cash and Credit in Mauritius', *The South African Journal of Economics*, Vol. 26, No. 3 (September 1958), pp. 213-21.

whose agents make a first initial payment in cash and thereafter hand over paper receipts for each lot of coffee as it is brought in, until such time as the whole shall have been sold upon the world market, when the receipts are presented for money. Small general stores in this coffee area allow credit to their customers, taking the receipts for security. This practice, which is explicitly illegal, is beyond the means of the smallest stores, whose owners tend to buy retail and sell at slightly enhanced prices. The rather more substantial storekeepers, however, both give credit and make cash loans against the security of the coffee receipts, which are also used to secure loans made by other (i.e., non-shopkeeper) individuals and even actually as money. Dr. la Fontaine,[22] who spent two years on field work among the Bagishu, describes how widely the network of debts is spread, especially just before the coffee harvest, 'when everybody owes money to everybody else'; she also agrees that, even though coffee receipts are used to secure the debts, a shopkeeper (or anyone else) would be unlikely to extend credit facilities to complete strangers, whereas on occasion he does give them to a well-known customer on personal trust alone.

We may ask how big a credit clientele any one shopkeeper in the Bagishu area has? Dr. la Fontaine's estimate is that a 'big' man may have as many as 20-25 credit customers. Yet 'almost everybody' takes advantage of these credit facilities. The inference is plain that there must be a fair multiplicity of general stores in this part of Uganda.[23] It is unfortunate that the complete census of Uganda, taken in 1948, has not yet been published, which makes it impossible to provide a numerical test for this inference.

CREDIT RETAILING: GHANA

Bauer's study of West African trade includes a passage which makes it clear that all the often multiple stages of merchandise trade between the importing firms and the ultimate consumer makes substantial use of credit. He gives no information about credit purchases by peasant consumers, however, and it seems likely that the extreme multiplicity of agents in the distributive trade in West Africa (which takes the form of an immense multiplication of petty traders rather than of identical general stores) is to be explained without reference to the number of credit customers any one retailer can be expected

[22] Dr. J. la Fontaine personal communication. I am indebted to both Dr. la Fontaine and Dr. Benedict for their willingness to allow me to quote from their answers to my questions about their field material from Uganda and Mauritius.

[23] The Bagishu apparently pay cash for small purchases and to hawkers, pedlars, and petty traders. They also pay cash, saved or borrowed, for big (i.e., Type A) purchases (e.g., bicycles). The credit arrangements described above are for such items as: tea, sugar, meat, kerosene.

to have.[24] We have already suggested that there is likely to be less demand for credit purchasing on the part of Ghanaian cocoa farmers who eat local produce than of, say, Sarawak rubber planters who eat imported rice.

Nevertheless, many Ghanaian cocoa farmers do make intensive use of credit facilities of other kinds, and it is to these that we turn now for our second examination of evidence which has bearing on the main theme of this paper.

LOANS: GHANA COCOA FARMERS

Evidence of the demand for credit is provided by the history of the Agricultural Loans Board which was set up in Ghana (then known as the Gold Coast) in 1950. 'In the space of less than two years 73,000 requests for or inquiries about loans were made to it. Nearly 30,000 [largely illiterate] farmers submitted formal applications on an eight-page form; they applied for a total of some £50 millions.' The Board suspended operations in 1953, having made loans totalling £1,320. The Minister of Agriculture stated that the government was now considering whether it might not be better to decentralize the machinery, looking round for some other body who might be in closer touch with the farmer from day-to-day, and who accordingly would be in a better position to know the standing of a particular farmer.[25]

The existing suppliers of credit are certainly in close day-to-day touch with the cocoa farmers. We have seen that these farmers do not, as far as we know, make purchases on credit accounts. On the other hand, they can and do borrow cash—usually in the form of loans against the security ('pledge') of land, usually land under cocoa. The details of these arrangements differ considerably from any we have so far discussed, but the question which is basic to the present enquiry can still be posed: namely, are the creditors in these transactions numerous or few in relation to the primary producing population?

Miss Hill describes the practice of pledging cocoa farms as follows: 'When a . . . cocoa farmer wants to borrow money for (say) six months or longer (usually longer) he often finds it convenient to do so by means of pledging his farm to a lender. The farm provides the lender with security for the debt, and the usufruct provides the borrower with a means to pay interest on the loan as well as, in many cases, with the means for repayment. Pledging . . .

[24] Bauer's description of credit trading extending even down to the petty retail stage refers only to market women selling on credit to clerks and other workers in government service or mercantile firms and gathering round the office doors to collect their debts on payday. See *West African Trade*, pp. 61-62.

[25] Hill, *op. cit.*, p. 70.

is a kind of indigenous mortgage system.'[26] Although a good deal is known about the relationships between debtor and creditor under this system, it is naturally not possible to indicate the average numbers of debtors per creditor for the country as a whole. Creditors do not lend themselves to providing this kind of statistical information, and practices vary from place to place. But 'in many areas the creditor who has had farms pledged to him by more than two or three debtors would seem to be very rare. The typical creditor perhaps has one or two farms pledged to him.'[27]

Here too, then, is a society of peasant primary producers in which there is a high demand for credit (here in the form of cash loans) and in which it seems that the proportion of creditors to debtors is high. Certain other points are also clear. For example, very few Ghanaian creditors are professional moneylenders. They do not make lending their sole occupation but continue to pursue other work, and as a result they are not a class apart. Indeed, it appears that they are even less a class apart from the local primary producers than the Far Eastern middlemen-retailers we have considered above, for most of the Ghanaian cocoa pledgees are themselves cocoa farmers, living in the same area as their debtors, and many of them are closely related to or very friendly with their debtors. Certainly it seems that what we have suggested may be the necessary condition that the creditor should be personally assured of his debtor's reliability obtains. In this case he needs to know also his debtor's land and its productivity, but Miss Hill suggests that there is an even more important consideration! 'I have never met a creditor who was willing to cope with more than a small number of farms: the supervision of the labourers is too much work.'[28]

CONCLUSION

The evidence from Ghana, and possibly also that from Uganda—though administrative control probably accounts largely for the apparent absence of credit facilities (or at least their failure to be reported) there—shows that the earlier implication that credit account purchasing, as found in Sarawak, Malaya, Hong Kong, and Mauritius, might be universal for peasant commercial producers, was incorrect. Peasants who live on home grown (or locally

[26] *Ibid.*, p. 48.

[27] Personal communication.

[28] Personal communication. In an unpublished MS., Miss Hill remarks further upon the rarity in the cocoa areas of the large creditor. In her experience the largest clienteles contained only about twenty people. The average sums borrowed were small. I am greatly indebted to Miss Polly Hill for allowing me to quote from her unpublished work and also for her personal communications and criticism.

produced) foodstuffs can subsist without recourse to credit purchase. Even they may use cash advances to tide them over the harvest period, however, and the Ghana evidence in general shows that when they reach a rather higher than subsistence level (which it is the whole trend—and aim—of commercial crop production to develop) they are likely to require loans of cash for expenditure of type A described above. Miss Hill has pointed out that it is the *poorest* Ghanaian cocoa farmers who do *not* pledge their farms. She adds, significantly: '*in their ability to borrow cocoa farmers are a favoured class compared with most other people*, favoured by the fact that they own something worth pledging and that there are those of their number who want to lend'.[29] The cocoa farmers having farms to pledge are in much the same position as houseowners in, say, England who have property to mortgage: they are by no means the poorest members of the community, nor are they usually considered unfortunate or worthy of special governmental assistance to help wipe out their debts.

Indeed, it might be suggested that the similarities between some of the methods of entering into a credit relationship in peasant producing populations and in the West are closer than might be expected. If a private individual here in England wants to borrow money or open a credit account, he too has to establish his credentials, and in the last resort this means that he too, depends on personal knowledge on the part of his creditor. This applies to loans from building societies and even from the banks, which do not have a multiplicity of branches stretching into quite small villages for nothing. It applies still more to the multitude of more or less 'private' mortgages negotiated by solicitors on behalf of their clients. It could be argued that this function of the local solicitor in England (together with others that also require his personal acquaintance with his clients) largely explains the otherwise rather surprising multiplicity of small legal firms existing in every small town in the country. There is certainly a very large proportion of creditors to debtors in these 'private' relationships.

Evidence from other primary producing areas is required, but in general it does seem that one concomitant of commercial production at this level and the rising standards of expenditure that go with it is a demand on the part of

[29] Unpublished MS., my italics. Miss Hill notes the reasons which induce a cocoa farmer to borrow money. In many cases loans were raised for expenditures of type A, but in many others they were to meet the expenses of a sudden 'calamity'. As Miss Hill hereself points out, however, calamities which can be recouped by monetary loans are more likely to happen to the relatively well off. A man may borrow to replace a damaged lorry or because he was unable to meet commitments (such as the payment of school fees) from which he was unwilling to withdraw, but a truly poverty stricken peasant does not own lorries or send his children to school at all.

the primary producers themselves for credit and/or loan facilities. These may take various forms, according partly to the types of expenditure involved and partly to the availability of capital and its location. From our point of view here the significant question is: from whose hands is this credit or loan obtained? I am not concerned with the question of the ultimate source of the capital, but with the direct relationship between the primary producer borrower and his personal creditor. It seems that there are three main types of source: local middlemen (produce buyers), local retailers, and each other.[30] In all these cases, no matter what the type of credit arrangement, there is a limit to the number of debtors per creditor. This limit is usually set by two factors: first, the small amount of capital available to the creditor; and second, the necessity for the creditor, who in the circumstances we are discussing nearly always has to act on his own sole responsibility, to have personal knowledge of the character and circumstances of his debtor.

It follows that there must be a relatively large number of creditors, and in those territories in which they are also produce buyers and/or shopkeepers a multiplicity of middlemen and shops.

[30] Some or all of these roles may overlap in one and the same individual. In Sarawak, middleman=retailer; in Ghana many a cocoa farmer is also a middleman in the cocoa trade and at the same time a creditor or debtor in the pledging system.

8. A Small Factory in Hong Kong: Some Aspects of Its Internal Organization*

The past twenty years have seen an industrial revolution in Hong Kong. Dependent largely upon the huge influx of capital, management, and labour that began around 1949. It has involved a complete change in the pattern of trade as the Colony's economy switched over from an entrepôt to an industrial basis. Already by 1965 more than 50 per cent of the employed population was engaged in industrial and construction work, and well over 90 per cent of the total exports consisted of industrial products, of which the large majority were taken by North America and Western Europe (Chou, 1966).

Two of the most striking features of Hong Kong's prodigiously rapid industrialization have been the remarkable diversification of its products and its dependence upon private enterprise. Cotton textiles and garment manufacturing, completely dominant in the early days, have now been joined by an ever-increasing range of export goods the very nature of which was unknown in the Colony a few years ago. They include plastic products, wigs, steel cutlery, beach wear, sports gear, optical and scientific instruments, and electronic equipment of all kinds. It is worth nothing that these are all products requiring a high degree of skill at least at certain stages of their production. As for private enterprise, all manufacturing industry in Hong Kong is essentially capitalistic. It is true that the public sector has regularly contributed about 30 per cent of the total annual domestic investment (Chou, 1966:74), but this contribution has customarily gone into administration and such traditional public works as roads, water supplies, and public building. In addition to this valuable contribution to the infrastructure, the government has also provided certain minimum controls over factory sites and the employment of labour, and has developed a number of advisory services, but beyond this it has explicitly and consistently refused to 'interfere' in either commerce or industry.

The typical factory in Hong Kong probably does not exist. The range from squatter huts housing outworkers for the plastic flower industry to

*Reprinted from *The Economic Organization in Chinese Society*, edited by W. E. Willmott with the permission of the publishers, Stanford University Press. © 1972 by the Board of Trustees of the Leland Stanford Junior University.

air-conditioned, electrically powered cotton mills is too great. In any case, the factory described in the following paragraphs was chosen not because it was typical but simply because it was available.* Further investigations may well show it to be unusual in many ways, but I do not expect it to prove unique. It certainly shared most of the characteristics mentioned above: it was privately owned, it turned out a modern product, and it depended largely upon immigrant capital and management.

The fieldwork on which this paper is based was intended to be part of a pilot study for what I hope to develop into a comprehensive investigation of industrialization in Hong Kong. Informing my approach to the whole topic was a wish to discern what, if anything, was specifically 'Chinese' about the socio-economic relationships involved. This is the aspect of the study that is followed up here. Broadly speaking, my conclusion is that in this factory the primary factors determining the structure and organization of relationships were the restraints imposed by the technical requirements of the process of production as such. These were straightforward, 'rational' requirements that left hardly any room for culturally differentiated *nuances* in performance. Only in those areas where the demands of the technology itself were not overriding was there room for variations in what I later call the 'style' of organization. Such areas were to be found in the relationships between the management and the workers, in some aspects of the relationships between workers, and, most significantly for the development of the business, in relationships at the level of the directorate. In this last set of relationships, however, other—probably universal—factors also came into play; notably a tendency, once the technological structure of the firm was assured, for leadership to move increasingly out of the hands of the technologists and into the hands of the managers and market men. These findings may give rise to a number of hypotheses concerning the process of industrialization in general. They may be particularly relevant to the question whether the kind of technological process carried on in a factory is related to its socio-politico-economic environment, specifically the degree of freedom that exists for the development of differences in 'style'. The relative efficiency of such stylistic differences, the possible concomitants of change, and so on, could also be examined on the basis of the kind of data reported here. Much of this is

*The information on which this paper is based was obtained during six weeks' fieldwork in the spring of 1968. I wish to thank the Directors of the Ford Foundation and the Southeast China Program at Cornell University for the great generosity which made it possible for a foreign scholar to travel to Hong Kong for this fieldwork; the Director of the School of Oriental and African Studies, University of London, for giving me leave of absence during the Easter Vacation; and, most of all, the directors, staff, and workers of the Kau Fung Glass Factory for their kindness and cooperation.

conjecture for future exploration, however. The paper remains essentially an ethnographic account of a single Hong Kong factory as it existed in 1968.

The progress of the firm has certainly been dramatic. Starting from scratch in March 1967, it received its first overseas inquiries (from Germany) after five months. During the few weeks of my fieldwork in April 1968, further inquiries came in from South Africa, South America, Canada, India, Indonesia, and Australia.

FACTORY LAYOUT AND ORGANIZATION OF WORK

The factory makes glass. It is a special kind of heat-resistant glass, very clear and strong. You can fill a flask of it with cold water, put it over a naked flame until the water boils, then take it off the flame and plunge it straight into a bucket of cold water, and it does not crack. Unlike the majority of goods manufactured in Hong Kong, this glass makes use of one locally available raw material, namely sand. All the rest are imported.

The process of manufacture is relatively simple. The various raw materials are weighed out, mixed in an electrically operated tumbler, and fed at regular intervals into one or the other of two large furnaces. Fed in as a kind of coarse powder, the mixture quickly melts and attains temperatures as high as 1,600° Fahrenheit. The liquid glass passes gradually through the furnaces—which are about forty feet long—to be drawn out at the far end like large blobs of colourless treacle on the ends of long brass and steel tubes. Skilled blowers grasp the tubes, spin them rapidly, and blow the blobs into the required balloon-like shapes. These are then quickly moulded in a two-sided, hinged metal mould and splashed with cold water before being taken by another worker to the annealing furnaces where they are stacked, at precisely controlled temperatures, and allowed to cool gradually over a period of twenty-four hours. Removed from the (now cold) annealing furnaces next day, the glass globes or funnels (or whatever) are finally cut with coal-gas flame cutters to the right size, polished, finished, and packed ready for export. At the time of my study, the whole process, from weighing the raw materials to sending out the finished product, employed just forty-eight men and women, of whom two were managing directors, two were paid white-collar managerial and secretarial staff, and forty-four were classed as workers.

In the process of production outlined above, each stage follows necessarily in order upon the last, the order of events being set by the very nature of the process. It follows that there is little room for argument and decision-making about the work flow. With enough space, a rational layout is almost unavoidable. By no means do all kinds of industrial production share this characteristic. Where the final product is not, as here, the result of a single, straightforwardly cumulative process, but rather of collecting and putting together a number of different components each of which is made separately, the work can be organized in many different ways. In such circumstances, an outside investigator might find that differences in the culture or the personality (or both) of management and labour were reflected in differences in organization. In glass-making the central process imposes its own ineluctable rationality, a fact of which the managers of the factory under discussion were very well aware. The problem they had to solve was to find enough space for this central process to be carried out and, having done that, to organize the flow of preliminary and final processes with as nearly the same rationality as possible. Culture or personality could make little or no difference at this level.

In diagrammatic form the flow of production comprised the ten stages, picutred in Figure 1, of which Numbers 4-7 comprise the central process and Numbers 1-3 and 8-10 the preliminary and final processes respectively. It will be noted that without sufficient storage space for the ready-mixed batches of raw material and for the cooled but not yet cut and finished glass products there could be no pauses between the successive stages. The diagram also makes the key position of the delivery stage (10) quite evident: the limited storage space made rapid clearance of the finished and packed goods essential. In this connection it must be remembered that space is one of the scarcest resources in Hong Kong; even if adequate space were available, it would not normally be economical to rent it merely for storing finished products.

Finding any space for the factory had, indeed, been one of the major

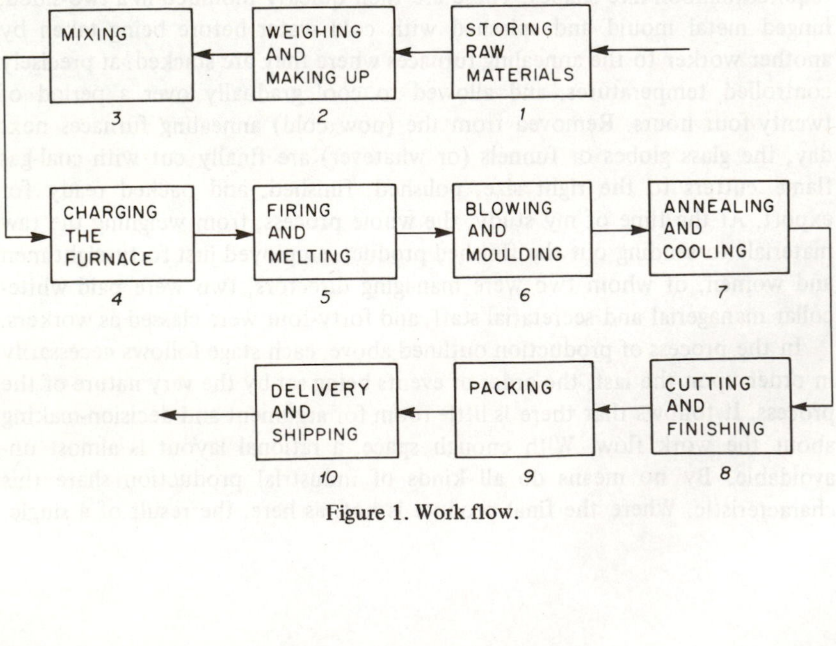

Figure 1. Work flow.

problems at the beginning. During the second half of 1966 the items of capital equipment being accumulated had to be stored for several months in a garage belonging to the brother-in-law of one of the directors. The only site available at first, the one still being used at the time of my fieldwork, was relatively cramped and not particularly convenient. It was an irregular rectangle, measuring 160 feet by 67 feet and situated about 300 yards from the main road. Access to this road was difficult because the side streets were narrow and steep. The problem of space was complicated by the Fire Brigade regulations, because stages 4 to 8 of the production process obviously required very high temperatures and the use of naked flames.

When I studied the factory, the layout was according to the plan shown in Figure 2. This plan shows clearly the 'natural' rationality of the locations chosen for the central stages of production—charging the tank (4), smelting (5), blowing and moulding (6), and annealing (7)—and the way in which the management placed the preliminary and final stages in relation to them. Stages 1-3 (storing the raw materials, weighing and making up, mixing) were arranged to take place close together and closely under the supervision of the managing director (*A*) in his office. The raw materials were stored at some distance from the main entrance through which they had to be brought in, but this was because it was even more important for the offices to be adjacent to the main entrance, and for them and the rest room next to them (in fact the sleeping quarters of Office Worker *a*) to be on an outer wall with windows for light and air, than it was for the raw materials to be stored near their point of entry. The position of the offices being fixed in this manner, the placing of the first three stages followed almost automatically from the managing director's need to oversee and participate in them. (Certain ingredients were kept under lock and key in his office, weighed by him on a delicate spring balance of his own design, and added only by his own hand.) The result was, however, that two workers had to carry each heavy batch of made-up raw material almost the full length of the building and through the packing section (9) to the tanks (4, 4a, 5, 5a).

Two other major defects of this layout were obvious to all. First, the clumsy trolleys that carried the glass pieces from the annealing furnaces to the cutting and finishing room had to be pushed too great a distance. Part of their route lay across the open-air passage, which was often obstructed, and where they sometimes bumped into either the batch carriers or those who were trying to load the outgoing truck. Second, the space available for packing was inefficiently small, and storage places were both inadequate and inappropriate for stacking the boxed finished products. This layout was, however, expected to be temporary: by June or July of 1968 at the latest the large tank (5) would have to be replaced, thus providing an opportunity for

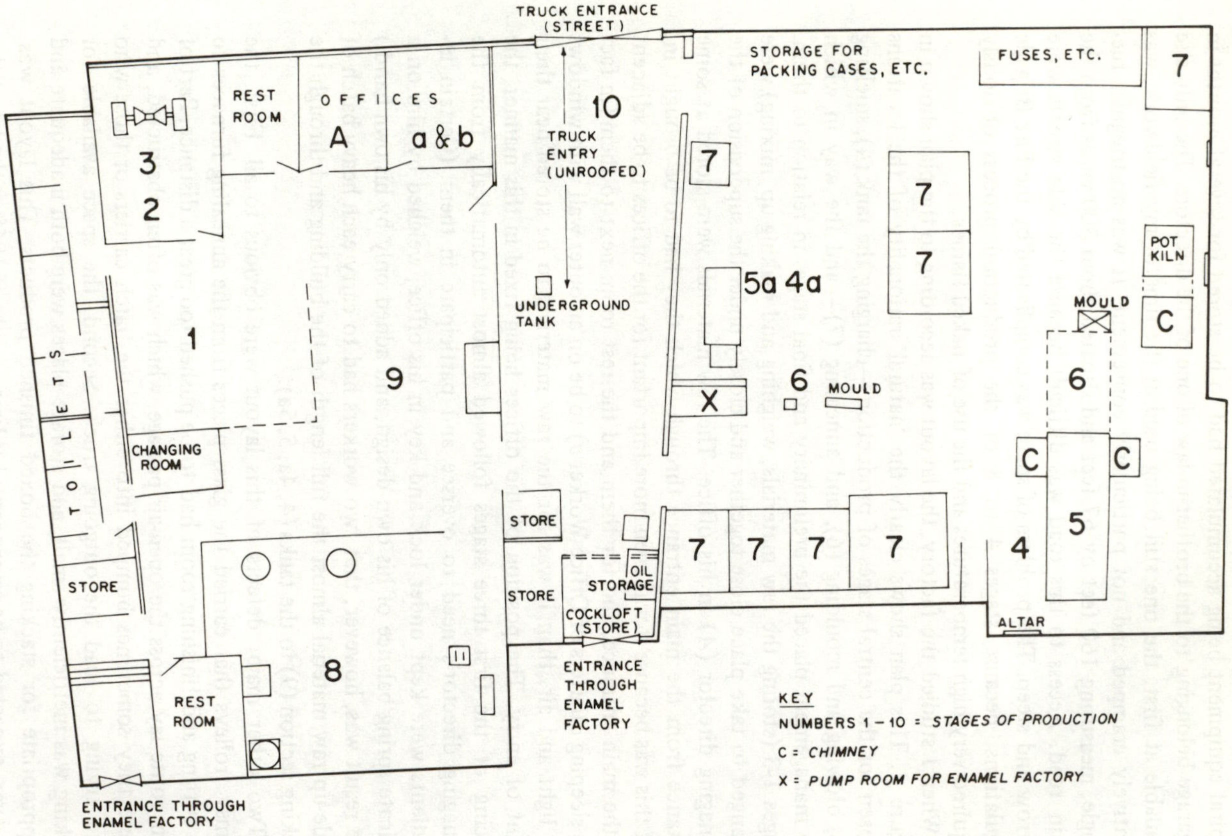

Figure 2. Floor plan of the Kau Fung Glass Factory, Hong Kong (1968).

replanning, and it was hoped that it would be possible at the same time to acquire more space. (After I had left the field, this did happen.)

The layout of the factory was, of course, only one aspect of the process of production. The other was the organization of the work. Here one of the most significant factors was the small size of the labour force and the consequent opportunity for face-to-face relationships at all levels.

During the period under review the formal structure of the factory underwent certain changes that will be described in a later section. Fundamental though they were and potentially of great significance for worker-management relationships, they did not alter the organization on the factory floor. This remained throughout essentially the same as when I observed it in April 1968. Figure 3 summarizes the simple, essentially rational, formal internal organization of the process of production.

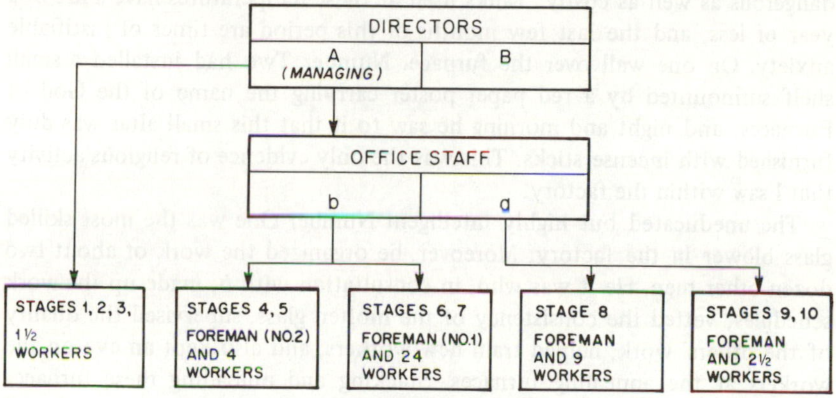

Figure 3. The organization of work.

Buying, storing, weighing, and mixing the raw materials were under the personal control of the managing director (*A*) who alone had full knowledge of the chemical processes involved (and claimed that certain essential ingredients were his personal secret). Making up and mixing took place in a room next door to his own office (see Figure 2), and were performed under his eye by a woman whose full-time job it was, assisted by a man who worked part-time in the packing section (stages 9 and 10). When not actually engaged in weighing and mixing, the woman swept, made tea, and so on.

Stage 4-7 all took place in the largest room, which housed the two smelting furnaces (tanks) and the annealing furnaces. The workers here were all under the general supervision of Office Worker *b*, but the work was actually directed by two foremen (known sometimes as 'Number One' and 'Number Two' in the factory) who were in charge of the shaping and cooling of the glass products and the smelting tanks, respectively. Superficially these two men could hardly have been more different: Number Two (the furnace man) was over fifty years of age, a well-educated man with a military background (he had held a commission in the Kuomintang army, and his brother was still an army officer in Taiwan); Number One, also a refugee, but only twenty-nine, was the nearly illiterate son of a tannery worker. Both were excellent and reliable craftsmen, with a quiet, confident manner, respected by workers and management alike.

The furnace foreman's responsibility was the more limitedly technical. He had constantly to watch the temperature, keep an eye on the level of molten glass, decide when to feed in more 'batch' and how much. (He was also skilled in the highly technical craft of building furnaces, of which more below.) At the very high temperatures reached in the main tank, mistakes could be dangerous as well as costly. Tanks used at these temperatures have a life of a year or less, and the last few months of this period are times of justifiable anxiety. On one wall over the furnace, Number Two had installed a small shelf surmounted by a red paper poster carrying the name of the God of Furnaces, and night and morning he saw to it that this small altar was duly furnished with incense sticks. This was the only evidence of religious activity that I saw within the factory.

The uneducated but highly intelligent Number One was the most skilled glass blower in the factory. Moreover, he organized the work of about two dozen other men. He it was who, in consultation with *b*, made up the work schedules, vetted the consistency of the molten glass, supervised the quality of the others' work, helped train new workers, and also kept an eye on the workers at the annealing furnaces. Stacking and unloading these furnaces were also skilled jobs. The workers concerned kept records of the number of completed pieces in each chamber and the dates and times each was sealed, writing this information on small blackboards fixed at the side of each furnace. These records were frequently checked by the office worker (*b*) in charge. It is important to appreciate the informal and generally friendly nature of these relationships. Neither Number One nor Number Two used an authoritarian approach, and *b* was forever strolling in and out of the furnace room, joking and chatting with the foremen and the workers in a quiet way.

On removal from the annealing furnaces the glass pieces were stacked on crate-like wooden trolleys to be trundled somewhat laboriously on small, metal-shod wheels across to the cutting and finishing room. This transfer and the final packaging were under the general supervision of the other member of the office staff (*a*), who also supervised the loading of the boxed glassware into the firm's truck and then delivered it to the purchasers or to the docks at Kowloon. The other part of his job was to handle all the consignments of raw materials, fuels, etc., as they came into the factory. Cutting and finishing the glass globes and vessels was done by nine workers (including a girl whose sole job was to stencil the appropriate trademarks on the pieces) under the supervision of a short, stout foreman who never seemed to stop working (or smiling). In this step of production, the workers used a series of coal-gas burners mounted on rotating stands. The foreman inspected each finished piece for cracks or flaws.

From the cutting and finishing room (8), the finished products were once more pushed laboriously by hand in the same clumsy trolleys, this time only to the packing room (9). Here, in much too cramped a space, they were individually wrapped in a single layer of tissue paper and packed into collapsible carboard cartons. Finally, the trademarks, the descriptions of contents, and the addresses of the consignees were stenciled on the boxes, which were then ready to be sent out. This work, under the general supervision of the 'outside' office man (*a*), was directly under the control of one male worker (dignified with the status 'foreman' in Figure 3) with full-time help from one woman and part-time assistance from the man otherwise engaged in weighing and mixing in the 'batch' room. As a matter of fact, however, the packing section, small though it was, was often occupied by a much larger number of people. Anyone not working at his regular task, including the office staff or even the directors' wives, could be seen from time to time helping out with wrapping and boxing. this stage (9) was, indeed, the least efficiently organized of the whole process—largely because of the lack of adequate space either for the packing operations themselves or for the bulky parcels once they were made up. A day's backlog in outward delivery (stage 10) meant near chaos in the packing department, which, being at the end of the production line, was in constant danger of being crowded out with finished products. I have already suggested that the high cost of space and the problem of finding it in the first place probably made this difficulty unavoidable.

For, and this was an important aspect of the built-in rationality of the work-flow, the nature of glass-making in this factory gave to the process of production not only a regular order but also a steady pace. There were two reasons for this, both of them conected with the tanks. On the one hand, it was, of course, necessary for the molten glass once drawn from the tank to be blown or moulded immediately, while it was still viscid, and for the shaped products then to be stacked at once in the annealing chambers so that the glass should be cooled at the correct rate. The significance of speed and accurate timing is obvious here. But time was also important at the other end of the tank, where it was necessary to keep the temperature and level of the molten material within fairly narrow limits for the sake of safety as well as efficiency. Level and temperature were checked once every hour, and both heat and the flow of raw materials adjusted accordingly. Thus the central production process created a kind of push-pull effect that regulated the tempo of the whole factory. As temperatures and levels dropped, more 'batch' had to be ready to feed into the tank, more weighing and mixing had to be done, and—ultimately—a steady supply of raw materials had to be maintained. (A temporary shortage of one particular ingredient during the winter of 1967-68 caused great anxiety and nearly led to a complete shutdown.) On the other side of the tank, in turn, the raising of the temperature and level meant that the blowers and moulders had to be ready to remove the molten glass, which once drawn out had to be dealt with immediately. The process once started, the tanks themselves acted as regulators to keep production going at a steady pace.

It follows that, as long as raw materials were steadily available, the tanks and other equipment were sound, and the chemical formula produced the desired results, there was as little room for decision-making in the strategy of organizing the work as in the planning of the factory layout. Moreover, with such small numbers of workers in face-to-face relationship, the daily tactical decisions about such matters as work schedules were in general arrived at by amicable mutual consent under the leadership of the three major foremen and the office staff. As far as the organization of work went, only two important matters fell outside the automatic control provided by the central process of production: namely, the recruitment and stabilization of an appropriate labour force and the development of adequate marketing outlets.

RECRUITMENT AND STABILIZATION OF LABOUR

Up to this point my argument has been that the organization of production in the glass factory was essentially rational in the sense that the layout of the factory floor, the order in which the stages of production took place, and the tempo of production were all ultimately regulated by the requirements of the process itself. Another way of putting this would be to say that the basic structure of the activities necessary for turning out the completed glass products was unaffected by cultural factors. From an anthropological standpoint the term 'universal' might be more illuminating than 'rational': there has been nothing specifically 'Chinese' about the organization as described so far—unless a strong tendency to use economic common sense is to be regarded as a peculiarly Chinese quality.

When we turn from the techniques of production to the problems of the recruitment and management of labour, however, we may find ourselves forced to consider local culture-linked factors. In other words, we may expect to be asked whether or not the methods used and the relationships set up reflect values and practices that can be described, however loosely, as 'characteristically Chinese'.

Before considering precisely what this phrase may mean, let us examine first the factory's stated policy about recruitment and the history of that policy, and then the general principles and practice of reward and management.

From discussions about recruitment policy with the two directors and both members of the office staff, three main points emerged. First, skilled workers such as glassblowers, stackers, and furnace men were scarce in Hong Kong. It was therefore essential to attract and hold them by offering higher wages, better promotion prospects and conditions, and more fringe benefits than other firms. The number of glassworks in Hong Kong was quite small, with the result that anybody employed in the industry for any length of time knew a great deal about the conditions and the personnel in all the other glass factories. Managing Director *A*, who had had previous experience in managing a glassworks and was known to be a brilliant technical man, was therefore able to do a certain amount of personal recruiting before the factory first opened. Nearly half the skilled men, including both leading foremen, came in this way. About a quarter came a little later, through personal contacts either with *A* or with the skilled craftsmen already employed. The rest appeared in response to advertisements posted at the factory entrance (see Table 1).

Table 1. Channels of recruitment, all recruits, Kau Fung Glass Factory, Hong Kong, March 1967 to April 1968

Channel of recruitment	Permanent (Primarily skilled)	Temporary (Primarily unskilled)
I Personal contact		
(a) By managing director	8	1
(b) Glass-industry grapevine	9	5
(c) Friend or neighbour	1	10
(d) Relative in factory	1	7
II Advertisement	8	41
III Unknown	1	6
Total	28	70

Note: See text for full distinction between the two categories of workers.

Now it is important to notice that in using his personal contacts and the glass industry's grapevine to recruit skilled workers, *A* was in fact employing the most efficient method available. In circumstances of absolute shortage of and high competition for particular skills, personal contact is often the best (if not the only) source of information and channel of communication.

Although *A* used personal methods, his criterion for recruitment was nonetheless universalistic: he wanted skill and knew how to assess it. None of the men who came from the factories in which he himself had previously been employed was linked to him by any of the usual Chinese particularistic ties, such as kinship, or school, being classmates, or having a common place of origin or dialect. Yet all the skilled men who had worked in glass factories before were recruited either by *A*'s personal invitation or through the glass industry's grapevine. Such men could be found only in existing factories: without them a new glass business could not even begin.

The second point the management stressed was a general one regarding the state of the Hong Kong labour market at the time. The shortage of skilled labour (by no means confined to glass manufactories) existed alongside a superabundance of unskilled labour. It was, they told me, the practice of unskilled workers to shop around, trying out this firm and that in order to find the best pay and conditions, for there was a sense in which unskilled workers could afford to be more choosy than the skilled men, whose opportunities were limited by the relatively small number of firms requiring their particular competence. As a result, they said, there was no problem of recruiting unskilled labour; an advertisement on the factory wall outside the main entrance would bring in plenty of inquirers. The problem was to keep them. This argument that the existence of a large, mobile pool of labour inevitably forces wages up was repeated to me several times by the management. It formed the basis of their policy of recruitment and reward for unskilled workers, the large majority of whom did in fact come in response to written advertisements posted outside the main entrance of the factory. Most of them were, therefore, not previously known to the management (directors or office staff), to the other workers, or to each other.

Table 1 sets out the different channels of recruitment for the ninety-eight workers who were on the factory's books at one time or another during the year March 1967 to April 1968.

A few comments on this table are necessary. First, the category 'friend or neighbour' may well overlap the category 'grapevine'. The entries here have been transcribed from my questionnaire replies as follows: if the worker said he had been introduced by a friend or neighbour the entry is under I (c); if he said he had worked in a glass factory before, it is under I (b) unless a specific statement was added mentioning the managing director as his 'introducer'. (None said both.) Second, several of the large number in the 'unskilled' category who said they came in answer to an advertisement may well have had their attention drawn to the advertisement by friends or acquaintances already employed in the factory. I did not check this possibility in the factory. I was, however, repeatedly assured by the office staff that 'most' of their unskilled recruits were in fact obtained by advertisement, and I myself witnessed about a dozen inquiries from casual passersby. Third, the categories 'skilled' and unskilled' themselves need some reconsideration. This appears in the immediately following paragraphs.

One striking feature of the first year's operation of the factory was the high turnover in labour, particularly in 'unskilled' labour. Whereas 22 of 28 'skilled' recruits were still employed in the factory at the end of the year (i.e. in April 1968), only 22 of 70 'unskilled' workers recruited during the same period remained. This difference, which bore out the directors' expectations expressed above, was probably closely connected with differences in the systems of rewards offered to the two categories. Before describing these, however, it is necessary to draw attention to the fact that the two categories were not in fact distinguished purely in terms of skill. As indicated in Table 1, the terms actually used in the factory, as elsewhere in Hong Kong, were not 'skilled' and 'unskilled' but 'permanent' and 'temporary'. It happened that all the fully skilled workers fell into the permanent category, but a number of the semi-skilled and one or two unskilled were also included there, whereas by no means all the temporary workers were completely unskilled. Allocation to the permanent category was made on the basis of a combination of criteria of which skill was the most important; but hard work, long service, and responsibility also counted. In addition to all the skilled blowers, for example, the permanent category also included the woman who worked full time at weighing and mixing the raw materials (stages 1-3) and the full-time male assistant in the packing section (stage 9).

The formal difference between permanent and temporary workers was that the latter were engaged on a daily basis, the former by the month. In addition, there were a number of fringe benefits for which only permanent workers were eligible. These included a meals allowance of $2 a day, a bonus scheme, sickness pay, eligibility (for single men) to reside rent-free in the firm's own hostel, and the opportunity to attend the firm's annual dinner and receive gifts of new clothing at Chinese New Year. A similar division between permanent and temporary workers obtains in nearly all Hong Kong's industries, although the benefits available to the former vary both in detail and monetary value. These 'extras' are widely regarded as an important part of the system of rewards, their explicit object being to encourage good workers to stay. It is for this reason that promotion to permanent status is open to semi-skilled and even unskilled workers. The management of the glass factory claimed that the difference in the rate of turnover between the two categories was closely connected with this incentive scheme. Temporary employees were having to be replaced every month, but permanent workers left only infrequently. There were at least four months in the year prior to my fieldwork in which temporary workers were lost faster than they could be replaced.

Conversations with permanent workers left me in no doubt that they very much liked the scheme, and consciously valued the increased security as well as the fringe benefits that their status commanded. It seems likely that in Hong Kong at the present time the system contributes to a greater stability of valuable labour than would otherwise be found in such a highly fluid situation. However, insofar as the skilled men were concerned specifically, their stability is as likely to be ascribable to two other mutually linked factors: the specific nature of their skills (which meant that there were very few other factories in which they could find equivalent employment), and their relatively high wages (they were the highest-paid glassblowers and furnace men in the Colony).

Wage differentials, always with the chance of an increase, existed within each category. Wages were calculated at daily rates, but paid out at sixteen-day intervals. There were two methods of calculating a day's work, both in effect a time rate, although the second was described to me in piece-rate terms. For most workers, a day's work was reckoned as ten hours; anything over that was paid at double rates. For the glassblowers and stackers, however, the idea was that a day's work consisted of the performance of a certain stint; once that was completed any additional work was payable at double rates. Since their stint had been calculated as requiring eight hours of work, theoretically they had the choice of working a shorter day than any of the other workers, or of earning more overtime pay than any of the other workers. In practice, they almost always choose to work more than eight hours.

Additional piece rates, in the strict sense, were paid to the two leading blowers, the foreman cutter, the foreman packer, and the two men responsible for taking the cooled glass products out of the annealing furnaces. These piecework payments, acting as a kind of foreman's reward, were shared out by the recipients among the members of their work gangs. For example, on April 28, 1968, the number-one glassblower received in addition to his fortnight's total of $407.75, a further sum of $62.15 for blowing especially big glass globes (used for fishermen's lamps) at $.55 each; it was then his responsibility to share this sum with the four or five other blowers who were skilled enough to assist him in this job.*

Permanent workers were eligible for three other regular monetary payments, some of which have already been mentioned briefly. These were as follows: $2 a day for food, a bonus of twenty-four extra days' pay a year,

*The currency referred to in every case is the Hong Kong dollar, worth approximately eighteen cents in United States currency.

and the special overtime rate of two-and-a-half times the ordinary pay for work done on any one of nine annual public holidays; namely, four days at Chinese New Year, Ch'ing Ming (April 5), the Dragon Boat Festival (fifth day of the fifth lunar month), May 1, the Mid-Autumn Festival (ninth day of the ninth lunar month),* and the day of the winter solstice. (It is perhaps worth noting that with the exception of May 1 these are all traditional Chinese festival dates.)

Daily rates of pay fell within the range $7.00 to $11.00 for temporary workers and $6.50 to $18.00 for permanent workers. (Because of the increase obtainable from the fringe benefits available to permanent workers, promotion from the temporary category normally involved an initial drop in the daily rate received.)

On one payday I observed (April 28, 1968) the average size of the fortnight's pay packet actually taken home was $122.00 for temporary workers and $230.00 for permanent workers. The actual pay of most temporary workers nearly approximated the average, but for permanent workers the range was much wider: the number-one blower, for example, received, as we have already seen, $407.75 (before piece-work money); the most recently promoted permanent workers, $136.90 and $149.00, respectively. But it is worth noting that, although the last two mentioned were on daily rates of only $6.50, only two of the temporary workers (on rates of $8.00 and $8.50, respectively) took home more. It is also worth noting for comparison that very many white-collar workers in Hong Kong at the time received monthly salaries of between $500 and $600.

Table 2 presents a breakdown of the fortnightly pay packets taken home by eight selected workers on April 28, 1968.

The system of rewards included quite frequent reviews of wages and the possibility of increases, especially for the permanent workers. There was no regular rule about this, but the system was operated on the basis of the personal knowledge and judgement of the office worker (*b*) in charge of the accounts, in consultation with the appropriate foreman and the managing director. The same applied to questions of promotion from temporary to permanent status. Table 3 sets out the daily wage patterns as they were in operation in April 1968. It shows at a glance the greater use of flexibility and pay increases for the permanent workers and the overall differentials between the categories and between males and females.

There is some evidence that permanent workers worked longer hours than temporary workers. My records of the payday calculations for April 28, 1968, indicate that the permanent workers worked an average of approximately

***Mid-Autumn Festival should be on the fifteenth day of the eighth lunar month—ed.**

Table 2. Take-home pay of selected workers, Kau Fung Glass Factory, Hong Kong, April 1968

Category and job, age and sex	Daily rate	Days worked (max. 16)	Overtime (days' pay)	Bonus days	Total days counted for pay	Meals money	Repayment of advance	Take-home pay	Remarks
Permanent									
No. 1 blower M/29	$18.00	16	2.875	2	20.875	$32	–	$407.75	Plus $62.75 in shared piece rates
Mixer F/44	7.00	15.5	7.5	2	25	32	–	207.00	Only female permanent worker
No. 1 furnace man M/51	15.00	16	4.5	2	22.5	32	$40	329.50	No. 2 on factory floor
Cutter and finisher M/16	6.80	15	5.1	2	22.1	30	–	180.20	Recently promoted
Temporary									
Cutter and finisher M/17	8.50	15.5	5.6	–	21.1	–	–	179.35	
Helper (carrying moulding) F/47	7.00	14	–	–	14	–	–	98.00	
Glass smasher M/26	10.00	12.5	–	–	12.5	–	$20	105.00	
Cutter and finisher F/21	8.00	11.8	1.75	–	13.55	–	–	108.40	

Note: The workers included in this table were selected not so much to typify the temporary and permanent categories as to represent certain other categories such as age, sex, skill, and status. The cutter and finisher appearing last in the permanent category should by my calculations have earned $180.30, but the figure shown was his actual pay.

Table 3. Daily rates of pay for workers by category and sex, Kau Fung Glass Factory, Hong Kong, April 1968

Daily rate	Permanent		Temporary	
	Male	Female	Male	Female
$18.00	1	–	–	–
16.00	2	–	–	–
15.00	3	–	–	–
12.00	2	–	–	–
11.00	1	–	1	–
10.50	2	–	–	–
10.00	1	–	2	–
9.00	1	–	–	–
8.50	–	–	3	–
8.00	–	–	6	–
7.50	–	–	–	2
7.30	1	–	–	–
7.00	3	1	–	7
6.80	1	–	–	–
6.50	2	–	–	–
Total	20	1	12	9

Note: Two female temporary workers were paid piece rates only for taking products out of the annealing furnaces. Here and throughout the remaining tables, these two workers are omitted from consideration, leaving a total of 42.

15.5 regular days out of a maximum of 16, and earned an average of about 2.5 days' pay in overtime work, whereas the temporary workers worked an average of approximately 14 regular days and earned an average of only about 1.2 days' pay in overtime work.

It is not easy to deduce from these data the extent to which the stability and industriousness of the labour force in this glass factory are to be connected with peculiarly Chinese patterns of reward and recruitment. The findings could also be explained by reference to universal economic considerations. The shortage of skilled workers made it inevitable that there would be competition for their services, and this in turn made for higher wages. The wages of the skilled workers were indeed relatively high, and made even higher by their fringe benefits as permanent workers. One wonders why it should have been considered more useful to cast these additional rewards in the form of bonuses and benefits rather than simply increasing the money wage. Two possible reasons come to mind, both of them at least partially culture-linked. The first is that workers in the Chinese context in Hong Kong today may value improvement in status almost as much as increase in income. This is a culture in which prestige still goes in the traditional way to scholars and white-collar workers. I have already stated that a skilled glassblower can earn more in a month than a typist—and this without including the monetary value of the fringe benefits. In Hong Kong today this is by no means an unusual state of affairs. Yet parents continue to demand the exclusively literary education that most Hong Kong schools provide, and unemployment and underemployment among white-collar workers and shop assistants continue to increase. Is it not possible to see the creation of a higher ('permanent') division of industrial workers as an attempt to provide some of the prestige normally denied the wage-earner?

The second possibility is that the attempt to draw certain (good) workers into closer connection, as it were, with the firm by providing fringe benefits may be an example of the often-remarked Chinese preference for multiplex rather than single-stranded relationships. There is a constant endeavour in Hong Kong to bind one's economic collaborators to one by whatever other ties one can activate: kinship, fictive kinship, friendship, *kan-ch'ing*, and so on. Almost any economic transaction except the most casual purchase tends to attract other, social, attributes; and where, as here, the transactions are between employers and employees, it is felt appropriate by both sides that these should be paternalistic. Such arrangements, regarded by the employees as a guarantee of security (as well as increased income) and by the employers as insurance against the loss of valuable workers, are typical in present-day Hong Kong. To that extent they may certainly be described as 'Chinese'. Paternalism of a similar general kind has, however, appeared at certain times in the industrial development of most societies, and it is possible that in part as least it may be a characteristic of a certain scale and stage of economic development rather than a specifically culture-linked phenomenon.

THE WORKERS: BACKGROUND AND ATTITUDES

In any social analysis of the early stages of industrialization, the background of the workers and their attitudes regarding employment may well be crucial factors. During the last few days of my six weeks in the glass factory, I was able to interview every worker. In addition to data (about kind of job, rate of pay, length of employment, etc.), I obtained information as to age, marital status, language, and provenance; how long each had been in Hong Kong, how much education he had, and what had been the occupations of his father and other close relatives. I also discussed with each one the number of relatives he or she still had in China, if any, and tried to assess attitudes about factory work in general and this factory in particular. My formal questionnaire, however, included only factual questions. I used no attitude tests. The individual interviews were supplemented by more or less daily observations, conversations, and eavesdropping during the whole fieldwork period.

The following tables and paragraphs summarize my findings. I am of course very well aware that the sample is far too small to allow any significant generalizations from the findings, even if it were possible—as it is not—to argue that this factory was 'typical'. The figures are given here primarily as a convenient method of presenting description; it is possible, too, that they may give rise to some hypotheses for testing in the future.

There is little need for comment on Tables 4 and 5. The age structure of Hong Kong's population, of which about 50% is nineteen years old or younger, was not closely represented in the factory. As might be expected, however, skilled workers were congregated in the younger classes; the unskilled

Table 4. Age of Kau Fung Glass Factory workers by sex and category, April 1968

Age	Permanent		Temporary	
	Male	Female	Male	Female
Under 20	3	–	3	4
20-29	9	–	4	1
30-39	3	–	1	2
40-49	3	1	3	2
50 and over	1	–	1	–
Unknown	1	–	–	–
Total	20	1	12	9

Table 5. Marital status of Kau Fung Glass Factory workers by sex and category, April 1968

Marital status	Permanent		Temporary	
	Male	Female	Male	Female
Single, including divorced and widowed	10	–	7	4
Married, spouse in Hong Kong	6	1	3	4
Married, spouse elsewhere	3	–	–	1
Unknown	1	–	2	–
Total	20	1	12	9

were scattered more generally throughout the age range. The youngest employee was sixteen years old. There were no consistent sex-related differences in the ages of employees. If one includes those whose spouses were not residing in Hong Kong (three in China, one in Indonesia), a little over half the workers were living singly. One of these was a widow with four children. Most of the single men in the permanent category were living in the firm's hostel.

The mother tongue of all but five of the workers was Cantonese. Of these five, one was from Kiangsi; one, whose first language was Bahasa Indonesia, was from Java; and one was a Teochiu-speaking immigrant recently from Vietnam (Cholon). All the others had been born either in Hong Kong or in Kwangtung Province; two of the latter said they were Hakkas. There was no discernible tendency for people to have originated from the same native place in Kwangtung. All the workers spoke Cantonese to each other. It should be added that none of the management was a native Cantonese speaker, and that the managing director spoke that language hardly at all, though he understood it perfectly well.

An analysis of the length of time each worker claimed to have lived in Hong Kong gives the results shown in Table 6.

Table 6. Length of stay in Hong Kong by category, Kau Fung Glass Factory workers, April, 1968

Residence history	Permanent	Temporary	Total
Born in Hong Kong	5	8	13
Came as a child pre-war*	2	1	3
Came about 1947**	4	2	6
Arrived 1950	3	1	4
Arrived 1951	–	1	1
Arrived 1954	2	–	2
Arrived 1955	1	–	1
Arrived 1960	–	1	1
Arrived 1961		2	2
Arrived 1962	2	1	3
Arrived 1963	2	2	4
No information	–	2	2
Total	21	21	42

*I.e. before the Japanese occupation in December-January 1941-42.
**I.e. at the end of World War II when many previous residents returned.

If we assume that only those neither born in Hong Kong nor living there before 1949 can be meaningfully classed as 'refugees', it is clear that just under half the workers fell into that category. It is interesting that they accounted for just under half the permanent workers, too. In other words, this factory depended for its workers, both skilled and unskilled, as much upon natives of the Colony and long-term residents as upon recent immigrants. This is partly to be linked with the connection between skill and youth already mentioned. Of the thirteen workers born in Hong Kong, ten gave their ages as 21 years or less. Only one of these was the child of a truly local family, his father having farmed ancestral land in the New Territories. All but one of the others, including the two (aged 28 and 46 respectively) who were born some years before 1949, stated that their fathers had been immigrants. There is, however, nothing unusual or new about this for Hong Kong's urban population, and it does not follow that the fathers referred to were all 'refugees'. On the contrary, in addition to the one youngster whose ancestors were all New Territories people, six stated that their fathers had come to Hong Kong before the Japanese occupation; the other five did not know when their fathers had arrived.

Because a history of recent immigration is normal for Hong Kong's urban population, it is probably not very useful to try to relate individual differences to date of arrival. These differences are more likely to be connected with such factors as level of education and degree of previous acquaintance with factory employment. This likelihood is explored in the following paragraphs and in Tables 7-9.

Table 7 shows that there was some degree of correlation between level

Table 7. Level of education by category and sex, Kau Fung Glass Factory workers, April 1968

Educational level	Permanent		Temporary	
	Male	Female	Male	Female
Post-secondary education	–	–	–	–
Secondary school completed				
3 years	3	–	1	–
2 years	3	–	–	1
1 year	1	–	–	–
Primary school completed				
6 years	2	–	3	2
5 years	3	–	–	–
4 years	1	–	1	–
3 years	4	–	3	2
2 years	–	–	–	–
1 year	1	–	–	2
No education	1	1	3	2
No information	1	–	1	–
Total	20	1	12	9

of education and permanent or temporary status, in that rather more workers in the permanent category claimed to have received rather more education than those in the temporary category. The correlation may have been largely coincidental—or if causative, only in the sense that the same qualities that would lead a person to seek further education might make him both more able and more willing to meet the criteria for promotion to permanent status. In any case, there are indications that the workers themselves saw very little causality in the relationship. None of the temporary workers whose ultimate ambition apparently was to become permanent workers reported that they intended further education. And the four workers who reported attending or intending to take classes—although three of the four were temporary workers who would have welcomed permanent status while at the factory—all aspired ultimately to become white-collar workers and leave factory work altogether. (These four were the youngest employee, who had just completed four years of primary schooling, and three others, one of them a woman, who had reached or completed middle school.) In this, they reflect the prevalent patterns of upward mobility in Hong Kong that were discussed briefly above.

It should be added here that all four of the managers (directors and salaried staff) had received at least some post-secondary education. Managing Director *A* had a Ph.D. from a European university.

Among workers under thirty there was little or no evidence of sex-linked differences in level of education attained.

With regard to father's occupation (see Table 8), there are few differences between the permanent and temporary categories, though a surprising number of the temporary workers were unable to give any information about their

Table 8. Father's occupations by category, Kau Fung Glass Factory workers, April 1968

Father's occupation	Permanent	Temporary
Profession or management	2	–
Farming*	7	6
Glass factory	1	1
Shop or small trade	4	2
Other**	2	5
'Retired'	3	–
No information	2	7
Total	21	21

*Includes one described as a 'gardener' and employed by the Urban District Council.

**Includes two factory- or office-cleaners, a beach lifeguard, a sailor, a tailor, a hairdresser, and a matshed-maker.

father's work. In most cases this was because the fathers had died many years before.

In the light of the previous paragraphs it is at first sight surprising to find two permanent workers, apparently uninterested in further education, with fathers in professional and managerial positions (teacher and agent in an import-export firm). This is explained by the refugee situation: both these workers were older men (they included the already well-educated furnace foreman, aged fifty-one) who had come down in the world.

It is worth remarking, also, the very small number (two) of factory workers and the relatively large number of farmers among the workers' fathers. Both factory workers happen to have been employed in the making of glass. Small, rather primitive, factories for melting down old glass bottles to make new ones have existed in Canton, Macao, and Hong Kong for at least several decades. It may or may not be a simple coincidence that in the only cases where fathers were in factory employment children have, in fact, entered work in the same kind of factory. Workers with farming fathers are not, as might perhaps have been postulated, all older people, but rather equally scattered through the age groups. The relatively large number of farming fathers probably reflects simply the fact that the industrial revolution in Hong Kong began less than a generation ago.

All but two of the workers in this factory were thus first-generation factory employees. More than half of them were also the only factory employees in their respective kin sets, probably a further reflection of the recency of industrialization in Hong Kong. As with father's occupation, there is no significant difference between permanent and temporary workers, or even between the sexes, on this variable. Only in examining the previous experience of employees do any such clear differences emerge (see Table 9).

Here are no farmers, only one non-urban type of employment, and a

Table 9. Previous employment by category and sex, Kau Fung Glass Factory workers, April 1968

Previous employment	Permanent		Temporary		Totals
	Male	Female	Male	Female	
Factory work—not glass	11	1	6	8*	26
Glass factory	7	–	1	–	8
Construction	–	–	1	–	1
Forestry	–	–	–	–	1
None	1	–	1	1	3
No information	1	–	2	–	3

*Includes one previous an outworker.

strong tendency for factory workers to remain in factory employment. The tendency is so striking (particularly for the women) that one can state firmly that this factory has not drawn its workers from a general pool of totally 'raw' recruits. On the contrary, with only one exception and despite the fact that Hong Kong's industrial revolution is so new that only two workers had fathers with industrial experience, every worker on the books in April 1968 had previously been employed in industry (if we include the one in construction). This finding gives some credence to the view that, despite all appearances to the contrary, Hong Kong's industry may be facing the possibility of a shortage even of unskilled labour. At the very least, Table 9 raises the question whether or not the prejudice against non-white-collar employment, which has been mentioned above (pp. 155-56), may be creating a kind of artificial labour shortage.

MANAGEMENT: THE SALARIED STAFF

There were only two salaried managing staff employees at the factory in 1968 (see Figure 3 above). Both had arrived in Hong Kong since 1949, and neither was Cantonese. Both were college-educated, and one spoke fair English. Both in their late twenties and unmarried, previously unknown to each other, they had each been recruited personally by one or other of the two directors.

Managing Director *A* had brought Managing Clerk *a* with him from the glass factory where they had both been employed. This man, who held a truck and car driver's license, was well acquainted with most aspects of importing raw materials and exporting finished products, and well known to most of the agents of the firms concerned. His job was mainly with these outside contacts. He was also charged with the general overseeing of the packing section in the factory, and the preparations for delivery. He was in no way related to *A*, nor did he even come from the same province or language group. Their original acquaintance was purely a business one. Both were, of course, aware that *a* owed his new position entirely to *A*.

Office Worker *b* was in charge of the accounts and records, and, under *A*'s direction, kept a watching eye over all the internal management of the factory not overseen by *a*. I have already described the pleasant, cheerful, friendly manner in which he discharged this duty. He also handled the petty cash, and presided over payday when, having worked out the wages due, he checked each sum with each worker individually and handed over the pay packets. He lived with his mother only a few hundred yards away, and except at night was almost constantly in the factory. As a result he was responsible for a large number of the more or less routine decisions, coping with minor crises, etc. At night, *a*, who had sleeping quarters in the factory, took this responsibility, but as work was not normally continued beyond 10:00 p.m., his position in this respect was less important.

Office Worker *b* had been offered his post by Director *B*, under whom he had already worked for about five years in the office of the publishing firm by which *B* was still employed at the time of my fieldwork. There was no previous relationship between the two men, nor did they come from the same province in China. (They did, however, both have 'gentry' backgrounds, as did also Managing Director *A*, Staff Member *a*, and the furnace foreman [Number Two].) *B* had selected *b* for his abilities: accuracy, conscientiousness, good humour, intelligence, reliability, and complete loyalty.

Nominally *a* and *b* each received $600.00 a month, but, as for this purpose a convention that there were fourteen months in a year was accepted, the actual sum each received was almost $700.00 a month. In addition, *a* had free lodging in the factory. Each received a free mid-day meal, taken with the directors if they were present (see below) and paid for out of petty cash.

In general status there was no doubt at all about the superiority of the managing staff. This distinction was both expressed and reinforced in many small ways. The office staff always wore collars and ties, and spoke Mandarin together, normally using Cantonese only when speaking to the workers, and then with a strong accent. The office staff and directors ate with the workers only on ceremonial occasions; normally the workers took their lunch at a nearby café, while the office staff and the directors lunched together at one or other of the excellent local restaurants. With the one exception of the furnace foreman, whose special case has already been discussed, the managers were very much better educated than the workers—a fact that was apparent in dozens of small unconscious mannerisms and in their overall bearing. Social distance thus evidenced appeared to be accepted by both sides as right and proper. Its impact was greatly modified by marked and, I believe, genuine friendliness in conversation, by paternalism coupled normally with great care over giving 'face', and by an explicit belief, held by both the managers and at lease those workers who had attained or aspired to permanent status, that as far as the firm was concerned their interests were the same.

MANAGEMENT: THE DIRECTORS

Basically simple though the process of glass manufacture is, it nevertheless requires a number of technological skills. One of these, the skill (and physical strength) required by the glassblowers, has already been commented upon. I have also mentioned the skill required for stoking the tanks and maintaining the proper loads and temperatures in them. A further very valuable skill, that of actually making the tanks, is closely linked with a fourth and most important skill; namely, a sophisticated knowledge of industrial chemistry and, in particular, of refraction. With the exception of glassblowing, these skills were all in the command of one man, Director *A*.

As the sole technical expert, *A* appeared to be indispensable to the glass factory. As noted above, he supervised the mixing of the raw materials, to which he added certain ingredients that he weighed behind the locked door of his private office. The formula was his own. The layout of the factory followed his plan. He allocated work tasks and devised schedules. Present almost every day, he took a minute interest in every aspect of the practical work, and he brought his two wives and their respective children with him to help in certain of the secret jobs. Both women also lent a hand with packing the finished glassware, as did anybody else who had a spare moment and felt so inclined.

The second director, *B*, knew virtually nothing about the technology of making glass. He was the public-relations man, the maker of outside contacts, searcher-out of markets, negotiator of credit; his was the task of arranging advertising and coping with licenses, fire regulations, relationships with buyers, and so on. He had interests in a number of other business enterprises of various kinds.

At this point it is necessary to go back about three years to the time when *A* first considered setting up a separate glass factory and *B* was looking for fresh fields for the investment of his financial and personal talents. At that stage (1964-65) *A* was certainly the key man. Without his skill, no glass factory could have appeared. At that stage, too, his personal contacts and credit in the glass business were also crucial. Through them he was able to borrow money, secure advance orders, acquire some of the necessary equipment cheaply, and recruit skilled labourers, some of whom he had previously trained himself. He also had a small amount of financial capital and personal contacts in the business community that made it easy for him to borrow money from the banks. He still needed more capital, however, and he also needed a kind of 'contact man' with drive and initiative to help find a factory site, organize advertising, and so on. *A*'s own assets were unique: he, and only he, could found and run a specialized glass factory. The skills required of the partner he needed were entirely generalized: *B* could have gone into any kind of business. It was in a sense purely by accident that *B* found himself engaged in manufacturing glass, and not plastic flowers or cotton vests or wigs or transistor radios. It should be added that both men were refugees, one from Central and one from North China, arriving in Hong Kong in 1949 and 1950 respectively.

Once the two men had agreed to enter into informal partnership (this was in 1965) the dominance of *A*'s role was complete. *B* helped find the site, negotiated a loan, borrowed trucks for transporting equipment, badgered the authorities for licenses, and so on, but all this was under the direction of *A*, who alone knew what was required technically, could put it into operation, recruit labour, and direct commercial contacts in the glass trade. Indeed, at this stage, and for more than the first year of the factory's operation (including the whole period of my fieldwork) *B*'s employment in the firm remained on a part-time basis. He did not take on full-time responsibilities until July of 1968.

Already after about six months' operation, however, once the factory was in steady working order, the locus of leadership began to shift. The change was accelerated when an advertising campaign was developed and foreign inquiries began to flow in. In their turn, *B*'s professional expertise and contacts now came into their own. In February 1968 a full-scale article on the glass factory appeared in *Hong Kong Enterprise*, a journal put out monthly by the Hong Kong Trade Development Council. It was a superb piece of commercial writing, with first-class photographs. Within two months it had stimulated inquiries and orders from every continent in the world. When I arrived in April 1968, the leadership statuses of the two men were more or less in balance.

Both men were fairly clearly aware of their competitive situation. So were the two members of the office staff and at least some of the workers, in particular the two foremen. It was here that *B*'s personality and social conscience, as well as his special structural position, became important. *A*, a reserved man without local ties, commanded little sympathy among the predominantly Cantonese workers. His necessarily strict day-to-day technological supervision of the delicate operations of his specialized process preparation and weighing of formula, temperature control, prevention of breakage, etc.) inevitably led to direct confrontations with careless individuals. His high technical standards, his 'foreign' upper-class manner, and his structural position as overseer tended to alienate even the key skilled workers he himself had brought to the factory at the beginning.

B, by contrast, had a Cantonese wife and spoke the language well. He had a disarmingly gay, friendly manner and a genuine concern for other people and their problems. He had also a much less intimate connection with the day-to-day running of the factory, no responsibility for the standards of work, and virtually no disciplinary function. With a joke for everybody, and a proven willingness to help anyone in personal trouble, he evoked a generally warm response all round. Moreover, the workers believed that *B* had obtained most of their increases in wages, and had succeeded in improving their fringe benefits, over *A*'s objections.

Probably the swing of worker allegiance from *A* to *B*, which was at its critical point at the time of my investigation, was structurally inevitable. In any complex technological system the role of the technical expert, thrown into day-to-day supervisory contact with the workers and compelled to maintain high standards, must have some disciplinary features. The organizer of the factory's outside contacts, on the other hand, can avoid this. Seeing the workers less regularly, controlling them hardly at all, he has no need to keep much social distance, and can afford warm friendliness. At the same time there is a constant tendency for the outside contact man, like *B*, to be seen to be active in the more popular aspects of worker management, such as recruitment and the initiative for improvement in working conditions and wages, for these are the two major functions that are assimilated to the 'outside' part of the factory's overall organization. When *A* fired a bad worker, it was *B* who found a replacement; whereas *A* was concerned with the maintenance of his furnaces, *B* knew that other factories had better lavatories, more valuable lunch vouchers, or bigger pay packets, and that his must be improved accordingly if his workers were to remain. It seems likely that the way in which *B* was beginning to take over the leadership from *A*, once the major technical problems had been solved, exemplifies a universal tendency in the second stage of a factory's development. In a small concern the two stages and tendencies are likely to be very clearly distinguishable, and when, as here, the 'outside man' has far the more winning personality, the outcome is not hard to predict: other things being equal, the technical man is likely to lose out, whereupon the factory's development will enter a third stage.

Early in April 1968, *B* began to put into operation a plan he had long been considering. His own statement was that it sprang directly out of his personal experience as a down-and-out refugee in Hong Kong in the early fifties. From that experience he had gained a passionate determination to help improve social conditions and a firm conviction that neither state control nor capitalism provided the answers he was looking for. In brief, his scheme was to provide for a kind of joint control of the business by setting up a private limited company in which, though he and *A* were to be the main shareholders, there should also be a number of other members with equal voting rights. The entire month was spent arguing the case for registering the firm as a private limited company and including in its membership the two office staff workers, and five of the workers from the shop floor, the shares of all these employees to be acquired in the beginning by free gifts of $1,000 each from *B*. It was also to be made known that any permanent worker could look forward to becoming a shareholder in the future.

As far as I have been able to ascertain, this was a unique development in Hong Kong. Although the practice of setting up registered limited companies, never very popular in the past, has been catching on quite dramatically in the last few years, none had, so far as I could establish, included salaried staff, to say nothing of blue-collar workers. *B* was enthusiastically proud of his plan, constantly discussing it and reiterating his hope that it might become a model not only for Hong Kong but for industrializing countries in general. In spite of *A*'s initial hostility, not only to the idea of worker membership, but also to the whole notion of forming a limited company, the company was registered early in May 1968 with a board of seven, consisting of *A*, one of his wives, *B*, the two white-collar staff members, and two foremen.

Such a radical restructuring of the legal framework of the factory's ownership raises a number of interesting questions, only two of which can be considered here: namely, the possible reasons behind it, and its effects upon the day-to-day organization of production.

The importance for economic development of an adequate framework of commercial and industrial law has often been remarked. In Hong Kong such a framework has existed for a very long time, but until fairly recently the particular aspect of it that enabled the creation of corporate and continuing legal entities (private limited companies) was seldom invoked. Very likely, so long as businesses remained family concerns, any possible advantages that might result from forming such a company were outweighed by the disadvantage of having to disclose shareholdings at the time of formation. The Kau Fung Glass Factory, however, like an increasing number of others today, was not a family business. We have already referred to the consistent tendency for Chinese businessmen in Hong Kong to prefer multiplex to single-stranded relationships. Confidence in Chinese business is so much a matter of multiplex relationships that, as I have said above, almost any transaction beyond the most casual purchase tends to take on social attributes. It is possible that men who lack personal relationships (as in the refugee situation was often the case), or who for any reason have entered into non-family partnerships (these are increasing at what is likely to be an accelerating pace), and who may also be influenced by modern values in favour of universalistic rather than particularistic relationships, may be motivated to look for legally binding contractual ties instead. Hence (so runs the argument put to me by a number of well informed official and unofficial observers in Hong Kong in 1968) the increase in the number of limited companies registered in the past few years—the glass factory among them.

This seems a plausible hypothesis. It certainly fits the situation under discussion. The two directors had no mutually binding particularistic obligations with which to cement their mutual interest in the factory, and, given their different personalities and dissimilar backgrounds, little chance of developing any. Moreover, both had been exposed in different ways to modern, universalistic values, and at least to a certain extent both accepted them (we have seen this at work in the firm's policy and practice about recruiting workers and staff). At the same time, both were aware that their mutual relationship was a precarious one, and each may have seen the entry into a legal contract as a possible safeguard, *A* after some initial hostility to the whole idea.

But this explanation does not account for the unique element in the new situation; namely, the inclusion of the salaried staff and some workers in the articles of association. Here the personal influence of *B* was decisive. Questioned, he denied having read any of the literature on co-partnership in industry or allied topics: the idea appears to have been genuinely original. He saw it both as a method of distributing power and as a way of binding workers and management more firmly together through the actualization of the belief that their interests in the firm were the same. He was explicit about all this, and I have no doubt that he was sincere. Nevertheless I suggest that the move also held certain strategic advantages for himself.

We have seen how, lacking technical expertise of the kind that had made *A* indispensable in the early stages, *B* had nonetheless acquired a balancing position in the directorate. From his point of view the formation of the limited company was more than just an attempt to perpetuate this situation, for by forming it in such a way that he himself controlled a majority of the votes, *B* made it possible for the firm to continue as a legal entity no matter what steps *A* might take. As time went on, the factory's dependence upon *A*'s technical expertise would probably grow less. It was possible to foresee a situation in which, if it came to confrontation (or the threat of confrontation), *A* might withdraw, leaving *B* in sole effective control.

STYLE AND ORGANIZATION: 'THE CHINESE WAY'

My period of fieldwork came to an end in early May of 1968, so all this is speculation.* What is quite clear, however, is that at the level of actual production the changes in the structure of ownership made little or no difference. This was partly because the layout and organization of the factory were already as rational and efficient as space would allow, and partly because the firm was still small enough for face-to-face relationships to exist throughout. This made it possible for workers and managers to be personally known to each other, and joint consultation had always been continuous and effective. This was no accident. *B* and *b* explained to me many times that personalized methods of management were much better than others because they

*I have since been informed that *A* did, indeed, leave the firm in December 1968. The salaried staff member *a* left at the same time.

permitted the giving of 'face' and so ensured mutual respect and self-respect. They usually referred to this approach as 'the Chinese way', and contrasted its economic effectiveness with what seemed to them to be the essential irrationality of the Western preference for impersonal, single-stranded relationships.

Until now the descriptive analysis contained in this paper has given little support to the notion that there was anything peculiarly Chinese about the internal organization of the glass factory. Layout, work flow, job allocation, labour recruitment, even most aspects of the workers' previous experience and background did not appear to be specifically culture-linked. Even among the managing staff and directors there were no particularistic ties of a traditional nature. Only the system of rewards by categories seemed to be somewhat unusual, and even that is quite common in other parts of the Orient. As a piece of organizational machinery, the glass factory may be said to conform more closely to a 'universal' than to a culture-specific pattern.

Nevertheless, and making full allowance for the fact that smallness of scale anywhere allows a personalized flexibility in management and encourages acceptable paternalism, there remain some features to which, taken together, the phrase 'Chinese way' can be meaningfully applied. They include beliefs about the value of education, the virtue of hard work, and the self-evident goal of economic self-betterment, shared by workers and management alike. This set of values was accompanied by an ingrained habit of giving 'face', in my opinion closely linked with the strong preference for multiplex rather than single-stranded relationships that has been mentioned in a number of contexts. It is my present hypothesis that insofar as it may be possible to isolate any aspects of the internal organization of this factory as uniquely 'Chinese', they will be found not in the structural framework or the organizational plan, but in intangibles such as these, none of which alone is specific to Chinese culture but all of which in sum constitute a peculiarly Chinese style of running economic institutions.

REFERENCE

Chou, K. R. 1966. *The Hong Kong Economy: A Miracle of Growth.* Hong Kong: Academic Publications.

Section III

Aspects of Socialization

9. Temper Tantrums in Kau Sai: Some Speculations upon Their Effects*

The following paragraphs are offered with considerable diffidence. The fieldwork upon which this paper is based was directed primarily towards the analysis of a socio-economic system as such.[1] As a result, the data on child development and adult attitudes which appear in my notebooks do so almost by accident. They were certainly not collected systematically with the object of testing the validity of hypotheses in social psychology. They did, however, appear to me to have some intrinsic interest at the time, and my thinking about some of the major puzzles in Chinese social patterns—in particular, the marvellous ability of Chinese to 'live in crowds and keep their virtue'—has been partly influenced by them. An unpublished version of this paper has already provoked some useful rethinking, and it is my hope that if a wider audience may be reached others may be moved to look further and more scientifically into these and similar matters. The ensuing observations are therefore offered simply as speculations for discussion. I should add that they apply strictly to one particular fishing village in the British crown colony of Hong Kong, but I believe that such truth as they may contain has a much wider validity for Chinese families in general.

The village, Kau Sai, is situated on an island in the eastern waters of the colony. This paper begins in the period 1952-53 when the population was about 450, nearly all of them living on small boats anchored just offshore. Ten years later there had been a number of changes, notably an increase of population to about 600, the beginning of a move to living ashore, the building of a fine new school (with three teachers and more than 100 pupils), and a generally marked rise in the standard of living. All these things were connected with the completion of the mechanization of all but one or two of the fishing boats, which had brought also much greater physical mobility, knowledge of the ways of the big city, and so on. I do not think there have been or are

*Reprinted with permission from Philip Mayer (ed.), *Socialization: The Approach from Social Anthropology* (London: Tavistock Publication Ltd., 1970), pp. 109-25.

[1] I wish to record my warmest thanks to H. M. Treasury Committee for the Study of Foreign Languages and Cultures (the Scarborough Committee) and to the London-Cornell Project for East and Southeast Asian Studies for making this fieldwork possible.

likely soon to be, concomitant changes in the patterns of child behaviour described here.

THREE KINDS OF TANTRUM

Both in the village and in Hong Kong generally I noticed very early that it was quite a common thing to see children, especially small boys—between the ages of, say, five and ten—in a screaming rage: lying on the floor or the pavement (sidewalk), kicking and screaming, red in the face and making no end of noise—an obvious tantrum, and nobody taking any notice. Usually these tantrums just petered out into sobbing, and the child finally picked himself up and went away; sometimes an elder brother or someone else, usually but not always a parent or sibling, would come and pull the child up, scold him and tell him to stop. Now in England I think it is true to say that children's tantrums tend to occur at rather younger ages and that they are much more usually a matter of adult concern. Either by comforting or by scolding the mother will usually try to stop her child screaming, and also it would, I think, be unusual for any adult to notice a screaming child and do just nothing about it at all—and this whether the child was any relation of his or not—whereas here they were just left to scream themselves out.

Later, I made a tentative classification of tantrums observed in Kau Sai village, as follows:

1. There was the kind of tantrum that occurred when a child felt himself left behind or deserted by his parents or others. This was especially common among the boat children who sometimes found themselves left on the shore while others went out to the boats—they were scared of being abandoned and they yelled their feelings very loud in order to make their presence known. This kind of tantrum happened to both boys and girls, and at any age from about three to six, seven, or eight; that is, from the time they were able to wander about on their own, and so run the risk of getting left behind, to the time they were able to scull a boat for themselves and so need not fear being left behind. This seems to me to be a very ordinary kind of rage: any small children fear being abandoned and react to situations in which they think this is likely to happen in much the same way—the only difference here was that the pattern of living on boats made this situation a little more common, perhaps, than it is in other kinds of community. I feel myself that this fact may have some effect on the personality development of the boat people as such, but that is not my present concern.

2. The second kind of tantrum consisted of the crying and stamping that a child might break into if he did not get what he was asking for immediately.

For example, a small girl wanting ten cents to buy sweets might stamp and shout until her father gave it to her just to keep her quiet. This again is not at all an unusual thing in any family where the children have been indulged. It was not a common type of tantrum in Kau Sai and is probably commoner in all societies among richer families who often have more time and opportunity to 'spoil' their children than have poorer ones.

3. The third type of tantrum was the one that interested me most. It was likely to affect both boys and girls, but boys more often. Though closely connected with the second type, it was not exactly the same in origin. For example, a group of small children is playing ball, a bigger boy comes along and kicks the ball away from them. The owner of the ball, a little boy about six years old, rises and runs after this bigger boy but fails to catch him. Finally, the bigger boy lets him have the ball back. The small chap, Ah Kam, picks it up again and goes off with it, but before he has gone very far an adult comes along and knocks it out of his hands. This causes laughter among the onlookers, and Ah Kam laughs too as he goes to pick up his ball once more. Later in the same morning he is playing with other children who have a skipping rope. Ah Kam tries to help to turn the rope for others to skip, but he is called away by his mother who wants him to bring the baby to her. A bit later still he starts playing at 'cooking'—with scraps of straw for firewood and broken-up pots for rice and dishes—with another group of his age-mates. This game goes on quite successfully for about fifteen minutes until along comes another adult who, with a sweep of his hand, knocks the pretence rice and the pretence pots and pans flying. The adult laughs and the children laugh too. By then it is nearly noon and Ah Kam is hungry, so he trots off to the shop to spend his ten cents on biscuits. After collecting them he runs out of the shop and collides with another child coming in. One of the biscuits falls on the ground and is smashed. Ah Kam also falls to the ground in an apparently uncontrollable rage. He yells for some time. Nobody takes any notice of him except perhaps to look in his direction once or twice. Gradually his sobs grow quieter until, after about ten minutes, he picks himself up, still clutching his biscuits, and wanders off sobbing to himself. His slightly older sister comes up to him and takes two of the biscuits away from him. He makes no protest. About twenty minutes later he is playing with the other children again—the tantrum apparently forgotten.

Now the points I want to notice are three:

1. In the first place, this third kind of rage springs from an accumulation of frustrating situations. Ah Kam, aged six, has already learnt to put up with a great deal of outside interference—he laughs at the ball being knocked out of his hands, for example—but he cannot yet put up with too much. In the

end he simply screams.

2. Second, these frustrations are some of them accidental (running into another child) and some of them apparently deliberately caused (knocking over the cooking game). This apparently deliberate interference in the children's affairs is not in any sense considered unkind or unusual in the village. The general adult attitude if expressed would be: these are only children and it doesn't matter.

(There is here, by the way, an interesting difference between English and Chinese views on children's sensitivity. When a child falls down or hurts himself in Kau Sai, nobody makes any fuss about him, though of course if there is serious injury there is considerable alarm and great care is taken. As a result, one may guess, of the lack of fuss, children who have tumbles and minor hurts seldom cry. They appear to know they will get no attention if they do. Western children tend to behave in just the opposite way, crying loudly and unnecessarily over the smallest injury because they usually get much attention from doing so. Western and Chinese adults' explanations of their differing behaviour in this matter are interesting. The Westerner says: because he is a child it is more difficult for him to bear pain, he has not yet learnt to control his reactions. The Chinese villagers I know say: because he is a child he does not *feel* pain as badly as an adult would, so there is no need to fuss. Once I asked a woman how she knew that children felt pain less than adults do. She said: 'But of course you don't feel pain so badly when you are a child; if you did you would remember, but look at this—she showed me some deep scars on her chest—'that happened when I was about two years old and it was very serious as you can see, but I can't remember anything about it at all. So it can't have hurt very much.')

But to go back to the adult's frustration of children: I repeat there is absolutely no intention of being unkind. Children's affairs are not considered important and the children themselves are naturally expected to share this view (to which there is only one exception: going to school is considered important). Nevertheless, everybody is interested in children, and everybody likes to watch them; they provide, indeed, a common form of entertainment and pleasure. The same is true of small babies, who are continually being played with and talked to. Many, if not most, fathers like to carry a small child around with them almost wherever they go—particularly, of course, a boy baby. Now this great interest in small children leads very often to a desire to provoke them to some reaction. In very much the same way as a small child himself when playing with a live animal will poke it with a stick just to see what happens, so adults who play with live children tend to like to poke them in the ribs just to get a reaction. It does not much matter what the reaction is: the baby may smile or he may cry, in either case he has *provided a reaction*, and the person who provoked him is satisfied. Thus very early indeed babies in the village are subjected to adult provocation of one kind or another.

This continues into childhood, but by that time there are two differences to be taken into consideration. First, the child is more likely to be aware of frustration than the baby, because the ways in which adults can provoke a reaction from him are different. For example, a baby may be asleep and an adult may wake him up. The baby has been provoked and he will cry but he will probably fairly soon go back to sleep. But a child may be concentrating intently and deliberately on some game which an adult destroys, and this is a much more consciously frustrating experience than simply being woken up out of sleep. Second, a baby suffers less than a child in this matter because a baby if crying will always be comforted, picked up, fondled, given the breast, and generally soothed down. The change to being left alone to cry oneself out comes at about two and a half years or so, and is probably closely connected with weaning and with the arrival of another child in the family—situations themselves likely to provoke distress in the displaced child, especially if he is a boy and has therefore been particularly well noticed before.

Thus the frustrations that appear to be deliberately brought to children of, say, three years old and upwards are not intended to be unkind; they are in some ways simply the ordinary expression of interest in children, but they are none the less often very painful in their effects.

3. The third point about these tantrums that I want to stress is that, as a general rule, the child is left to cry himself out. Normally no one goes to deal with him either by scolding or by comforting. It is my belief that one result of this is that the child fairly quickly learns that such rages bring no reward (just as crying after being physically hurt does not pay), and it is probable that at the same time he also learns that he can expect no sympathy from others in his private despairs. As a result the village children I know do seem to learn remarkably quickly to accept frustration, and to be peculiarly self-composed and in emotional matters self-reliant.

Although I have said earlier that tantrums occur rather later than in my experience with English children, they do not continue past the age of nine or ten.

So far the data; now for the speculation. The following arguments are not of a kind that is fashionable at present among either social psychologists or social anthropologists. It does not follow that they are entirely without validity. At the very least, speculation upon them may provoke others to develop more adequate hypotheses. I therefore wish to examine here the possible connection between the observations just recorded and certain other observed features of village social life, namely: the relatively problem-free period of adolescence; the strict playing-down of aggression; and the ability to live in extremely crowded conditions.

ADOLESCENT ADJUSTMENTS FOR BOYS AND GIRLS

First, then, I should like to postulate that there may be some connection with later individual development. The village of Kau Sai contains a community in which problems of adolescent adjustment appear to be minimal, especially for boys. There were in 1950-53 a number of circumstances relevant to this: children grew up with a clear idea of exactly what their place in the socio-economic system was to be; they lived always in the very midst of the cottage-industry type of fishing business which occupied all their neighbours and in which they themselves took an active and useful part from a very early age; the necessary skills were acquired gradually and at home; marriages were arranged when the children were about sixteen years old. Thus there were virtually no alternatives offered to adolescents, no choices they could make, and for boys there were no sharp discontinuities at any stage. As far as skills were concerned there was a gradual assumption of adult roles with increasing maturity and physical strength, and none of the necessary skills were beyond the achievement of any ordinary individual; as far as status was concerned, the ceremony of marriage conferred adulthood publicly and without any doubt; and early marriage gave adolescent sexual activity both limitation and legitimation. These are all structural features that point to a relatively stress-free adolescence. The period of greatest emotional strain, for boys at least, appeared to be much earlier—in the tantrum years from about five to ten.

The pattern for girls was different, for the obvious reason that they experienced the complete, sometimes traumatic, discontinuity of leaving home at marriage. Because of this, they were usually given clearly to understand—from the time they could understand speech at all—that they were 'goods on which profit is lost', which gave them from the start a position very different from that of their brothers. Generally less indulged when very young, and earlier introduced to responsible domestic tasks, girls appeared in 1953 to accept their frustrations more readily than did boys. I certainly observed fewer tantrums in girls, and they seemed not to persist beyond the age of five and six. The major problem for girls at adolescence was, of course, adjustment to the new family after marriage. I have very few observations to offer on this, beyond the obvious point that there were considerable differences between, say, a marriage with the boy next door (this is a mixed surname village)[2] and a marriage into an unknown family living at a distance, and, of course, between different individual mothers-in-law. A few (very few) recently married girls did try to run away, but a young bride is very unlikely to have anywhere to run to, and most accepted their new situation with much the same apparent readiness as that with which they had accepted their earlier frustrations. Perhaps these latter served the useful purpose of providing habituation. At any rate there is no doubt in my mind, after many conversations, that village girls were enirely realistic in their attitude towards their own situation, accepted it as inevitable, did not (I am speaking of a time about ten years ago) question its essential rightness, but did know that with luck, the successful production of children,[3] and the passing of time they too might have a more prestigeful, somewhat more restful, and much gayer future to look forward to.

To a lay observer all this appears to be a reversal of the usual developmental sequence. Both sexes exhibit in adolescence a marked degree of emotional control, in other words a successful adjustment to their structural situation. Is it fanciful to regard this as, in part at least, an outcome of the earlier period of stress and frustration which both undergo though in rather different ways? My own inclination is to argue that there is a connection but that it is in no sense causative. The psychological stability of the adolescent period in Kau Sai is to be explained in the situational terms I have just listed, including, at the time of which I am so far writing, the lack of alternative choices and the relative prosperity of the fishing industry there (a youngster is assured of a reasonably good living if he stays at home). At the same time, the kinds of childhood experience that most adolescents have undergone have led them to suppress the outward manifestations of emotional frustration and not to expect any deep emotional sympathy from others. They have also, of course, been deliberately taught the rightness of familialism and of the whole going concern into which they have been born, and, once again, at this level too, no alternatives have been put before them. They are therefore psychologically fairly well adapted to accepting the actual situation when it develops. It must be remembered, too, that adolescence in Kau Sai brings very real satisfactions, for it is during the age-period fifteen to twenty that nearly all members of this community marry and begin their economically

[2] The traditional rule that marriage may be contracted only between persons of different surnames is strictly adhered to. Many villages in S.E. China are 'single surname' (i.e. localized lineage) villages, containing only bearers of one patrilineally inherited surname and their wives.

[3] Not simply sons; they deeply desire girls, too, especially among their older children, for a daughter can give really useful help with the everlasting domestic work at least eight years sooner than a daughter-in-law.

productive careers, thus entering into the two most highly valued of the universally available statuses in traditional Chinese villages.

In the summer of 1963 I went back to Kau Sai. I noticed no changes in the parental treatment of children. The same temper tantrums could be observed. Indeed, it was laughable to see the younger brothers of today's strapping young married adolescents repeating their elders' behaviour patterns in almost identical ways. But there had been some changes in adolescent behaviour, if not in general then for certain individuals. Four girls had married, rather later than would have been usual ten years ago, *landsmen* of their own choice; five boys had gone away to work for wages ashore. In other words, the possibility of choice had now appeared. With it also had come a new school and, for the first time, an education which made it possible for some of the new choices to be taken up. Nowadays young people do discuss the alternatives to accepting arranged marriages and staying at home to work in the family business. A girl who leaves the community still does so only on marriage, and gains much the same status as she did before—or, because she can now more easily marry 'up',[4] a better one. A boy who leaves is less likely to marry early. He gains independence, but may well lose economic advantage, at least for a time. He may, perhaps, return to the family fishing business later on and settle down, or he may not. In any case he faces a period of uncertainty which does not exist in the village. It seems to me that his childhood experiences fit him just as well for that.

If I have dwelt overlong upon adolescence this is simply because it is a subject not yet much discussed in the Chinese context. The other two topics I wish to draw attention to have been more frequently described.

THE AVOIDANCE OF VIOLENT BEHAVIOUR

As I have explained elsewhere (Ward, 1954, 1965, and 1966), village organization in Kau Sai (which is a small community in which there have never been any 'gentry' and both the standards of living and the sources of livelihood are more or less identical for all members of the population) is markedly anarchic. Leadership roles are shunned rather than sought, and on the one annual occasion on which organized leadership is required (at the annual festival in the 2nd moon) leaders are always selected by lot at the village temple. To push oneself forward in an open effort to dominate others is considered wrong in much the same way that any openly aggressive behaviour, including verbally aggressive behaviour, is considered wrong. One of the actually most influential men in the village is one of the most retiring, and he owes his

[4] The water-people form the lowest category in the Hong Kong stratification system.

influence (the existence of which he denies) largely to this fact. He has never been known to quarrel with anyone, and has several times been held up to me as an example of good character because of this. His reputation was enhanced rather than the reverse during the period immediately preceeding family partition,[5] when fairly frequent noisy arguments broke out between his brothers; whenever this happened he quietly, and in obvious distress, absented himself and went to bed.

But then the phrase 'I was so angry that I went home to sleep' is one that I have heard more than once, and from different people of both sexes. Withdrawal from a situation in which aggressive feelings are likely to break into open expression is highly approved behaviour, and a good temper and a controlled tongue are among the most valued personal qualities. A good deal of the local gossip centres upon these qualities and a young person who lacks them, or whose horoscope or other magical properties indicate their absence, is difficult to marry off.

All this is part of what appears to many Westerners to be an exaggerated fear of violence. Children are constantly told not to fight each other and are quickly restrained if they do. There is absolutely none of the 'hit him back next time' kind of advice, but rather a warning to keep out of the way or run a bit faster. Adults who show signs of coming to blows are separated at once and the theme of one of the most usual lines of criticism of foreigners is the appalling violence of their behaviour.

Actually, quarrels or any sort of open expression of aggression between Kau Sai villagers appear to be exceedingly rare. There is no local mechanism for dealing with them, and it is unthinkable that any Kau Sai person should take another (or indeed anybody) to court. Potential hostility is not usually allowed to develop into open aggression, and is constantly played down. Young men in their late twenties, or even thirties, whose fathers still exercise complete authority over them, may grumble to an anthropologist, but they are careful to see that no one else overhears them. Brothers whose joint property is still undivided may squabble in public, but usually only after drinking; and everyone hastens to point out that drunken words carry no real significance. Within the village these are the two sets of relationship most loaded with potential hostility.

Relationships with non-Kau Sai people tend to be thought of in terms of general potential hostility mitigated by special circumstances. For example, the villagers of X across the water are nearly always described as being bad people, quarrelsome and thieving, yet there has been continued intermarriage

[5] I.e. the division of property among sons which takes place, usually, some time after the death of their father.

between the two settlements and probably every individual in Kau Sai has close and amicable ties of both kinship and friendship with some individual(s) from X. Similarly, the local Hakka-speaking Chinese in general[6] are said to be 'no good'; again, it is significant that this is elaborated in terms of their alleged quarrelsomeness and thrusting. Most of the landsmen (including fish dealers) with whom the Kau Sai fishermen come into contact locally are in fact Hakka, and all fishermen in Kau Sai do have particular Hakka friendships. This distrust of other people when seen generally as groups, along with a willingness to accept close ties with particular individuals from those groups, goes along with what I have described elsewhere (Ward, 1965) as the lack of intergroup relationships between communities as such and the development of a series of dyadic relationships between Kau Sai individuals and non-Kau Sai individuals.

One consequence of the lack of intergroup relationships as such at the village level is that there is no local mechanism for dealing with disputes if they do arise. From time to time thefts of nets are reported in Kau Sai; usually the villagers of X are blamed, but there is no machinery for dealing with the matter other than through formal complaints to the police and through the courts. It is needless to say that no one follows this course. But the lack of machinery for the local settlement of disputes, together with the believed-in inaccessibility of the courts, means (as Smith remarked in his study of Chinese villages years ago: Smith, 1890) that there is very wide scope for the local bullies. In fact, the Hong Kong Marine Police maintain a close patrol in local waters and frequently visit outlying villages, but even so nets can be stolen with impunity, temples are robbed from time to time, and memories of successful piracies are very much alive. Every fishing boat carries sticks of dynamite, and these are not always used only for the (illegal) stunning of fish. The fear of violence is by no means without foundation.

CONCLUSIONS

What has any of this to do with temper tantrums in childhood? I can give only a common-sense suggestion: we have here a structural situation which offers few effective sanctions against aggressive behaviour; the people appear to rely mainly upon the successful repression of aggressive impulses within each individual. This is secured during the period of socialization partly by direct verbal teaching, partly by physical restraint, and partly, though not I

[6] The two major indigenous languages in Hong Kong are Hakka and Cantonese. Cantonese dominates in both numbers of speakers and prestige. The fishermen speak a dialect of Cantonese but are in other respects usually considered lower in the local prestige ranking than Hakka speakers.

assume by conscious intent, through the kinds of childhood experience of frustration and the failure of aggressive behaviour to obtain its objectives that I have described above. There may well be other contributory factors.

But except for particularly meek individuals (like the admired man of influence previously mentioned, who in most English villages would probably be the object of amused derision) it is impossible to rely solely upon the internalization of the values of non-aggression. As a result, the maintenance of public order is likely to be rather a chancy business.

Self-control may break down for various reasons. Some of them are psychological. For example, individual consciousness may be, as it were, in abeyance—in drunkenness, for instance, or hysteria (including mob hysteria). It has, of course, often been remarked how relatively peaceable Chinese drunks are, which suggests that the control of aggressive behaviour is pretty deeply imbedded. Nevertheless, I have frequently observed that people in Kau Sai and elsewhere are afraid that a drunken man may turn nasty; a careful watch is usually kept on a man who is drinking, and drunken quarrels do sometimes occur—only to be hushed up and explained away as quickly as possible by everybody else. It may well be that the very fact that aggression is so much played down makes people the more afraid of it. There being virtually no legitimate outlets for aggressive behaviour and few effective external sanctions against it, once the internal controls do break down it can get quickly out of hand, and so there is good reason to be afraid. Herein may lie some of the explanation of the extreme violence of an aroused Chinese mob. Contrariwise, the relative ease with which a riot can be brought under control may possibly be partly due to the ease with which the internalized controls take over automatically once the hysteria has been checked.

Obviously there must be many individual personality differences. Some people are quick to take offence, and some tempers do flare up easily. The point is, however, that in Kau Sai everyone rallies to prevent a quarrel if possible, and even the offender himself deplores the lapse once he is restored to equanimity (or sobriety).

But it is obvious, too, that this cannot be the whole story. One cannot fall back upon 'personality differences' and temporary failures in self-control to explain such recurring phenomena as, say, banditry, clan warfare, or oppression by unscrupulous officials. Even the incidence of village bullies and other local delinquencies of the kinds I have already mentioned has been far too regular in traditional China to be entirely accounted for in terms of individual psychological peculiarities. Either the argument so far has no general validity and people in other parts and strata of Chinese society do not exhibit the same degree of control as in Kau Sai or something more than a psychological explanation is required. I am inclined to think that both these objections have some truth in them.

Kau Sai people are boat-people,[7] and the boat-people of Kwangtung and Fukien have long been a despised group, at the bottom of most local systems of stratification and hitherto largely without wealth, education, or connections with the ruling elites. Moreover, being water-dwellers they are potentially completely mobile; it is always possible for them to up anchor and run away. For these reasons they probably are an extreme case. Few other groups in China are likely to show such a high degree of non-aggressiveness. On the other hand, even a Kau Sai fisherman would not disapprove of, say, the use of firearms (or, lacking them, sticks of dynamite) against pirates—provided only that it was successful and did not provoke still more trouble.

Are we to say, then, that aggressive behaviour is considered deplorable only because it is likely to provoke retaliation? Rather I would suggest that this way of posing the problem is mistaken. Instead of concentrating upon some supposedly unitary concept called 'aggressive behaviour', as this paper has done so far, it would be more useful to switch our attention from the actor to the situation, and to argue that, whereas in certain situations any kind of aggressiveness is thought wrong, in others some kinds of aggressiveness may be considered correct though possibly inexpedient. Kau Sai people themselves do not say 'we deplore violence' or 'we try to inhibit agreession'; rather, they say 'we fishermen are desperately afraid of trouble' and 'we people of Kau Sai are just like brothers and sisters and so we do not quarrel'. The first of these sentences refers to their situation *vis-à-vis* non-Kau Sai people, clashes with whom might provoke 'trouble' (perhaps a lawsuit, perhaps future retaliation, perhaps further squeeze—there is a large range of possible trouble); the second refers to their situation at home—strife there would not provoke trouble in the same ways, it would just be bad in itself, making community life insupportable. For the boat-people, and indeed for the majority of Chinese most of the time, open manifestations of aggressiveness against outsiders must nearly always have been unwise, but there were quite a number of other groups in traditional China to whom this disability did not apply. Those who, for whatever reason, could oppress outsiders with impunity often (usually) did so. In so far as childhood training and experience did succeed in inculcating self-control of aggressive behaviour, it seems that this could be relied upon only within narrowly limited situations.

The last topic I should like to raise for discussion is the fascinating and astonishing Chinese ability to live successfully in conditions of overcrowding which would drive most other peoples to crime and/or despair. A foreigner is usually struck first by the, to him, intolerable overcrowding of such towns as

[7] Often called 'Tanka', a term used only in S. E. China; see Ward, 1965.

Singapore, Hong Kong, and Shanghai. He tends to put it down to something called 'the early stages of urbanization', talks about 'population explosions', and wonders at the apparently successful adaptation the populace has made. But, generally speaking, crowded conditions and an almost complete lack of privacy are as typical of the villages and, of course, of the boats as of the towns; Chinese peasants who 'become urbanized' are usually moving only from one kind of crowding to another.[8]

No doubt this does go far to explain the seeming ease of transition from rural to urban living (and often back again), but we are still left to wonder what are the factors that make such crowding tolerable anywhere. And here it does seem that there may be a much more direct connection with childhood's temper tantrums and their treatment than any we have so far been able to uncover, for it is at least plausible to suggest that early habituation to frustration and interference may do much to make possible the kind of living on top of each other that is so common. This and the playing down of aggressive behaviour, which we have already discussed, probably also contribute to the remarkably low crime-rates typical of even the most densely crowded Chinese communities.

But there is a further kite here that I should like to fly. I earlier referred to my observation that village children seemed to be peculiarly self-composed and in emotional matters self-reliant. I connected this on the one hand with their experiences over temper tantrums and on the other hand with their apparently unstressful adolescence. But I mentioned also that young men going to town faced at least an initial period of uncertainty such as did not exist in the village, and suggested that their childhood experiences, by giving them emotional self-reliance, fitted them well to cope with this. Whether or not I am right in connecting emotional self-reliance with the kind of treatment given (or, rather, not given) to temper tantrums, there seems to be no doubt that it is a marked feature of Chinese personality structure. And it seems at least very likely that it contributes significantly to the success with which Chinese adapt themselves to new circumstances—whether these involve moving into a bed-space in a tenement crowded to the brim with strangers, or migrating overseas, or accepting extremes of social change at home.

REFERENCES

Doolittle, (Rev.) Justus. 1865. *Social Life of the Chinese: With Some Account of Their Religious, Governmental, Educational and Business Customs and Opinions. With Special But Not Exclusive Reference to Fuhchau.* New York.

[8] And traditional towns were no less crowded than modern ones; see, for example, Doolittle's description of Fuchow in the mid-nineteenth century (Doolittle, 1865).

Smith, Arthur H. 1890. *Village Life in China.* New York.

———. 1894. *Chinese Characteristics.* New York.

Ward, Barbara E. 1954. 'A Hong Kong Fishing Village'. *Journal of Oriental Studies* 1(1). Hong Kong.

———. 1965. 'Varieties of the Conscious Model'. In M. Banton (ed.), *The Relevance of Models for Social Anthropology.* A.S.A. Monographs 1. London: Tavistock Publications.

———. 1966. 'Sociological Self-Awareness: Some Uses of the Conscious Model'. *Man* (N.S.) 1(2):201-215.

10. The Integration of Children into a Chinese Social World: A Preliminary Exploration of Some Non-literate Village Concepts*

This short paper attempts to explore the meaning of three Cantonese words as they were commonly used by villagers in the New Territories of Hong Kong in the fifties of the present century. The village in question was (and is) very small, occupied today almost exclusively by ex-water-dwelling Cantonese speakers.[1] At the time of which I am writing, the population was about 500 in all and included some 100 Hakka speakers, who lived in stone houses strung out along the water front, and approximately 400 Cantonese-speaking fishermen who lived on boats moored (when not engaged in fishing) at permanent anchorages just off the shore. The data on which the following paragraphs are based come mainly from notebooks and diaries which record the social anthropological studies which I carried out (mostly by the method of so-called participant observation) during two quite prolonged periods of stay in the village (from February 1952 to September 1952 and from December 1952 to August 1953) and a number of shorter visits between July 1950 and February 1952.[2] I have made many subsequent visits.

*An earlier version of this paper was read at the 1979 Annual Conference of the Hong Kong Psychological Society.

Reprinted with permission from the *Bulletin of the Hong Kong Psychological Society*, No. 4 (January 1980), pp. 7-17.

[1] The majority of the fishermen claimed to have derived, some four to six generations before, from Tung Koon 東莞 County, Kwangtung Province. Linguistic studies have confirmed this origin. The Hakka were more recent arrivals. I do not employ the term 'Tanka' 蛋家 for the fishermen for two reasons. The first is that they themselves dislike it, being convinced (rightly) that it carries derogatory connotations. They call themselves by an occupational term (i.e. fishermen, 漁民) or sometimes use the expression *'ngoh tei shui sheung yan'* 我哋水上人 ('we water surface people'). The second reason for not using the term in this paper is that it is often believed by landsmen (both Chinese and non-Chinese) that the water-dwellers do not speak Cantonese. This is an error. The vast majority of the water-dwellers and ex-water-dwellers of all occupations in Hong Kong speak Cantonese. A minority originated from further north and speak Hoklo. A very few, only, speak Hakka. See also John McCoy, 'The Dialects of Hong Kong Boat People: Kau Sai', in *Journal of the Royal Asiatic Society: Hong Kong Branch*, 5 (1965), pp. 1-19.

[2] Throughout the period 1950-53 I was supported by a generous grant from H. M. Treasury Committee for the Study of Foreign Languages and Cultures (The Scarborough

In order to clarify my approach to the subject of socialization in a Chinese context, I think I should stress that I write as a social anthropologist untrained in psychology[3] and, of course, as a foreigner. It is relevant to add that the intensive fieldwork I carried out in 1952 and 1953 was done in Cantonese without interpreters. No one in the village spoke English. The debt that this paper owes to Dr. D.Y.F. Ho for his article entitled 'Traditional Patterns of Socialization in Chinese Society' (*Psyche* 1976-77, pp. 27-39) is very great indeed; I am equally indebted to him for another article in which he rightly points out some of the dangers and errors to which foreign observers in any culture are prone. I can only ask Chinese readers to believe in my good will and accept my apologies for my mistakes, and I beg them to allow me to learn from them when (as is likely to be only too often the case) they disagree with my interpretations or think that they should be modified, extended, or curtailed.

Dr. Ho's paper on traditional patterns of socialization dealt mainly with the ideas of educated people as they have been expressed in writing. By contrast, this present paper is about the usage of certain Cantonese words as I heard them spoken at various times during my fieldwork. The words I have in mind are: 教 *kaau*, usually translated 'teach', but possibly more closely akin to 'instruct'; 養 *yeung*, which is more or less equivalent to 'care for', 'look after', perhaps 'rear' (U. S. 'raise'); and 學 *hok*, for which 'learn' is the most common English translation.[4]

教 *kaau* is probably the easiest to interpret. As Dr. Ho points out, for traditional Chinese writers, like most traditional non-Chinese writers, *kaau* was the only recognized way of training children, whether by percept or by straight instruction children had to *be taught*. Reading, writing, history, and moral education—all were to be gained from instruction. Certainly the

---

Committee) which was set up shortly after World War II with the task of beginning the reinstatement of Oriental and other studies in Britain after the long period of closure during hostilities. I am deeply grateful to that committee.

[3] Unlike their American colleagues, British anthropologists normally have no professional exposure to either psychological or psychoanalytical concepts, though in a few British universities students of anthropology are given courses in social psychology (but then usually only as one option among a number of others). This difference reflects the strong sociological bias of British anthropology (British anthropologists call themselves social, not cultural, anthropologists) which contrasts markedly with the much wider, more eclectic, and in some schools basically psychological approach in the United States.

[4] In this paper I follow the form of romanization used in *The Student's Cantonese-English Dictionary* compiled by Bernard Fr. Meyer and Theodore F. Wempe (Kelly and Walsh, 1935 edition). Because of my own experience of the frustrations of trying to read and understand papers which include Chinese characters but do not give their romanized pronunciation, I have decided to include both character and romanization throughout.

non-literate or barely literate villagers of whom I am writing agreed. It seems likely that most of the other people in the world today (and almost certainly throughout history) share this point of view, but there are a number of respects in which the Chinese attitude (or, rather, the combination of values that supported the attitude of the villagers about whom I am writing) appears to be unique.

The first and most important of these, in my opinion, was the value given to work, which carried with it a corresponding denigration of any activity that could be described as 'non-work', including, of course, play. I have described elsewhere[5] some of the observations I made on this topic in the village. After having stayed there for about six months I returned to England for a short period of leave. Coming back again, I naturally brought gifts for my hosts and their families. Naturally too (from my own ethnocentric point of view), the gifts I brought for the children were toys. The parents were very polite about this but it was not at all difficult for me to realize that in their eyes I had made a serious blunder. At that time these village children had no toys except for the short-lived paper figurines (紙紮公仔) that were sometimes stripped from the elaborate paper shrines (花炮) after the annual village temple festival. From time to time the children did try to make crude toys for themselves, and occasionally they engaged in quite complicated make-believe games with them, but such activities were not viewed with any seriousness by anybody except the participants, and even they had become inured to having them verbally ridiculed or physically swept aside by any teasing passer-by. In any case, a count of the ways in which children spent their free time put chasing games well ahead of play with any kind of artifact—with the sole exception of playing-cards (Chinese and Western) with which both boys and girls, usually in separate groups, imitated their elders' gambling.[6] Sometimes (though seasonally, and then only rarely in those days) they flew small, flimsy paper kites.

The points I want to emphasize here, however, are not the relative poverty in imagination and variety of these children's play but the attitude towards it of the grown-ups, which inevitably the children themselves began early to assimilate. Although it is true that the children's activities provided one of the most important forms of spectator enjoyment for adults who happened to have leisure, it is also true that there was very little such leisure, that children were expected to share in adult work as well, and that at any time play might be interrupted—either because there was a job of work for a child to do or,

[5] B. E. Ward, 'Temper Tantrums in Kau Sai', in P. Meyer (ed.), *Socialization: The Approach from Social Anthropology* (Association of Social Anthropologists Monographs. London: Tavistock Press, 1967).

[6] In the fifties they gambled for bottle tops; in the seventies for ten cent pieces.

as already indicated, because some passing adult felt the whim to break it up. The only exception to the general rule that children's activities were essentially unimportant applied to those who went to school and had homework to do. Schooling and study were considered virtually equivalent to work, and children practising writing for the next day's lessons were relatively free from interruption.

The Chinese enthusiasm for schooling is probably greater than that of any other people in the world. The historical reasons for this are obvious and well known. Some of its modern manifestations in Hong Kong include the scramble for places in kindergartens, the ever earlier age of sitting for entrance examinations, and the sight of three- and four-year-olds doing homework. For ambitious Chinese parents (and what parents are not ambitious for their children?) these are normal matters. They certainly occur also in Singapore, among Chinese elsewhere overseas, and among Japanese. They are equally widely deplored, even (perhaps most?) by the very people who have expended most energy in putting their own children through the hoops, but it is hard to see how matters can be changed. Parents who regard the ladder of education as the one fairly sure route to gaining or sustaining a high standard of living in the modern world are being no more than realistic, but if that were the only cause of the intensity of competition in Hong Kong we should be left without an explanation of why presumably equally ambitious parents in other equally crowded cities in other cultures do not usually appear to push their children into the school system either so young or so urgently. Where the Chinese (and to a large extent the Japanese) appear to differ is in two other matters: first the long tradition of value for education not only because it was the way to worldly advancement (though it certainly was that), and not only for its intellectual content and training of the mind (as in the European tradition), but above all for its moral component. I do not know how far it would be correct to argue that in traditional Chinese thinking in general an uneducated man could not, by definition, be in the full sense a good man, but from my notes on conversations with my uneducated village informants I gain the very strong impression that this was (and, I think, still is) their point of view. Education was therefore considered of the utmost importance for its moral value, and by no means solely because it might get one a better job.

The second and, in the practical sense, more intransigent reason why Chinese parents want their children to start school early is, of course, the intrinsic difficulty of learning the written language. No other script except Japanese makes such demands upon memorization or takes so long to acquire, and the fact that Japan has an even more competitive educational system than Hong Kong should at least make us pause before condemning parents here whose children face substantially greater linguistic problems.

At this stage it may be objected that even granting that the above arguments have validity they are not likely to have had much significance for essentially uneducated people such as the villagers of whom I am writing. Though in a sense this must be true, it remains equally true that these 'essentially uneducated' villagers were perfectly capable of discussing the same arguments and I am convinced that they fully accepted what they regarded as the ideals of Chinese culture and civilization as their own ideals, while at the same time knowing that they themselves did not—and could not—live up to them in practice. They frequently asked me why I was taking the trouble to study the ways of life in such a village as theirs: 'You ought really to have stayed in town and learned from the educated people. . . .' The fact that they had had little or no schooling in no way detracted from their high estimation of its value, both moral and pragmatic.

But the use of 教 *kaau* was not confined to school teaching. The word was employed also for instructing children in the performance of everyday economic tasks connected with fishing or farming (the Hakka women did a small amount of cultivation and reared pigs) or household jobs, like cooking and sewing. My impression, however, is that most of these tasks were more 'picked up' by the children through imitation rather than actually 'taught' by instruction. I shall therefore come back to them later when discussing the use of the word 學 *hok*. One particular piece of behaviour was always most carefully 'taught', however, and at an extremely early age. It is often overlooked how early training in social skills begins in all cultures. As soon as their toddlers are learning to talk at all, English mothers anxiously start instructing them; so do Chinese mothers. The English mother constantly presses her child to say 'please' and 'thank you'. 'What do you say, dear?' can be heard over and over again—at table, in the home, the streets, the shops—whenever the child is the recipient of any small gift, or service, or good; and the same question recurs with equal insistence whenever the child makes a request of any kind and omits the symbolic 'please'. Children who fail in this matter shame their mothers. Chinese mothers worry about social shame in a very similar way, but over a different skill: not 'What do you say, dear?' but '叫 *kiu*' (literally 'call', here meaning: 'Use the right term of address and greet this adult politely'). 'Here is your father's eldest brother, greet him properly . . . *kiu*'; 'This is Mrs. Chan greet her properly . . . *kiu*'. And even the tiniest children just able to speak put their little hands together and lisp: '*Ah baak*' ('father's elder brother') or '*Ch'an t'aai t'aai*'. And mother can relax. Both English and Chinese mothers grow tense in this social situation; particularly in front of strangers or significant others, children *must* perform correctly. In the village this was the earliest form of 教 *kaau* to which a child was exposed and its importance should not be underestimated. A social skill was being taught in a real social situation, and with it implicitly the beginning of an understanding that one lived and had one's own place in the set of moral relationships that was the village. It was, perhaps, the first deliberately taught step towards the integration of the village child into his future social world.

But what about 養 *yeung*? With this word the villagers appeared to denote a very wide concept for which English has not one single verbal equivalent but only a number of different words each somewhat specialized in usage. For example, an English villager might say of a neighbouring stock farmer: 'He *breeds* cattle'; of a young mother: 'She *looks after* her children'; of his own flock of sheep: 'The old ewe died, so we had to *rear* (or bring up) the lambs by hand'; of a friend with a market garden: 'He *grows* vegetables'; of his unmarried sister who now lives alone: 'She *cared for* our old parents until they died'. Here are six distinct verbs. The Hong Kong villagers used 養 *yeung* for all six meanings. One would often hear '*yeung tzu*' 養豬 (breed pigs), '*yeung tsoi*' 養菜 (grow vegetables), '*yeung lo tao lo mo*' 養老豆老母 (care for old parents), and of course '*yeung tzai*' 養仔 (rear, or bring up sons).

With reference to babies, 養 *yeung* included feeding, dressing, changing, bathing, carrying about, and generally looking after them, but *yeung* did not come to an end with infancy. Though its quality and contact altered, and older children themselves took part in 養 *yeung* their younger siblings, 養 *yeung* continued to some extent all through the period of childhood (that is, up to marriage) and perhaps for males, in a sense, it went on throughout life, unless they left home and lived separately away from their families. For females, on the other hand, there was traditionally a sharp break when they left home at marriage and thereupon entirely ceased being the object of 養 *yeung*, becoming instead actively engaged only in providing it for members of their husbands' families. A married young women would not be 'cared for' again until she became a successful old grandmother much later in her life.

Thus, actively providing 養 *yeung* was mainly a female role, and mainly the task of females between the age of marriage and grandmotherhood (at that time in the village, say, between about 16 or 17 and 50 to 55). The recipients were males and females younger and older than the providers. However, so far as very young children (mainly but not exclusively boys) were concerned, men also often played an important 養 *yeung* role too. Whatever the old gentry ideal about a father's aloofness, in the village one often saw a man carrying a small child about, playing with it, kissing it, fussing over it, and generally just enjoying it. Indeed it sometimes seemed to me that for a number of village children possibly the major part of the sheer, unmixed warmth of adult love that they experienced when they were very small came from the closely intimate relationship that many of them had with their fathers. This was not 教 *kaau*, it was 養 *yeung*.

We read often of the distant nature of the father-son relationship in traditional China, and of its quality being one of respect rather than affection. In gentry families, and others in which fathers did not have contacts with their young children this is likely to have been the actual as well as the approved situation, but for village families and others in which fathers did have such contacts one can speculate that patterns observed in recent years in Hong Kong may well have also been obtained previously. We know that despite the ideal that families should be large and extended only about 10% (or less) of families at any one time actually attained the ideal. Thus in at least 90% of families in, say, the Ch'ing dynasty China fathers must have had quite close contacts with their young children. Did these early contacts in those days have any of the same quality of warmth and affection that they appeared to have in the village in the fifties? If so, did this have a significant bearing on later relationships between fathers and their children? And if so, does this indicate that there may have been important differences between gentry and non-gentry male personalities? I have described in another article[7] the period of withdrawal of paternal indulgence that appeared to affect boys in the village at around seven years of age. This is, of course, about the age when fathers in traditional settings (and the village was still such a setting) began to teach their sons their trades. Thus, at about this age, fathers switched from a 養 *yeung* role to a 敎 *kaau* role. The two were strikingly different, and the effects of the change may well have been as lasting as they were dramatic.

Before discussing it further, however, it may be useful to consider the third concept I wish to introduce here: namely, the concept referred to by the term 學 *hok*. Like 養 *yeung*, 學 *hok* too has a wide set of connotations. Usually translated 'learn', 'copy', 'imitate', 學 *hok* can also mean 'follow after' or 'take after', as in the English expression: 'She takes after her mother', which can refer equally to a child's looks or behaviour or character and personality. In one very common usage 學 *hok* is simply the reciprocal of 敎 *kaau*: the teacher teaches, the child learns. But 學 *hok* has wider implications for the child's behaviour too. In connection with both 養 *yeung* and 敎 *kaau* the child is an object; action lies with adults. In connection with 學 *hok*, however, the child is the subject. It is true that 學 *hok* often means no more than 'learn by heart' or 'copy', but after all many things are best learned in that way, and even learning by heart and copying involve some self-motivated activity. The fact that villagers were well aware of this was proved to me by the type of explanation they always gave for success or failure at school and out-of-school learning. A quick learner was not normally described as intelligent (聰明 *tsung ming*) but as *'ho k'an lek'* 好勤力 (very diligent, or very

[7] B. E. Ward, *op. cit.*

hard-working)—a moral quality for which the child himself was held to be responsible and in which he could be encouraged by parental (or schoolmasterly)exhortation and discipline, though seldom (if ever) by reward.

My note books give evidence of the word 學 *hok* being used also for learning from experience. Here the contexts I have recorded are all of rather older children or young adults discovering, usually painfully, that carelessness (for example in threading bait onto sharp fishhooks, or putting fuel on the kitchen stove) did not pay. I have no record that leads me to suppose that the villagers had any belief that very young children learned anything (consciously or unconsciously) from the experiences they underwent during the process of 養 *yeung*. On the contrary, although my evidence is that the villagers did use 學 *hok* to cover the idea of learning from experience in the case of older children, I am sure that they did not think that very young children learned in that way. I have to admit, however, that my evidence for that statement is inferential only. For this reason I give some of it in detail, as follows:

During the period in which I lived in the village in 1952 and 1953 the housewife in the family with whom I stayed became an intimate friend. One evening, I dared to ask her how she had acquired the mass of deep scars I had several times noticed on the skin just above her breasts. 'Oh that?' she said, 'That was a lot of bad boils I had when I was very young.' I asked if they had been very painful? 'Oh no,' was the reply, 'of course not. I was too young. Everybody knows that very young children don't feel pain as much as adults do.' This was a surprise to me. In my own English village the belief is exactly the opposite: there small children are thought to feel pain more than adults do; that is why they cry so loudly. I therefore asked her how it was known that very young children did not feel pain? 'That's simple,' she said, 'if I had felt the pain when I had those boils I would have remembered it; but as I do not remember it at all, obviously I felt no pain.' Later, when I asked others the same question, I received the same response. Small children, it seemed, were believed not to feel pain.

As I watched the behaviour of adults and older children towards the very young, I began to discern a pattern that seemed to me to fit with this belief. Very small children (babies, toddlers) were a constant source of pleasure and spectator attention and they were usually greatly loved, but they were treated very much as 'objects'—watched, commented upon, provoked, carried about, played with, rather like toys. A baby on its mother's back might be fast asleep; an adult or older sibling passing by might stop to look at the baby, make a comment about it, and then might give it a strong poke in the side, just to see what the reaction would be (or so it seemed to me). When the baby woke up and cried (as nearly always happened) the provoker would laugh—not at all unkindly, but in the happy way one laughs when one's expectations are fulfilled—and walk on. Unless she were very busy and therefore irritated by the interruption, the mother would laugh too and rock the baby to sleep again or give it the breast. My in-built ethnocentric reaction of feeling sorry for the baby and indignant at this treatment was shared by no-one else in the village.

It is from an accumulation of incidents of this kind and from the general adult impatience with children's play that I mentioned earlier that I infer that, in the minds of the villagers, babies, toddlers, and young children were thought of very much as objects for which and to which things could be done, not—that is, not yet—themselves active agents, still less initiators of interaction. In this view (if it is indeed the view they held) the villagers would be in agreement with most of the rest of the world—even, until recently, with many social psychologists as is attested explicitly in the book by Martin Richards from which the title of this paper was adapted,[8] and implicitly by the very word 'socialization' itself, which implies that children are 'socialized', in the passive mood, the active 'socializers' being others, and usually adult others at that.

The question then arises: if in the villagers' eyes very young children were 'objects' in this sense, at what stage were they considered to become capable of being 'subjects'? Perhaps that is not the most helpful way of phrasing the question. As I have indicated earlier, although the bringing up of very young children is primarily a matter of 養 *yeung*, not 教 *kaau*, there are some matters that are taught when the child is very young indeed. The example given was teaching the proper rituals of greeting (it is interesting that these are social requirements, taught in real social situations). With greater knowledge about the acquirement of a mother tongue, I might have tried to discuss that too. Thus it seems that the distinction to be drawn is perhaps less between the ages at which 養 *yeung* or 教 *kaau* are respectively considered appropriate in a general sense as between matters which can be (or ought to be?) taught (教 *kaau*) earlier or later. There were also differences in the treatment given to the different sexes: girls started being taught household tasks (or perhaps they were simply encouraged to imitate [學 *hok*]) at a very early age; boys had the more abrupt break between a longer period of more-or-less pure 養 *yeung* experiences and the moment when they were considered capable of starting to learn the skills of men. Thirty years ago in the village this break did not necessarily, or even usually, involve the boys (still less the girls) in going to school as well; now it does. But school age for both sexes and the age at which boys began (and begin) to experience different treatment

[8] M. Richards, *The Intergration of a Child into a Social World* (Cambridge: Cambridge University Press, 1976).

from their fathers are about the same. One might suggest the hypothesis that the main reason why boys could enjoy a longer period of relative irresponsibility was simply that in a society with a rather clear sexual division of labour they could not realistically be expected to start picking up specifically male skills until they were ready to spend fairly considerable periods of time away from their mothers. Where schooling is concerned the same consideration applied equally to both sexes.

Be that as it may, by the age of six or seven a village boy was a small-scale adult, expected to work, able to learn (學 *hok*), subject to instruction (敎 *kaau*), though also still a recipient of a degree of 養 *yeung* from his mother (though not his father any longer) and, as I have suggested above, likely to remain such recipient from the women of his family throughout his life. For a girl the progression was more gradual, but more complete. The sharp change in the attitude of the parent with whom she made her sexual identification was not experienced by a girl. Instead she was from the earliest age under steadily developing pressure to take part in adult female occupational tasks, learning them mainly by imitation in real social situations in interaction with her mother and other female members of her household who were all themselves part of the same social situations. By six or seven she, too, was a small-scale adult, better equipped at that age for her roles than her brother was as yet for his, and no doubt partly as a result of this, often given more responsibility.[9] Thus little girls emerged more quickly and less traumatically than little boys from the state of being mere objects of 養 *yeung*, and partly because their adult roles were (as they are) largely concerned with providing 養 *yeung* for others their emergence was more complete. Then years or so later they would face a break more drastic than anything in their brothers' lives when they married and left home for good.

The extent to which modern changes in the practices connected with 養 *yeung* (which I have not investigated in any detail in this paper) may affect the experiences of very young children in Hong Kong, and therefore the development of their personalities, is as yet unstudied. One can only speculate about some of the possible effects of, for example, the nearly universal change to bottle instead of breast-feeding, the discontinuance of the practice of carrying babies on their mothers' backs (at least in public), and so on. At

[9] The common (and common-sense) observation in many cultures that girls are often more 'mature' than boys of the same age may perhaps find a sociological basis in this argument. In the article already mention (note 5 above) I drew attention to the age at which temper tantrums seemed to be most frequent in the village and the sex of the children who had them. The discussion here reinforces the explanation I put forward there as to why temper tantrums appeared mostly after the age of seven years and in boys.

the level of social interaction and the expected performance of roles, probably the most significant changes for both sexes are connected with the coming of free education and the development of occupational roles outside the family-household. In the village today all children of school age are at school, girls as well as boys. Girls still learn their domestic roles at home very young, but they have less time to perform them, and they spend long periods of time being instructed in other than 養 *yeung* activities by people (usually men) who are not family members. And they can now earn money. The phenomenon of the earning daughter is a new thing in Hong Kong society as a whole; its effects on family structure, on marriage and the evaluation of girls (and, by reaction, of boys too) and their up-bringing are likely to be a great deal more profound than is sometimes realized.

But modern changes as such is not the focus of this short paper which has tried to explore some of the traditional usages of the three Cantonese words 養 *yeung*, 教 *kaau*, and 學 *hok* as they were exemplified in one village in the New Territories about a quarter of a century ago. I do not know how far (if at all) the verbal usages of a small group of largely uneducated villagers in the New Territories of Hong Kong in the mid-twentieth century can be taken as indicative of earlier 'traditional' verbal usages in general. I put them forward here for what they are worth, as a preliminary exercise in what could become a more sustained examination of the ways in which local people integrate their children into their social world, and as a complement (albeit far less accurate and less scholarly) to Dr. Ho's article and a compliment to its author.

Section IV

Modernization and the Status of Women

11. Men, Women and Change: An Essay in Understanding Social Roles in South and South-East Asia*

INTRODUCTION: WORDS AND CONCEPTS

It is important to explain at the outset what this book does not do. We have already insisted that it is not a study of the emancipation of women in the feminist sense and that it is not intended to be an academic treatise but a book for the general reader. Though it is certainly not our intention to discourage professional social scientists from reading it, we have not written particularly for them. Yet this is a sociological work. Aimed at a wider public than usual, it is nonetheless concerned with matters of sociological interest, treated in a sociological framework.

The general reader should therefore beware. This is not a psychological study, nor is it concerned with sexual relations in the narrow sense. No doubt a complete analysis of the changing roles of the two sexes should cover a study of the ways of making love and of mutual psychological adaptations. This book does not include these things. It takes its stand upon social facts and discusses only sociological differences between the sexes—in other words: the division of labour, of interest and of status.

What exactly we mean by these terms will appear in due course, for the final *caveat* we wish to enter concerns our use of words. Though intended for the common reader, the language of this book does not, is not meant to, conform entirely to common usage. This requires some explanation.

It is one of the difficulties of the social sciences that they have not, in general, produced a special technical language. Unlike, say, botanists or physicists, who use terms peculiar to their own subject matter and therefore relatively easily definable, social scientists rely in the main upon the use of words already current in ordinary speech. Hence arise many misunderstandings —and much of the layman's mistrust. For the sake of accuracy it is, of course, essential for social scientists to try to pin-point their usages, to narrow them down so that the referents are as nearly as possible clear and unambiguous. But common speech is nearer poetry than science, its tendency usually

*Originally published in Barbara E. Ward (ed.), *Women in the New Asia*, pp. 25-99.

towards wider connotations and evocative rather than indicative meaning. Thus many of the words social scientists use—'family', for instance, or 'social class' (to take but two examples)—have extremely wide, if not positively vague, connotations in everyday speech. As a result, a layman's reading of a professional sociologist's article on, say, the family in the class system of Western Germany, may be sadly distorted if, with the ordinary poetic overtones of everyday speech in mind, he fails to grasp the essential limitations of scientific terminology. Faced with an article on plant genetics he may also encounter difficulties, but they will not be those of over-familiarity with the terms used. Though to non-specialists the proliferation of 'jargon' at times appears excessive, there is a sense in which social scientists may envy the natural scientists' technical vocabulary.

For our present purposes, however, it is enough to let the reader be warned. Technical usages are explained in the text, and their limiting nature should not be forgotten.

The concept of 'social role'

There is, however, one particular terminological warning that must be made here. In this book the term 'social role' appears in the sub-title and, frequently, elsewhere. This is a quite specific technical term referring to the expected kinds of social behaviour associated with a particular social position. Thus the position 'teacher' is associated with a role which includes all the activities of teaching and also a number of other associated items of expected social behaviour—usually a middle-class standard of living, often a certain demeanour, and so on. Similarly the position 'unmarried adult daughter' in English society today is associated with a certain expected role which includes willingness to live within reach of her elderly parents, or with them if they are old and incapacitated, and to take over their full care and a large measure of their financial support if necessary.

These two simple examples should make it clear that the sociological concept to which the term 'social role' refers is an artificial construct. We are not talking of the social behaviour of any individual 'teacher' or 'unmarried adult daughter' (or 'businessman', 'father', 'clergyman', 'civil servant', 'teenager' or what you will). Instead, we are constructing types, and labelling them with the kinds of behaviour considered appropriate to each one. Considered appropriate, that is, by local and contemporary pleople. 'In Russia today the role of doctor of medicine is thus and thus'; 'In India the role of village welfare worker is to do this and this'; 'Among the Malays the role of father includes that and that'—and so on.

A number of sociological writers use the term 'social status' as a correlative to 'social role'. 'Status' in this phrase refers not primarily to a placing in a graded order of power or rank or esteem, but to 'position' in the sense in which that word has been used in the preceding paragraph. Thus one can talk of the 'status' of teacher, of adult unmarried daughter, businessman, father, and the rest. Because of the almost inescapable suggestion of grading which is attached to the word 'status' in everyday speech (which most sociologists also have in mind in using the word in other contexts) this is a difficult usage to maintain. We do not, therefore, use 'status' in this way (if a word other than 'position' in this general, non-grading sense is required, the Latin *locus* might be more appropriate). When, earlier, we referred to differences in the status men and women, we used the word in its more common sense. Status in this chapter thus refers simply to placement in a graded order of access to power and legal and economic independence. This is the usage which appears, for example, in the title of the United Nations' Commission on the Status of Women. (In talking of placement in a graded order of esteem, as distinct from—though, of course, often correlated with—power, we use the term 'prestige'.)

Readers who wish to follow up the concept of social role in more detail may be referred to the short bibliography at the end of this volume. For the present only three further points need to be made. First, it is clearly possible for one individual to take several roles. The derivation from dramatic usage is obvious, and each man not only in his life, but even in each day, plays many parts. 'Father', 'farmer', 'churchman', and so on; these are not mutually exclusive roles. It is not difficult to list the various different roles in which any given individual—oneself included—appears from time to time. Nor is it difficult to see that whereas some roles are, like those just mentioned, merely mutually compatible, other roles are actually inclusive of others—whether necessarily or by custom. Think, for example, of the number of roles comprised under the label 'mother'. This is a point to which we return later on.

But if some roles are compatible and others inclusive, still others are obviously incompatible or even mutually exclusive. One cannot, for instance, act as teacher and as pupil at the same time. This would be a sheer contradiction. On the other hand, nothing in either physical necessity or social custom prevents one from switching fairly easily from one of these roles to the other. It is otherwise with, to take extreme examples, either a Roman Catholic priest or a Hinayana Buddhist monk who breaks his vows of chastity. There is no physical bar to his being both priest (or monk) and parent; but the religious bar is absolute. Thus social sanctions can, and indeed often do, make incompatible what physical possibility has not divided. This question of the compatibility of social roles is crucial to our argument below.

The second point we wish to stress is closely connected with the foregoing, and equally obvious. We express it here as a generalization: the more complex the society, the greater the number of social roles that exist, and, in general (though this requires qualification, as we shall see) the greater the number of social roles available to each individual. In a very small-scale, simple band of primitive hunters and gatherers all men must be hunters and gatherers; for, with the exception of those of kinship and of rather rudimentary leadership, there are no other roles available. This, again, is an extreme example, but it illustrates another point to which we shall have to return below. For the new nations of the Orient are those whose social structures, for centuries already highly complex, are daily growing more and more so, through industrialization and its concomitants, and therefore those in which new social roles are daily emerging for both men and women.

Social role and social change

This, indeed, is one of the most striking features of current social change: the proliferation of possible roles. New kinds of paid employment, new types of leadership, new opportunities for the development of new skills of all kinds —these are some of the concomitants of industrialization and urbanization, political independence and development, and technological and educational advance. For the individuals who inhabit the new nations of the world, this is one of the most significant and often exciting factors of their lives: social roles which did not exist before are now becoming available.

At the same time old roles are changing. All the chapters in Part II of this book, particularly the autobiographical chapters, draw attention to the many patterns of behaviour accepted as proper and normal in the past which have drastically altered or which are in process of being recast.

Here, too, the concept of social role can aid our understanding. We have stated that in talking of roles social scientists are talking of types, not individuals. It is more accurate to say that we are talking of norms, that is matters which the consensus of reasonable opinion in any particular social group considers correct or appropriate. It is important to note that social roles are abstracted not from actual behaviour but from opinion about what behaviour ought to be. In other words, in this instance the social scientist does not watch what one hundred teachers do and construct the social role of teacher from that, but discusses with both teachers themselves and others what teachers ought to do, watches the reactions, verbal and other, to what teachers in fact do (and say), and constructs the role from the outcome of these discussions and observations. (It would be inaccurate but not altogether misleading to say that any particular social role is compounded from all the current prejudices about the particular social position to which it is attached.)

But—and here is the nub of the third point to which we wish to draw attention—prejudices are not immutable. If the actual behaviour of most teachers (to continue with our same example) begins to deviate from the hitherto accepted norm, it is likely that in time the norm too will change; similarly in certain circumstances changes in norms may lead to changes in behaviour. Thus—as in the drama—there is room for individual interpretation of roles, and a successful new interpretation of an old role may well be the starting-point of one kind of social change. Where such new interpretations are the result of conscious planning (whether based on general principles for social betterment or personal self-interest, or a mixture of the two) they may be copied by other people or not, according to circumstances and the innovator's powers of leadership. But probably, more often than not, a new interpretation of an old role is simply the accidental outcome of *ad hoc* adaptations to changed circumstances. If such changes affect many people similarly and more or less simultaneously, a kind of consensus of individual adaptations is likely to emerge, and remain more or less fixed as the new norm for the time being. So-called 'static' societies are those in which the role patterns have remained relatively stable for a considerable period of time; in developing societies roles are constantly being added to and reinterpreted.

It must not be thought that we wish to contend that the phenomena of social change can be explained entirely in terms of a theory of social roles. This is very far indeed from being our standpoint. But we do wish to suggest that the concept of social role can be useful in the kind of enterprise which we are engaged in here. By making it possible to distinguish between an individual and the roles he plays it allows us to escape from the difficulties inherent in popular psychological types of explanation, and thus makes genuinely sociological comparison between personal relationships in different societies possible.

In our own everyday social life we constantly find ourselves erecting stereotypes of the kinds of behaviour we consider appropriate (or 'proper') to certain kinds of persons. Indeed, as we have seen, it is largely from the consensus of such stereotypes that a social scientist constructs the social roles we have been discussing. But there are two essential differences between the social scientists' 'roles' and our own 'stereotypes'. The scientist abstracts his roles objectively by recording the norms held by the people of the society he is studying, and having abstracted them he regards them simply as patterns, models of behaviour which individuals occupying certain social positions are expected to follow while acting in these positions. For him as sociologist they are merely roles, not moral imperatives. For ourselves, the contemporary people under observation, it is different. Our stereotypes come from the teaching and learning which have been our constant experiences since birth in our own particular social environments. They are largely subjective: the believed-in justifications of our own attitudes. They are not merely roles, distinguishable from the individuals who play them, and valid only for particular positions in social life; instead many of them are highly charged with moral value and attached firmly in our minds to the personalities of individuals. Thus where the social scientists speaking as such might say: 'In this society the teachers' role is thus and thus . . .', we, speaking as ordinary contemporary members of that same society, would say: 'Teachers are—and ought to be—thus and thus . . .'. In other words, we are usually prejudiced; the concept of social roles can help us not to be so.

It is probably the main justification of a symposium of this kind that it may help us to emerge a little from the cocoon of our preconceptions, including our own culturally derived stereotypes about what are truly 'masculine' and what 'feminine' social roles—and also about what are really 'Eastern' and what 'Western' patterns of living.

CLEARING THE GROUND: THE DANGER OF OVERSIMPLIFICATION

To make any sort of sense of the welter of information and opinion that can be collected on such a challenging topic as ours it is essential to attempt to sort out the various factors at work and analyse their differing, though interdependent, significance. As far as the sociological understanding of personal relationships is concerned we believe that analysis in terms of new and changing social roles is one of the keys. But we are still left with the questions: Whence the new roles? Why the changes?

It is always easy to talk in a general way about the causes of this, that or the other example of social change. According to prevailing fashion, one can blame something called 'Westernization', or something else called 'urbanization', or 'the breakdown of religion', or 'the collapse of the traditional family system' and so on. But all these are no more than question-begging phrases. Simply calling the processes of change and their results 'Westernization' (for example) does next to nothing towards helping us understand them.

Indeed, it may be positively misleading. Historically it is, of course, a fact that recent and contemporary changes in Oriental societies have been connected with the period of Occidental economic and political dominance. But except in some strictly economic and political spheres, and where Western educational institutions have been unusually influential, it is probably true to say that comparatively little is directly and simply ascribable to Western influence or Western example. The relationship is more complicated than that. Thus to use the term 'Westernization' as an explanation is to introduce a false simplification. Orientals, if they do not resent it, may shrug their shoulders; but Occidentals, vaguely flattered, are often lulled by it into an unrealistic dream of elder-sisterly understanding—for we think we know what Western patterns are, and therefore we tend to look upon ourselves as the fore-ordained guides and patrons for 'Westernizing' Orientals. But patronage is always morally dangerous—especially for the patrons—and doubly so when based upon false premises. It is not only that the peoples of the East may not want to follow Western patterns (and, as our contributors show us, they often do not), it is not only even that they are increasingly (and rightly) rejecting our self-assumed leadership: it is also that many of the changes that are taking place have very little to do with 'Westernization' in any direct sense at all.

Similarly with 'urbanization': undoubtedly the rapid development of huge modern commercial and industrial towns all over the Orient has had and is having profound effects upon almost every aspect of economic and social relationships, including political and legal relationships, family grouping and the upbringing of children; but present-day changes are various, their starting-points different, and their explanation by no means solely to be sought in the modern surge of population towards the towns. Analysis must be more subtle than this.

Again, 'religion', 'the traditional family system'—these too are blanket terms. Religious beliefs and rituals and the effectiveness and range of application of religious sanctions are by no means uniform even within the borders of a single nation in which a single faith is officially proposed. Between different nations the differences may be manifold and profound. Christianity in Italy is not the same thing as Christianity in Sweden, nor is the Buddhism of Ceylon to be equated with the Buddhism of the Overseas Chinese; and it should go without saying that Moslems, Hindus, Buddhists and Roman Catholics—all of whom are to be found predominating in different Asian States—have very different approaches to such matters as family structure and the status of women.

As for 'the traditional family'—more nonsense is talked about this, both in the East and the West, than about almost any other subject. What was it? Who lived in it? Was it everywhere the same? How did it relate to the laws and customs governing property, marriage, the wider kinship system, politics and the economic division of labour? These and similar questions have to be answered before one can make valid pronouncements about the effect (or even the fact) of its decline. But how often are they even asked?

One of our troubles is that, Easterners and Westerners alike, we are too quick to put up straw figures, stereotypes of social patterns and cultural forms (as well as social roles) which we label 'Eastern' and 'Western' respectively. We forget the enormous variety within the West, let alone the even greater variety within the much larger East. We forget, too, that most

Europeans—and similarly most Asians—are ignorant of their neighbours' customs and traditions. We generalize from our own experience of the one or two places we know something about to the very many places of which we have no experience and know nothing at all. And we all forget that social patterns and cultural forms are never simple and never develop along single-line tracks, but are always complex and always mutually interdependent in a multiplicity of different ways.

The chapters in the main body of this book (Part II below) demonstrate both the complexities of change and the variety which exists in the countries of South and South-East Asia. (And almost incidentally, among other things they make it quite clear that the cherished Western notion of typical Oriental womanhood is an illusion.)

Nevertheless, when all that can be said about variety and the falsity of blanket explanations has been said, it remains true that the chapters in Part II of this book do also show remarkable similarities: the same themes do recur. Similar technical, economic and political changes and above all similar educational advances appear in nearly all of them. And the effects of these things do seem to tend in the same direction, towards similar patterns of urban in place of rural living, wage- and salary-earning in place of self-subsistence, buying and selling of factory-made goods in place of home handicraft production, universal suffrage and a national bureaucracy in place of colonial administration or absolute monarchy, modern schools and universities in place of traditional religious and home education, and so on and so forth. Not that all these tendencies are everywhere apparent at the same rate, nor that none of them has anywhere appeared before—towns are far older in Asia than in Europe, and a system of advanced competitive examination for entry into the national bureaucracy had already existed for a thousand years in China before it was taken as a model for Great Britain in the nineteenth century—but their scale, their widespread nature and the particular type of technological and economic system which underlies their present-day manifestations are new. The novelty is not least in the universality of the changes and their world-wide interconnectedness. What in the past were largely separate civilizations, though never completely isolated nor without influence upon each other, are becoming in the twentieth century ever more closely connected by the single network of economic and political relations which now enmeshes the whole world. At the same time their own economic and governmental systems are all being remade after a limited number of Western-type models.

Were we then wrong to denounce explanation in terms of Westernization? In so far as the large-scale economic and governmental institutions of the present day—together with the technological features which enable them to work—are European in origin and form, the whole world may be said to have become Westernized. But it is still true to say that the effects of the working of these large-scale Western-type economic and governmental institutions (and their world-wide interconnections) upon the everyday lives of ordinary people and the personal relations of men and women can only be ascribed indirectly to Western influence. Moreover, because of such things as original difference in culture and social structure and variations in the speed and intensity of economic and political change, they are not felt everywhere in the same way. At this level, to speak of the whole world becoming Westernized is to beg all the questions this book is designed to investigate.

Moreover, the West, too, is changing. 'Westernization' no longer has meaning as an explanation for a general process in which the West itself is also caught up, by reason of the interconnectedness of world events which, paradoxically enough, is greater now than in the colonial era, and because Western institutions themselves are altering. We are all in this together. Is it this, perhaps, which gives us today an opportunity for mutual understanding that has never really existed before?

Be that as it may, the ground has now been cleared for the next steps in our argument. These are as follows: first, an examination of some of the ways in which the rather similar new institutional developments in South and South-East Asia are opening new roles and new opportunities, especially for women; second, an examination of some of the ways in which these new features are affecting older institutions and bringing about changes in traditional roles—particularly the family roles of women; and finally a discussion of what may be the factors which make changes in the relative role patterns of the two sexes easy or difficult, acceptable or otherwise. The argument refers in particular to South and South-East Asia, but its general applicability is much wider, and we do not hesitate to point the comparisons.

NEW INSTITUTIONS AND NEW ROLES

Social change is no respecter of persons. Hardly any of the profound changes which have been occurring in South and South-East Asia have in themselves discriminated between the sexes. The trend towards urban living, for example, although it usually draws in men first, nevertheless also affects women (and children) whether they follow in their turn to the towns or stay behind in the villages. Improved health services, DDT spraying, inoculation and so on are not available for one sex only, nor are lowered death rates with their results in population pressure sexually selective. Most political, economic and religious changes are similarly impartial. Only a few special measures—women's suffrage, girls' education, the provision of maternity services, for example—have been deliberately devised for a single sex, and all these, together with recent legal alterations in such matters as marriage and inheritance, inevitably have repercussions upon men as well.

Nevertheless, existing differences in roles have necessarily meant that changes affecting all equally have not affected all similarly. The rich respond differently from the poor, town dwellers differently from country people, women differently from men. Our brief is to direct attention primarily to the women's response, and in this section we concentrate upon the ways in which these general changes are opening up new roles, or the potentiality of them, for women.

Obviously we cannot cover the whole canvas, but we shall select from the general changes certain aspects which appear particularly significant: modern medical measures, improved communications, increasing urbanization, new openings for paid employment, education, political emancipation and legal change. Our illustrations will be drawn primarily, though not exclusively, from the evidence provided in the articles which follow.

Modern medical measures

We have pointed out that the changes brought about in human social life by the application of modern medical measures are not limited to women's affairs only; nor, of course, are they unique to Asia. Many of the effects of postponing the age of death which are now beginning to appear in the East were first consciously experienced in Europe and the United States about a hundred to a hundred and fifty years ago. My husband's great-grandfather died in 1870. He left among his effects a small locket in which was framed the picture of a weeping willow tree embroidered entirely in seven different shades of fine golden hair, from the heads of the seven of his brothers and sisters who had died before reaching the age of ten years; several of the remaining thirteen died in adolescence. He himself successfully raised six children, one of whom was my husband's maternal grandfather who lost only one of his five, and that in battle. The daughter who was my mother-in-law bore one child only; we in our turn have two.

The same story appears over and over again in the history of middle-class Westerners in the last hundred years. Their families in the later nineteenth century were unusual not in the numbers who were born but in the numbers who survived. After about two generations of this, parents no longer in constant dread of bereavement started to control the number of births.

So far, as Ted Smith's article points out, only Japan in the whole of Asia shows a similar trend towards slowing the rate of population growth. Whether or not other Asian nations will follow suit is a matter of open debate; certainly, as Barbara Cadbury explains, much is being done to encourage them to do so.

At the level of national (and international) policy making, control of population growth is largely a matter of economic or military calculation. For individuals, too, economic thinking is often paramount though in a different way. Small-holding farmers who depend upon their children for increasing production naturally want large families, especially if they live under a family system which keeps adult children at home, or still more, one which maintains property (especially land) undivided for as long as possible. Wage-earners, particularly white-collared salary-earners who see a need for educating their children, do not want too many dependents. The validity of this argument is commonly borne out in the experience of family planning clinics whose *clientèle* is predominantly from the white-collar classes and above (though standards of education, availability of clinics and degree of acceptance of Western-type medicine also play a part in determining who shall attend and where). The evidence of the articles in the body of this book points to a future development of contraception on much the same lines as that which has taken place in the West, though some of the populations concerned are larger, and the time lag may be considerable.

This is a new thing in the world. Its full effects on the role of women are not yet clear even in those countries of the West where it has been longer apparent. But undoubtedly it is one of the crucial factors. For the first time in human history there is a promise of potential freedom from the physiological and social effects of the more or less continuous period of pregnancy, parturition and lactation which, with numerous miscarriages, has been the lot of the majority of women between the ages of about 15 and about 50 in all societies.

And the babies they do have need not die.

This, too, is crucial. A modern Westerner reads the pathetic inscriptions on the tiny graves which are scattered throughout the old burial grounds of Europe with pity; most modern Easterners would read them with a sympathy born of experience. One of the most striking differences between conversations with women in most parts of the West and most parts of the East today is that in the West one says: 'And how many children have you got?', in the East: 'How many have you reared?' Increasingly, as the former question becomes safer to ask in Asia as well—and this is happening—the roles of mother and wife will be affected by a new freedom from fear.

Moreover, this has been fear not of personal bereavement only, but of failure in marriage in the present and lack of support in the future. Foong Wong's article gives a telling account of a situation which is common in most extended family systems, such as exist in India and Pakistan and among the Chinese, for example: a wife must bear children (in patrilineal systems, such as these, especially sons) in order to justify her position in her husband's home. Children who die are almost as little use in this respect as children unborn, and certainly a widow without children to support her may be in a desperate plight. In countries like Burma, Thailand, the Philippines, where the true extended family does not obtain (except among some minority peoples) there is still a need for children to justify a woman's position in marriage (marriages in which there are no children are far more likely to end in divorce) and to support her in her old age. Modern medicine saves very many of the babies who formerly would have died and family-planning clinics can help restore fertility to couples who previously would have remained barren.

These are matters of peculiarly personal concern to women. Together with men they share also, of course, in the other benefits of modern preventive and curative medicine. And here the countries of South and South-East Asia are probably more greatly affected than the West, for 'the West' is on the whole a temperate zone, whereas the regions described in this volume all fall largely within the Tropics where diseases have been more lowering and more difficult to eradicate. Freedom from malaria, for instance, is one of the greatest boons that the twentieth century has brought. Cholera still strikes, but it can be controlled; leprosy can be cured; the typhoids become less and less common as sanitation improves; yaws can be easily eliminated. The list could be much longer. Dr. Smith's article describes how death-rates have already been falling—often dramatically.

But Dr. Smith's article also tells us something else about current death-rates in our region, namely that they are somewhat higher for women than for men. Here is a measurable contrast with the West. In most economically developed countries the number of adult women exceeds the number of adult men, and it is well known that the actuarial figures for a woman's expectation of life are higher than those for a man's. However, it does not follow that this difference between East and West is evidence of a low valuation of females in the East. Despite some popular beliefs, there is no demographic evidence that female infanticide anywhere in the region makes a noticeable difference to the sex ratio of infants and small children. Indeed, infant mortality in India, for example, is believed to be higher for male than for female babies. It is possible that among people whose family system shows a strong patrilineal bias girl children may not be given quite the same care as their brothers, but any such discrimination, in so far as it still exists, is likely to be of diminishing importance. It is much more likely that slowness in adopting modern methods of midwifery is to blame, whether because of their inadequate supply or from prejudice—and this is an area in which prejudice dies hard, as Begum Amna Gani points out. Compared with economically developed countries, relatively large numbers of women do still die in child-birth. But this is likely to be a temporary state of affairs.

What new social roles have all these developments brought? (Their effect upon old roles, particularly those of wife and mother, is discussed later on.) In the first place there are new opportunities for employment. Doctors, nurses, midwives, medical assistants of all kinds, social workers in the fields of health and nutrition, pharmacists and so on are required in increasing numbers, together with the host of other technologists and administrators and the developed system of communications without which a modern medical service cannot operate. In most of these occupations women (including at least five of our own contributors) are to be found as well as men, though, except in nursing, in lesser numbers. (It is interesting to notice a recent regulation restricting the numbers of women medical students in Bangkok because they were fast outnumbering the men to the detriment, so it was thought, of the future of the Thai health services.)

The role of 'healer' is, of course, not a new one; traditionally in different countries it was performed in varying ways, often closely connected with magical and religious rituals, sometimes by men and sometimes by women. Madame Lévy and Dr. Nayer both describe the high esteem in which their fathers' and grandfathers' healing powers were held. Nevertheless the full apparatus of modern medicine is a break with tradition, and the modern occupations of doctor, nurse and so on are the framework of what are essentially new roles for educated men and women in South and South-East Asia.

But those who become nurses or doctors are few. For most people the effects of modern medical measures upon their social roles are indirect. Freedom from ill-health (including the burden of continuous pregnancy and the bearing of too many children) and from fear of early death can lead to the reinterpretation of old roles in the family and the opportunity to develop other new roles outside it. Already in the West women are beginning to think in terms of a 'third period' of life in which, the tasks of motherhood completed, they still have time to re-enter the world of employment. The current campaign to draw married women in the United Kingdom back into the teaching profession is only one example. But we return to this and other aspects of what has been called 'the dual role' of women later on.

Communications

Pramuan Dickinson describes graphically how a journey which took her grandfather two months by elephant and her father a fortnight by train and on foot can now be accomplished in a few hours by fast motor-car. Romila Tharpar draws the moral that modern means of travel have been one of the most liberating influences upon women whose mothers were in full *purdah*. Eileen Arceo-Ortega and Subadra Siriwardena explain how driving their own automobiles makes it possible for each of them to combine successfully the roles of housewife, mother and professional educationist. Very many of our contributors have travelled the world around in search of higher education, on professional business, or for pleasure. Like modern medicine, modern transport is a kind of enabling measure making new roles possible and forcing the reinterpretation of old ones through the freedom which it confers.

This kind of freedom—to go about easily, speedily, over long distances, and if necessary by oneself—is a new thing in the world's history; not unique to Asia. It has been well said that even Napoleon's armies could travel no faster than Julius Caesar's—or, for that matter, Akbar's or Ghengis Khan's. The writer's own grandfather was born in the first heyday of railway building in England (the first, that is, in the world); her father watched the early motor-cars proceeding, as by law they were bound to do, behind a man walking with a red flag, and later saw Blériot fly the English Channel; her mother made social history in the West of England by being one of the first women to ride a motor-bicycle—in 1922. (Her son cheered Major Gagarin when he visited London in 1961.) Thus the development of modern transport is almost as recent in the West as in the East. The difference is one of degree only—and anyone who has been caught in the rush hour traffic jams of Bangkok or Manila or Calcutta might be forgiven if he doubted even that!

In some of the countries of our region (notably, from the evidence of our contributors, Burma and Thailand) women have apparently always had relative freedom to travel on their own affairs; in others (notably India and Pakistan) it has not been so. It is particularly in these latter countries that Dr. Tharpar's point that modern methods of transport have been indirectly one of the most influential factors in the practical emancipation of women is well taken. Traditional customs are not always easy to maintain on modern vehicles, distance from the familiar social environment may make them seem unnecessary, even ridiculous. Dr. Sushilla Nayer describes how her mother used to keep full *purdah* while travelling by train; a complicated business, requiring among other things a large staff of servants. There is a station on the line from Bombay to Delhi through which large numbers of the Indians resident in East Africa pass on their way to and from that continent. The women know it as 'Anand-raise-the-veil' or 'Anand-lower-the-veil' according to whether they are journeying towards their ancestral villages in India or their newer homes across the sea.

It is not necessary to labour the obvious points about travel broadening the mind, helping to break down ethnocentricity, leading to new personal contacts, economic and educational opportunities, even inter-marriage. Our contributors make them very clear.

But travel is only one part of the modern system of communications. Not only people, but goods and ideas too are being distributed more and more widely. Clothes which once had to be hand-made (even to the spinning of the threads, as Madame Le Kwang Kim explains) can now be bought ready-made; pots and pans can be of plastic and aluminium; soap, cosmetics, medicaments, surgical plaster, even comfortable and hygienic sanitary towels, are easily available almost everywhere; foodstuffs, once laboriously planted, weeded, harvested and processed by family hand labour, can be bought ready wrapped in the stores. There is electricity and piped water. These things are by no means true for all the people of our area, not yet; but they are for many. And their effects upon the lives and roles of men and women and the way they spend their time are profound. (Moreover, they are among the several modern developments which are making the lives of Easterners and Westerners more alike—and, therefore, presumably mutually more comprehensible.)

As for ideas—the spread of books and newspapers, and the telephone, radio, cinema, and television (already in 1961 popular television is a regular feature of life in Hong Kong, Manila, Bangkok, Singapore) marks a whole series of social revolutions. In education, the arts and entertainment their influence is obvious, producing new knowledge, new concepts, new and modified social attitudes, new ways of passing time, and new openings for employment. The husband who refused to countenance the education of women 'because my wife might learn to write and read love letters from other men' saw only a very small part of the complications that improved communications would bring. Perhaps the most striking tales of family change among those which follow in Part II of this book are those written by women university graduates whose own grandmothers, even mothers, were illiterate.

The surge to the towns

In 1953 something quite new happened in the Chinese fishing village of Kau Sai, which lies on one of the many islands in the territory of Hong Kong: several fishermen sent their daughters to school. Previously this had been the privilege of sons only. But in the early 1950s Kau Sai was becoming prosperous. Some of the fishing junks were fitted with diesel engines; catches were larger and more regular, incomes higher. With higher incomes, wives and daughters, as well as sons and grandsons, wanted to buy things. The city had plenty of things to sell, but to find the shops you needed to be able to read —read the shop signs, the street names, the figures on the buses and their destinations. Modern communications were all laid on, travel and goods were at the women's disposal—but first they had to be able to read.

In the village literacy was not necessary; town living, even town visiting, was difficult without it. The schoolgirls of Kau Sai illustrate very neatly the interdependence of the many different factors in contemporary social change.

More than that, they illustrate also the surge towards the towns. Between

1951 and 1959 four young fisher boys left the village—prosperous though their families undoubtedly were—for work in the city, and one girl was lucky enough to marry a townsman. This, which made her the envy of every other woman and the ideal of every schoolgirl in the village, meant that she went to live in a windowless cubicle about 9 feet long and 5 feet broad, whose hardboard walls reached a height of about 7 feet and which was flanked by six or seven similar cubicles with whose occupants (together with those who slept in the passageway) she now shares a common kitchen-*cum*-lavatory about 10 feet square. The fourth floor of the tenement which contains this cubicle is reached by a steep, straight stairway, a yard wide, down which all refuse—including night-soil—has to be carried, and which, being no tenant's property, is no tenant's business to keep clean. The tenement is, of course, only one in a street of such buildings, and in scores of such streets. There is a standpipe for water about a hundred yards away. The good fortune of this girl, who now has two children both under three years old, is still the talk of her old friends in the village. She has achieved their highest ambition: she lives in town.

What has she gained? In the eyes of her friends and herself two precious things: freedom from the ceaselessness of toil in the village, and access to glamour and excitement. Both the 'push' from the country and the 'pull' to the towns are here reflected. There is no doubt that in most countries peasant rural life is an endless round of physically demanding work. Chinese fishing families are perhaps an extreme example, since they live always (men, women and children) on their boats and many of them work far into the night; moreover they are driven all the time by the constant desire to make good in the material sense. By no means all the other nationalities in South and South-East Asia share this motivation, and, without it, most of them, living in a climate and environment which do not force absolutely continuous effort, do in fact lead a less strenuous life. Nevertheless, even for them, the work is usually demanding and unending; often especially so for the women who, in addition to the inescapable daily chores of child care, cooking, cleaning, collecting water and firewood, laundering, and other domestic duties, usually have the more continuous, if less arduous, tasks of agriculture laid upon them —planting out, for instance, and weeding.

In the towns those tasks disappear; water comes from a tap (what is a hundred yards or so down the street compared with a quarter of a mile or more on rough village path?); food can quite often be bought ready cooked; charcoal and firewood are in the market; there is electricity. All this and glamour too: things to see, shops to look at, the cinema, a fire engine, buses, crowded pavements, curious foreigners, rich people, perhaps processions for funerals and weddings. The fascination of town life for the imaginations of peasant women is not hard to understand.

The question how far their expectations are fulfilled can hardly be answered. For the fisherman's daughter from Kau Sai they undoubtedly were. Though to middle-class Western eyes she may appear to have exchanged a healthy open-air life in some of the most beautiful scenery in the world for an overcrowded slum, she is a truly happy woman. She told me so; and I could see that it was true. But for the pavement sleepers of other parts of Hong Kong (or Calcutta, or Bombay, or elsewhere) I cannot say. Overcrowding, unemployment, slum housing—these are common in all large Asian cities and there are probably many who wish they had never left the land. But we do not always see the alternatives. We need more information, more factual studies of the relative advantages of poor town and poor country living and the actual reasons behind the decisions to migrate.

Moreover it is as misleading to think solely in terms of poverty and overcrowding as it is to ignore them. Asian towns have their well-to-do inhabitants too. Furthermore, in Asia as elsewhere it is town life that gives the greatest opportunities for recreation, cultural activities of all kinds, education, diversified employment—after all, as the derivation of the word shows, towns are the seats of civilization. And, as Professor Karim points out, as often as not they are also the places in which it is easiest for traditionally secluded women to emerge from *purdah*. None of our Asian women contributors can be described as a mere countrywoman.

In this they are atypical. Dr. Smith tells us that, apart from city-states like Singapore, the proportion of the total population living in towns containing a population of 20,000 or more nowhere in our region exceeds 22 per cent, and the average is not much above 10 per cent. In North America it is (1950) 42 per cent, in Europe (excluding Russia) 35 per cent, in the U.S.S.R. 31 per cent. One of the difficulties in the way of mutual understanding between East and West is that the overwhelming majority of Asians are villagers—or small-town dwellers—still.

Nevertheless it is certain that there is a surge towards the towns in Asia, and that it is increasing. The figures in Table 1 were among those presented to a joint United Nations/Unesco seminar in August 1956 on urbanization in Asia and the Far East.

It is equally certain that the change from rural to urban living is accompanied by profound changes in social roles. What this may mean for traditional family roles we discuss below; the development of new types of role in towns is one of the topics we consider under our next headings.

New employment

When economists discuss increasing urbanization in terms of a 'pull' to the towns or a 'push' from the country they are referring to opportunities for making a living. Most of the new (that is, non-traditional) concerns are in the towns, and despite much serious urban unemployment and poverty the continuing processes of economic specialization and industrialization to mean that the towns offer a multitude of new jobs. For most men, whether 'pushed out' or 'pulled in'—or, more commonly, a bit of both—going to town and looking for work are more or less synonymous.

Table 1. Trends in percentage of the total population in towns of 20,000 inhabitants or more, 1910-51

Year	India	Federation of Malaya
1910	5.1	8.3
1920	5.4	10.1
1930	6.3	12.2
1940	8.2	–
1947	–	17.0
1951	12.0	–

Source: *Proceedings of the Joint United Nations/Unesco Seminar on Urbanization in the ECAFE Region, Bangkok, 8-18 August 1956*, edited by Philip M. Hauser (Calcutta, 1957), p. 103.

This is not necessarily true of women. Indeed, it seems likely that most of the migrant women who seek employment in the towns of Asia do so rather as a response to the economic necessity they find pressing upon them after they have arrived than as their intended goal on arriving. We must beware of equating the numbers of women living in towns with the numbers in employment: on the one hand, many women (and, of course, many men too) are employed in the country and, on the other hand, in both town and country many are not employed at all.

The recorded numbers of gainfully employed women are in fact always less than the total female population in any given place. This is not only because, as with men, a fairly large proportion consists of people who are either too young or too old to be included, but also because the tasks which engage most of the time and energy of most women everywhere are not included in the statistics of economic activity. Housework in one's own home is a job which has no money value put upon it; it is therefore excluded from the statistics and classed as 'uneconomic'. This fact, which complicates every discussion of the division of labour between the sexes, tends also to depreciate the social contribution of women—difficulties which could be avoided if it were possible (as surely it should be?) to set a money value upon housework at home (and, also, one might add, upon the strictly productive work of bearing and rearing children, which is likewise regarded as an uneconomic activity).

Be that as it may (and proverbial comment notwithstanding), the fact remains that most women do not 'work', including usually a large proportion of those who are of working age. In the United Kingdom, about half of the women between 15 and 59 are thus economically inactive; in India, of women aged 15 to 56, 58 per cent are inactive; in the Philippines, of women over 10, 60 per cent are inactive. Comparable information does not exist for the other countries of South and South-East Asia, which is especially unfortunate since (as will become clearer later on) the common Western assumption that women in all Oriental countries have a similar position is far indeed from the facts.

In any case, we are not so much concerned here with the extent of women's employment in general as with their employment in such ways as may be expected to bring about role changes. For some assistance with this topic we can turn to such statistics as do exist on the distribution of women workers between the three sectors of the economy: agriculture, industry, services, and on their distribution by status as employers and workers on their own account, unpaid family workers, and employees.[1]

Table 2. Percentage of female labour force in each economic sector

Country	Agriculture	Industry	Services
India	82	7	11
Federation of Malaya	79	8	13
Pakistan	82	9	9
Philippines	44	23	33
Thailand	90	2	8

Two points stand out: first, the high proportion of women employed in agriculture; second, the predominance of service over industrial employment. The first point reflects the preponderance of agriculture over industry in all contemporary South and South-East Asian economies. It also suggests that a

[1] For Tables 2 and 3 and much of their interpretation, we are indebted to a paper presented by Sir Alexander Carr Saunders to the thirty-first meeting of the International Institute of Differing Civilizations (INCIDI) held in Brussels on 17, 18, 19 and 20 September 1958, and published in the report entitled *Women's Role in the Development of Tropical and Subtropical Countries* (Brussels, 1959), pp. 500-516. The figures are taken from an article, 'Women in the labour Force', *Internatonal Labour Review*, Vol. LXXVII, No. 3 (March 1958).

large proportion of the employed women of this region have not left the countryside. The second is a feature of the industrialized West as well, but the kinds of services performed and the conditions under which they are carried out are usually different. It is perhaps worth recalling that 'services' include commerce and transport as well as domestic service.

Further light is thrown on these points by the figures in Table 3.

Table 3. Distribution of the female labour force by status (percentage of total)

Country	Employers and workers on own account	Unpaid family workers	Employees
India	26	60	14
Federation of Malaya	29	23	48
Pakistan	83	2	15
Philippines	11	60	29

In fully industrialized countries the proportion of women classed as employers and workers on their own account never reaches 20 per cent; in the United States, Canada and the United Kingdom, it is around 5 per cent. In other words, in those countries where industrialization has gone furthest, relatively few women are employers or workers on their own account, more than 90 per cent of the female labour force being engaged as employees. This is partly because of the greater number of women workers engaged in manufacturing, but also partly because the services in such countries tend to be organized on a larger scale. In less industrialized countries quite a large proportion of the women working in traditional ways in agriculture are employers or working on their own account, as would be expected; it is less often remembered that relatively many of the women engaged in trade or business are of this status too. This is especially so in Thailand (and also Burma, the Philippines and Indonesia which are not on this list). But these are traditional, not new, roles in these countries. When to those facts is added the probability that a large proportion of the women who are listed as employees are in fact domestic servants (another traditional occupation, and one which has dramatically decreased in importance in the West), it will be seen that probably the great majority of the gainfully employed women in South and South-East Asia today have not entered new kinds of employment at all.

But some undoubtedly have, and not only in towns. Agriculture has its own non-traditional side, particularly in plantation work which employs very large numbers of women especially in Ceylon, Federation of Malaya, Indonesia and parts of India. This accounts for the big discrepancy between the proportion of women workers in agriculture (79 per cent) and the proportion engaged as unpaid family workers (23 per cent) in Malaya, for example.

Plantation employment is rather a special case. Although certainly not part of the indigenous traditional economies, it has in most places now been going on for a fairly long time, and in any case being mainly rural and often engaging whole families at a time, it might be expected to bring about less fundamental change in the lives of the women engaged in it, and their families, than occupations which require a move to the towns. On the other hand, many plantation workers are immigrants, or the descendants of immigrants, from overseas (like the workers of South Indian origin in Ceylon's tea and Malaya's rubber plantations). And however true it may be that rural women of the poorer classes have almost everywhere and almost always taken part in their families' agricultural work, there are important differences between being a wage-earner working for someone else, and being a co-worker in your own family enterprise.

Nevertheless, it is when the wage-earning takes place in a completely non-traditional occupation in town that there are likely to be the greatest number of other differences too. And though the proportion of Asian women so affected is small, the number is not—and it is rapidly increasing. We should be exceedingly unwise to underestimate its extent, or play down its significance.

A great deal has been written about the effect of the change from subsistence agriculture in a stable village setting to wage-earning in the slum conditions of many modern towns. We have been told how the family ceases to be a unit of production, and how the bread-winner becomes for the first time a hired hand paid as an individual; how the dependants, who have hitherto been co-workers in a joint enterprise, find themselves in a new and lower status and how they may even be left behind in the villages; how when women, too, become wage-earners the disruption is even greater, children are not properly cared for, sexual morality is weakened, and the traditional family system undermined if not destroyed. This is hardly an exaggeration of a familiar line of argument.

There is some truth in it. Subsistence agriculture, which is the traditional occupation for the large majority of people in our region, is often bound up with the existence of closely integrated groups of kinsmen. It would not be surprising if, when individual wage-earning took the place of shared productive labour, some of the cement holding such groups together were removed. In the next section of this chapter (on changing family roles) we examine the relative viability of different kinds of family and kinship structure in this respect. But it does not need an excursion into kinship theory to demonstrate that by no means all the traditional Asian family systems are in fact so fragile as some writers believe. We have already noted the traditional role of women as traders in Burma, Thailand, Indonesia and the Philippines. These women have long enjoyed an independently earned income. And it should go without saying that all the countries of our region have had traditionally differentiated economies, such that money rewards for work have a long history for large numbers of men everywhere. Yet it is not suggested that these things have undermined the traditional family systems. (There is, however, ample evidence that the traditional family systems in the countries where women have freely engaged in trade are very different from those, of, say, India, or Pakistan; but that is just the point at issue.)

Reading some of the literature on urbanization and industrialization in Asia, one cannot help feeling that it has been written by Westerners suffering from a deep-seated, possibly unconscious, romantic yearning for a rural Golden Age in which the climate is always balmy, the season always just after harvest —and electricity and running water are not far away. It is true that the social cost of urbanization and industrialization has usually been extremely high. It is true that housing in rapidly expanding towns is often poor, insanitary and overcrowded. But we have already suggested that agricultural poverty and overcrowding may be at least as hard to bear. Experience shows that given industrialization (and only then) the extreme conditions of both rural and urban wretchedness can be mitigated. And may it not be these, rather than wage-earning, which are the significant factors in family break-up where it occurs?

Where women are concerned it is probably not wage-earning as such but the necessity of working to fixed hours which is more important in bringing about changes in interpretation of roles and patterns of family living. Hours of work on family agricultural plots, in traditional small-scale trading and cottage-industry, even, to some extent, in plantation work, are flexibly adaptable to the worker. A modern factory, big store, transport business, office, or school has a fixed time-table and pay is usually according to hours worked. People who have prior obligations to housework, catering, cooking, and, above all, children, find this extremely difficult, and very tiring. Only those who for economic reasons must, or for domestic reasons can, are likely to seek out employment of this kind. If this is so, then it helps to explain why it is that in several countries of our region, it appears to be commoner to find gainfully employed women among the poor and the fairly well-to-do, uncommon to find them from the middle ranges, or, of course, the very rich. Where the women of the poorest classes work from necessity, those of the next higher income groups tend to stay at home, partly because domestic work demands their presence, partly because social prestige for their families may depend upon their being different in this respect from the poor. The upper strata who can afford to give their girls both education and freedom from domestic tasks can also afford to ignore this particular badge of social prestige. (Indeed, for them prestige often comes more from having highly educated daughters or wives engaged in professional work and imbued with ideas of service to the community.) In some of the more highly industrialized countries of the West there is now a much wider scatter throughout the socio-economic scale.

But this difference in social class distribution goes with another difference; in the West a very large proportion of working women are unmarried; in the East nearly all are married. And this applies not only to traditional occupations and plantation work where the flexibility of time-table might be expected to facilitate the employment of married women, but throughout. (Widows, and women deserted by their husbands, who have children to support are an important minority, of course, everywhere.) This is not altogether surprising, for in some countries—notably, but not exclusively, India and Pakistan—girls marry young, and almost everywhere arranged marriages (usually implying the careful chaperonage of young women) are still the normal practice and spinsters hardly exist. Only among the later generations of town-dwellers in the East is there a tendency for girls to marry later and, with a higher standard of education, to seek a job as soon as they are old enough to work.

We may surmise from this that more differences between Western and Eastern patterns are likely to disappear in time. For if Eastern girls are beginning to marry later and go to work earlier, Western girls are beginning to marry earlier and stay at work later, and fewer and fewer are remaining unmarried. It is now not marriage which forces a girl's retirement from paid employment in the West, but the arrival of babies. The significance of child care in this respect is further demonstrated by the recent tendency noted widely in the West for married women to return to work after their children have grown up. We have already linked this with the increased expectancy of life and the decreased expectancy of pregnancy. We could also link it with the mobility of population which often denies a mother the support and help of nearby relatives, and with the decline in the number of domestic servants. All these are developments which are very likely to follow in Eastern countries later on. Will it also follow that there, too, the majority of the female labour force will be either pre- or post-child bearing? Or will other methods of organizing domestic work and child care—together, perhaps, with more flexible working hours, or less restricting housing programmes—be developed on a large scale? And will recognition be paid to the economic contribution of the childbearing years?

These are crucial issues in any discussion of the division of labour between the sexes and the changing roles of women.

They are crucial also in any consideration of the status of women in employment. Table 4 shows how small is the number of women in higher grade posts in our region.

This is a many-sided subject, to which we return in the later sections of this essay. Here we simply draw attention to one practical obstacle to successful participation in the professions and to promotion which affects men and women unequally: the years during which a person of talent and ambition consolidates his knowledge and skill, builds up his reputation and makes his important contacts are just the years in which a woman with children is most fully occupied at home. It is not an accident that so many Western women in high positions and in the professions have been spinsters. Up to now few Asian women have had seriously to face the choice between marriage and a career. Both are possible as long as domestic servants are easily available, or relatives are at hand, though even with good domestic help a professional woman with young children still has the problem of reconciling two responsibilities.

Nearly all our women contributors refer to these matters. Many are beginning to wonder what their daughters and grand-daughters will decide to do, for they are well aware that given small families of father, mother and unmarried children, isolated from close relatives, unable to engage domestic servants, and with a tradition that each family lives, eats, and brings up its young children separately, there is a genuine incompatibility between the role of mother and the role of professional worker or higher grade executive.

But this cannot be the sole obstacle to women's participation in the professions and promotion or our table would not show such marked contrasts between different countries. It is clear that proportionately it is much more than ten times easier for a women to enter these occupations in the Philippines than in Pakistan. Thailand, Singapore, India, Ceylon and Federation of Malaya—more or less in that order—lie between these two extremes. Our readers are invited to read the articles in the body of this book (especially those written by professional women) with the object of finding out why this should be so. We ourselves offer certain hypotheses in the remaining sections of this essay.

Note on equal pay

In 1960 the United Nations published a special pamphlet (E/CN/6/341/Rev. 1) on equal pay for the two sexes. In an appendix to this appear summaries of the measures taken in seventy different countries to give effect to the International Labour Office Equal Remuneration Convention and Recommendation of 1951. In almost all of them (the notable exceptions are South Africa, Australia and the Sudan) governmental and/or trade union policies endorse

Table 4. The proportion of women gainfully employed expressed as a percentage[1] of the total number employed; selected countries and selected occupations[2]

	Philippines (1960)	Thailand (1960)	Burma (1953)	Federation of Malaya (1957)[3]	Ceylon (1957)	Singapore (1957)	India (1951)	Pakistan (1951)
Total employed population	35	40	27	23	24	18	16	6
Agricultural and related occupations	25	52	22	27	27	27	18	6
Non-agricultural occupations	50	29	28	16	20	17	14	5
Professional, technical and related occupations	39	52	23	22	28	34	4(?)	4
Managerial, administrative and clerical occupations	5	17	9	0.09	8	9	4(?)	0.5
Sales and related occupations	57	44	48	27	11	10	10	3
Manufacturing occupations	61	28	31	12	25	16	14	6
Service occupations	61	51	15	10	24	37	19	8

[1] These percentages were calculated to the nearest whole number from round thousands. They are only approximate.

[2] Original figures were obtained from the most recent (as dates) census reports for each country, except the Philippines for which the data were taken from the *ILO Yearbook of Labour Statistics, 1960.*

[3] Malays only.

Note: Comparisons must be treated with caution because the criteria for allocation to occupational divisions, and for the category 'gainfully employed', are not always identical in different censuses. The figures for India, Burma and Thailand require special mention: the Indian census of 1951 employed a new method of classifying occupations from which the above figures were compiled with as near accuracy as possible; the Burmese figures refer to a sample census of 252 Burmese towns only; the Thai figures were calculated from data from two administrative divisions (*changwad*) only, one urban and one rural.

the principle of equal pay and seek to extend its application. Up to 15 October 1960, thirty-four governments had ratified this ILO convention, among them India, Indonesia and the Philippines. No other South Asian countries appear on the list of ratifications, but neither do over a dozen Western countries, including the United Kingdom and the United States.

It is, however, only fair to point out that ratification implies accepting the principle of equal pay, application of the principle does not automatically follow; moreover, failure to ratify does not imply rejection of either the principle or its application. The practice of paying equal reward for equal work regardless of sex is, in fact, more common in some of the non-ratifying than in some of the ratifying countries.

From our present point of view, however, the significant facts are that all South and South-East Asian governments endorse the principle of equal pay, and nearly all of them apply it in the public administrative and other services while at the same time endeavouring to promote its application in the private sectors of employment.

Two further points should be noted: first that sex-linked pay differences are common for unskilled and semi-skilled work in all countries where they exist at all; and second, that a relatively larger majority of women than of men workers are in unskilled and semi-skilled occupations. This also is true everywhere.

Modern education

If there is any single point on which our contributors are all agreed, it is the immense significance of education. This is not surprising. Although our region has been the seat and cultural domain of all the classical civilizations of India, and the sphere also of Chinese and Arabian influences (both long ante-dating the contacts with Europe, which themselves began as many as 400 years ago), most of the ordinary people have remained illiterate. Education in the formal sense was the privilege of a limited proportion of the population, to which, though with quite numerous and often notable exceptions, women did not usually belong.

There was, of course, nothing peculiarly Oriental about this. Universal education was nowhere even envisaged much before the twentieth century. Only advancing industrialism, ready to take virtually whole populations into its employ and depending for its further development upon vast numbers of relatively educated consumers, has begun to make general literacy (and numeracy) an economic necessity. This has been a recent occurrence even in the West, which was the cradle of industrialism. And even there the education of women has everywhere lagged behind.

There are certain rather obvious difficulties in the way of estimating a country's degree of literacy, but even if we allow for these we still have to admit that there are large variations not only between the industrialized and the non-industrialized nations of the world but also within each of these two categories. The report published in 1959 by the International Institute of Differing Civilizations, which we have already quoted, gives the following proportions of non-literate women in the total female population: Ceylon 46 per cent, Thailand 64, Federation of Malaya 84, India 92. In Viet-Nam, we are told, 30 per cent of those who have received at least primary education are female; in the Philippines, more than 40 per cent. The statistics for Indonesia are less definite, but it is reported that no more than 35 per cent of the total population were illiterate in 1958. From evidence that girls are less freely given access to education in Indonesia than boys, we have to assume that the ratio of females in this 35 per cent is high. The figures for Pakistan appear in a different form; in 1956 enrolments in all Pakistani places of education taken together were: males, 4,893,265; females, 566,834 (rather less than 11 per cent).

Although Pakistan's is the extreme case, it is clear that women are everywhere at an educational disadvantage. The Philippines goes nearest to affording equality in this, as in most other, respects. Our other countries lie at successive points along a continuum of which these two represent the respective poles.

One attempt at working out some of the possible social correlates of this variety appears in the political section of this essay. It omits, however, several important features which are particularly relevant to education: for example, governmental policy (and in the case of colonial governments the influence of contemporary metropolitan views on the education of girls) and the demands made by the economy for large numbers of literate female workers and consumers. Broadly speaking, the economic demand for female education is only now beginning to become apparent in South and South-East Asia. Furthermore, it is not to be expected that industrial development will occur evenly, or that existing differences will be quickly eliminated. In the Philippines women already and traditionally do most of the shopping; in traditional Pakistan they do virtually none. It is noteworthy, too, that India, which is without doubt industrially the most advanced of our countries, still has one of the highest rates of female illiteracy.

What have already told about the fisher-girls and boys of Hong Kong show well enough the desire for literacy. Some of its potential effects upon traditional roles are also discussed elsewhere. The demand for it creates the new roles of primary school teachers, mass education workers and so on, and beyond these it acts as a kind of lubricant for almost all the other changes we discuss. It is probably fair to describe it as the enabling measure *par excellence*.

But industrialized countries have already found that literacy is not enough.

The achievement of universal primary schooling (which we are, for brevity's sake, equating with the achievement of general literacy) has been followed by the development of universal secondary education. Here, too, the Orient is beginning to follow suit, but as yet there is everywhere a much smaller proportion of pupils in secondary than in primary schools and a still smaller proportion of these are girls. Once again there are national differences, the Philippines, where 44 per cent of the secondary school pupils are females, being well ahead of the rest (Ceylon 30 per cent, Thailand 28, Viet-Nam 25, Cambodia 16, India 13).

In so far as we are considering the approach towards universal education—whether primary or secondary—we are considering something which is in a substantial sense much less of a novelty for boys in the East than in the West. In Ceylon, Burma, Thailand, Cambodia, Laos and indeed anywhere where Theravāda (Hinayana) Buddhism is practised, all boys traditionally enter the monasteries for a shorter or longer period before attaining manhood. This novitiate includes training in the scriptures, with the result that in these countries all boys have long had the opportunity of becoming literate. Girls, however, had to depend upon such teaching as their brothers, fathers, husbands or other male relatives were willing to give, for no monk is permitted any personal relationship with a female. In Moslem areas (and in addition to the predominantly Moslem populations in Pakistan, the Federation of Malaya and Indonesia there are quite large Moslem minorities in every country of our region) a somewhat similar custom obtains for scriptural training in the Holy Koran, which is often given to girls as well as boys. It would therefore be quite untrue to say that universal education is in every sense a new thing in the East.

Nevertheless, in content and aims and in its ideal extension to both sexes equally modern education is certainly very different. Literacy is no longer sought mainly for the sake of reading holy texts; and going to school nowadays is an important step towards personal advantage in this world as well as the next. Even if widespread formal education is not the new idea to South and South-East Asia that it is to the West, its modern manifestations are quite unlike the traditional ones.

Much the same can be said about higher education. In so far as this is thought of as the training of *élites* rather than an extension of general education it—or something like it—has long been familiar in our region. What is peculiar to the modern situation is not that such a training exists but that its content is vastly changed and its scope vastly extended, both as regards more and new subjects of study and as regards a greatly enlarged student body. And for the first time this now includes women—again only a little later in the East than in the West. This is something really new.

Here, indeed, is one of the crucial points for studying the emergence of new roles for women. To what extent are they now being trained intellectually to enter the *élite*? It is common knowledge that there is no country anywhere in which the number of women receiving post-secondary education is as great as the number of men. It is worth pointing out, too, that the highest proportions of women students are not always found in the West, for Burma, the Philippines and Thailand, in each of which women make up about 36 per cent of the total number of post-secondary students, are among the most progressive in this respect in the world.

Table 5 shows the increases which occurred in four countries of our region in the ten years following the Second World War compared with figures from six selected Western countries (including the four major colonial powers of our region) for the same dates.[2]

Table 5. Changes in number and proportion of women students enrolled in institutes of post-secondary education[1] for the academic years beginning in 1945, 1950 and 1954, in selected countries

Country	1945			1950			1955		
	A	B	C	A	B	C	A	B	C
Ceylon	133	8.1	–	387	14.7	5.1	664[2]	16.0	7.9
India	20,844	9.8	6.2	43,185	11.2	12.1	83,751	12.4	26.4
Philippines (public institutions only)	965	42.9	5.3	2,749	42.6	12.5	–	–	–
Thailand	2,908[3]	15.5	17.0	2,522	8.4	13.9	9.554	36.5	47.1
Netherlands	3,245	14.9	35.0	4,346	15.4	43.0	5,152	17.4	47.9
United Kingdom	17,907	33.4	36.4	19,904	22.7	39.5	20,420	24.6	40.3
Sweden	3,048	21.7	45.9	3,942	23.3	56.2	6,387	28.5	87.9
France	40,211	32.6	102.8	47,260	33.9	113.2	58,534	33.8	135.3
U.S.S.R.	–	–	–	–	–	–	967,600	51.8	483.0
United States	585,431	41.7	418.4	724,609[4]	29.4	485.7	791,234	34.4	487.2

[1] A=Number of women students enrolled; B=Percentage of total enrolment; C=Number per 100,000 of total population.
[2] 1954.
[3] 1946.
[4] 1949.

[2] The figures for this and the following two tables have been taken from lists supplied by the Statistical Department of Unesco to the International Federation of University Women. All references to countries of our region have been included.

It is clear that the expansion in numbers of post-secondary students is fairly general, and that this has included in many countries an expansion not only of numbers but actually of proportions of women students. (It is noteworthy that this has not always been true in the West.) Nevertheless women are still in a minority, usually very much so. Most of the several reasons for this are discussed elsewhere. The strictly educational factors include the late entry of women into the field of formal education of any kind, the still very much smaller number of girls than boys in primary and secondary schools, and the various special curricula for girls which are often directed mainly towards preparing them for their traditional roles in the home at the expense of their intellectual advancement. This is not the place to pursue these and the other educational arguments further. They are well known. It may, however, be worth suggesting the probable value of a controlled inquiry into the question of whether the segregation of the sexes in education is compatible with equality.

Table 6 refers not to the numbers of students but their successes. In the countries of our region the proportion of women receiving degrees is higher than the contemporary proportion of women to men students. The answer to our former question is, then, that women are now being given *élite* training, but almost everywhere in small numbers. If education alone was the criterion for entry, we should expect to find many fewer women than men in the professions, and in executive and managerial positions in general.

Table 6. Degrees and diplomas awarded to women students in the years 1950 and 1954, in selected countries

Country	1950		1954	
	Number awarded to women	Percentage of total awarded	Number awarded to women	Percentage of total awarded
Burma	74	27.0	189	30.2
Ceylon	–	–	90	20.6
India	7,329	12.4	10,483	13.1
Thailand	140	56.0	179	46.7
Viet-Nam	10	14.7	35	11.4
Netherlands	352	12.4	395[1]	12.1
Sweden	657	20.9	2,297	31.7
France	5,465	33.8	1,051	37.8
United States	123,861	27.9	122,954	34.9

[1] 1953

But we should not expect the discrepancy to be as great as it is. Even in the Philippines where girls have very nearly equal educational advantages and there are, as we have seen, remarkably large numbers of women in the professions, administration, and relatively high posts in commerce and industry, the really leading positions are almost all held by men. A comparison between Table 7 and the two preceding tables shows what differences exist between the proportions of women who appear as students and the proportions who appear as teachers in post-secondary institutions.

Table 7. Numbers and proportions of women teaching in institutions of higher education, 1950 and 1954, in selected countries

Country	1950		1954	
	Number	Percentage of total	Number	Percentage of total
Burma	51	20.9	181	37.8
Ceylon	13	5.8	12	4.9
India	2,053	8.7	2,976	9.9
Singapore	5	5.5	. . .	. . .
Thailand	108	18.7	179	24.6
Philippines			–	39.3
Japan	3,097	6.5	4,358	7.2
Sweden	45	3.0	44	2.6
United States	44,492[1]	23.4	. . .	. . .

[1] 1949, including administrative staff.

Note: The figures for Japanese, Swedish and United States institutes of higher education are included for comparison. The relatively lower proportion of women employed in these than in some of the institutes of our region will not pass unnoticed.

. . . Data not available.

The discrepancies between these figures and those in Tables 5 and 6 make obvious what we expect already: that selective processes additional to those of educational attainment are at work. The fact that the differences between the countries of our region on this list follow much the same kind of graduation as we found in the preceding section of this essay—with the Philippines, Burma and Thailand standing at the opposite pole to India and Ceylon—makes it seem likely that these other processes are fairly constant. We discuss this further below.

Political emancipation

It is often forgotten how recent is the achievement of political equality between the sexes. Fifty years ago only one country in Europe (Finland) had granted women the vote, and certainly no Western woman could hold political office except for those very few who in certain exceptional circumstances happened to inherit royal positions. Today no country in South or South-East Asia discriminates between the sexes in this respect. Where the right to vote exists at all (and that is almost everywhere) it is held equally by women and by men, and in almost every State all political offices are similarly open to both sexes. Whereas in European Portugal and Switzerland women are still in 1961 denied the right to vote in national elections, Ceylon in 1960 elected the world's first woman Prime Minister.

This is a revolution indeed. There are many questions one could ask about it. For our present purposes we will confine ourselves to two: How has it come about? What does it mean in practice?

For the first question, the most striking thing for a Western observer is the relative ease of the revolution. Not for the East, it seems, the rigours of a militant campaign, but simply a quiet and quick advance. Indeed, one can often hear ladies in South Asia decrying what they regard as the hysterical excesses of the Western (particularly the British) feminist movements, whose small and short-lived (but spectacular and long-remembered) militant branches are so often wrongly assumed to have been representative of the whole, and whose historical and sociological backgrounds were very different from their own; whose success, moreover, undoubtedly influenced theirs. Despite quite considerable national variations in background, and in the speed and effectiveness of advance, it seems likely that the relative smoothness and rapidity of the political emancipation of women in Asia may be largely ascribed to the immediately prior (in some cases contemporary) success of the feminist movements in the West. The table showing the chronological order in which voting rights were granted in different countries (appended to Dr. Romila Tharpar's article) should be studied in this connection.

But it is not necessary for us to dwell on chronology; Romila Tharpar deals with it brilliantly. What we are concerned with here is sociological analysis. So, of course, to a considerable extent is she. She mentions the relevance of types of family structure and religion, both of which we examine again here, and points to the connections between the movements for women's education and women's emancipation both in the West and the East which we have also mentioned. She shows, too, how to some extent Western experience was paralleled in the East, for much as the two world wars in Europe, so the anti-colonial struggles in southern Asia provided opportunities for women to play roles which had not been open to them before, and thus to demonstrate their capabilities and prove themselves actively welcome as fellow fighters with men. It is not surprising that in such circumstances national emancipation and female emancipation went hand in hand, or that in those places where political rights had already been given to women by the colonial powers they should not be rescinded but rather enlarged.

It would not be surprising, either, if once national independence had been gained there should have appeared some reaction against the new political status of women, at least in countries where their previous subordination had been most marked. Dr. Vreede de Stuers (quoted by Dr. Tharpar below) has drawn attention to just such a reaction in Indonesia. But time has been too short to tell whether it will have much success there, or whether something similar may appear elsewhere too.

On the whole, it would seem rather unlikely. Though women may well have to overcome great difficulties in winning office or promotion, perhaps more so in some countries than in others, the general trends of world opinion —and, much more important than that, of world economic development which more and more requires the contribution of women both as workers and as consumers—makes it unlikely that there will be a general return to second-class citizenship for women as a category.

This opinion of ours implies an important distinction between actually holding political office, on the one hand, and simply exercising the full rights of ordinary citizenship, on the other. It is obvious that for the majority of both men and women office is in any case unattainable, but as long as the number of girls at school remains markedly less than the number of boys, as long as they continue to leave school earlier, attend less regularly, or receive a different quality of education, so long will there be proportionately fewer women likely to enter office than men. The exercise of the franchise is quite another matter. Nowhere in our region are educational qualifications required for this, and, in any case, 'wisdom' in voting cannot be measured except by untestable opinion. The only valid measurement is the number of people taking the trouble to cast their votes, and such figures as exist for the countries in our region so far show a marked consistency between men and women in this respect.

There are other differences. Whereas voting is an individual's personal concern, holding political office is a matter of exercising power over others, and the necessary qualifications for that cannot be inculcated in schools alone. People who are expected from earliest youth to submit to the demands of others and not to assert domination, given few or no opportunities to build up personal followings or practise the exercise of authority, may be expected to find it difficult to develop the traits required for active political life—the more so if they have to compete in a world populated mainly by those to whom they have been taught to defer and who, at the same time, expect their deference and have not suffered the same disabilities. This, which is the common situation of any politically subordinate people, is aggravated if the individuals concerned live largely separated from one another in such a way that they meet too seldom to make their common organization possible, or if the roles they play are so limited that they get little practice in wielding power even amongst themselves. All these disadvantages—and others which we will leave aside for the present—apply in a greater or lesser degree to women in different countries; but the franchise having been granted they are relevant much more to the holding of office than the casting of votes.

We shall return to this distinction, and mention others, a little later.

Now, in some parts of our region the roles traditionally open to a woman were very few in number, and almost all incompatible with the assertion of power. As 'daughter', 'daughter-in-law', 'wife', even 'mother', a girl living in a patrilocal extended family household, with few or no property rights of her own, has virtually no power. Such would have been the situation in the traditional three-generation family households of Hindu India, Moslem Pakistan and Confucian China. And for a respectable girl there were no other roles available. The limitations implicit in this situation were narrowed still further by the conventions which insisted—still insist, in many cases—upon *purdah*, backed by religious sanctions, as in Pakistan and parts of India, or at least upon careful seclusion backed by the full force of moral disapproval (not to mention foot binding) as in the gentry families of pre-1911 China. Granted seniority, sons, long life and a strong personality, a woman might expect to reach a position of authority in her husband's household later on. She might even come to exercise almost complete control—within the home. Outside it her traditional power was always officially nil, though indirectly by working upon the men who came under her domination at home (or, if she was not of the respectable class, elsewhere) she could possibly exercise considerable influence. Only in the most exceptional circumstances, however, could exceptional characters have any decisive effect upon political life. Information, contacts, experience, all were lacking; neither training nor opportunity was present.

Today opportunity (in the shape of formally granted rights) is open, but where schooling is still inadequate and the traditional attitudes pertaining to the type of family we have just described are changing only slowly, training often lags behind. It is probably not an accident that out of all the South and South-East Asian peoples for whom the patrilocal extended family was traditional the women who have so far shown themselves most politically advanced come from the upper-middle and middle classes of India, and, in rather lesser numbers, Pakistan. These are the classes in which modern education has made most headway, and where family structure has been much modified, as we shall see; they are also those where women took an active, often leading, part in the struggles for national independence. Dr. Nayer and

Dr. Dube both underline the significance of this practical training.

By contrast, political consciousness is apparently less highly developed among Overseas Chinese women. Both Ann Wee and Foong Wong mention the modifications of traditional Chinese family structure brought about in Singapore by the effects of migration, urbanization and the influence of British colonial law, and it is well known that schooling there is widespread, even for girls; but these things alone have clearly not been enough, or Ann Wee could not have described Chinese women in Singapore as being uninterested in politics as she did in an article published in 1954 in the book, *The Status of Women in South-East Asia*, edited by Dr. A. Appadorai. At least until more recently than that they have had little practice in active political campaigning.

Where the traditional kinship structure did not produce patrilocal extended family households, where there is no tradition of *purdah* or close seclusion, or where recent political history has followed different lines, the situation is different. In Burma or Thailand, for example, women have long held property in their own right, and often managed it, and have been accustomed to handling business of many kinds on their own behalf outside the family circle. Our figures of women retail traders in these two countries make this quite clear. Members of small, simple (or 'nuclear') two-generation family households usually with near relatives living close at hand, these Asian women have been subjected neither to the overriding rule of mother-in-law as in India or China, nor to the overriding demands of domesticity, as in the West. The number of roles open to them having long been relatively large, 'the vote' is not regarded as the necessary precondition and guarantee of other kinds of freedom, which it undoubtedly was (and probably still is) in most countries of the West. Moreover Burma's attainment of national independence was not preceded by a long country-wide campaign of anti-colonial resistance in which women could learn the practices of political activity, and Thailand is the one country of our whole region which never came under colonial rule at all. In each of these countries, too, the franchise was granted fairly freely (and early). Considerations such as these probably go far towards explaining the relative 'apathy' towards political affairs which our contributors report. If our diagnosis so far has been correct, we are now in a position to suggest a number of hypotheses to explain how it came about that out of the very various conditions prevailing in the different countries of our region have issued apparently very similar, smooth and rapid revolutions in the political status of women. However, before doing so we must clarify our use of terms a little further.

We earlier drew a distinction between holding the franchise and holding political office, both of which are comprised in the idea of emancipation. We now draw attention to two further usages: the first refers to a general level of freedom to engage in social and economic as well as political activity without restriction or supervision; this is the most generalized usage. The second refers to a degree of active political awareness, such as would be implied if one heard it said: 'Of course, only the women who have actually joined in [such and such political organization or activity] can be said to be truly emancipated.'

There are thus at least four quite separate notions included under the one label 'emancipation of women'; it is not useful to confuse them. In the following analysis, which has relevance for all four, they are distinguished as: the holding of the franchise, the holding of office, ability to engage in activities outside the home, and level of political awareness, respectively. With the exception of the last, all are easily measurable in terms of the numbers of women taking part. The level of political awareness can only be gauged by opinion, though the extent of women's membership in organized political associations could perhaps be used as a more objective measure were full data on the subject available.

Let us now consider the countries we have already discussed briefly. If we set aside the common modern factors (such as Western-type education) which differ mainly only in degree throughout, we can isolate three other main sets of conditions which appear to have relevance for all four kinds of emancipation.

First, there are sociological conditions: in Burma and Thailand the social structure of family households, their location and the division of labour between the sexes have traditionally tolerated the relative mobility of women and their engaging in occupations outside the home. In these countries we found a minimum of opposition to their being granted the franchise at the same time as men, but very few women are in political office and there is a generally rather low degree of political awareness. On the other hand, the present-day level of ability to engage in activities outside the home is still high—as witness the figures we have already quoted. In India, Pakistan and the homeland of the Overseas Chinese, by contrast, family structure and the traditional division of labour and responsibility between the sexes largely immobilized women except in the lower economic ranges. Equal franchise was not granted early in these societies, nor is the general freedom to engage in occupations outside the home even yet very marked. Among the Overseas Chinese the political apathy we might expect from such conditions does appear, but in India and Pakistan this is not so. There, albeit overwhelmingly among the upper-middle and middle classes in the towns, there is a relatively high level of political awareness and India at least can even show a relatively large number of women holding political office.

To explain this apparent contradiction we must turn to our second set of conditions: namely, historical. The active part that Indian and Pakistani women, especially—but not exclusively—of these social classes, took in anti-colonial struggles is sufficient to account for their political awareness. It is also probably the explanation for the relatively high number of women in office in India, and the ease with which the franchise was granted after Independence in both countries. A cynic might suggest that it was a series of lucky chances which brought the hardships and opportunities of anti-colonial struggle to just those countries whose women most needed them.

He would have to add, however, that they appear to have been less successful agents of change in Pakistan than in India. To explain this difference we refer to a third set of factors: religion.

We do not follow the lead of most previous writers on the position of women in the Orient who have, almost without exception, emphasized the paramount significance of religion. We find this unsatisfactory partly because the differences in this respect between the major religions of the region are often not clearly explained, and partly because it tends to mask other factors which we consider sociologically more significant. It is always sociologically unsound to argue as if social facts were derived from religious beliefs and rituals and did not exist in their own right. There is enough evidence from other parts of the world to show that the two basically different types of traditional family structure we have just mentioned as pertaining respectively to India, Pakistan and China, on the one hand, and Burma and Thailand, on the other, would have had their own characteristic effects upon the status of women in these countries quite irrespective of the prevailing religious systems. The various divisions of Hinduism and Islam and the mixture of Confucianism, Taoism and Buddhism, which was the religious background of traditional China, deeply influenced the social systems in which they have flourished, but they did not produce them. Perhaps we should add that we do not argue the other way (namely, that religious beliefs and rituals are simply a product of social structure) either. The relationship is one of subtle mutual influence, differing with different religious and social systems, and at different historical periods.

These differences are important. Although it is always to be expected that traditional religious attitudes will reflect and support traditional social practices and will probably be rather slow to change, the degree and effectiveness of their conservative influence differ considerably with differences in dogma and ecclesiastical organization. This is not the place, nor have we the space, to develop this argument fully, but very briefly stated it is that of the four major religions found in South and South-East Asia, only one, Islam, is inevitably resistant to change in general, and change in the position of women in particular.

Hinduism, despite its close hold over family and marriage, its special ideals of womanhood, its theories of caste and pollution, comprises an essentially flexible system of dogma, inclusive rather than exclusive, in which there is room for a huge variety of interpretations and many sects. Its long perspective, with its cyclical view of history as an endless rhythm of good and evil and its doctrine of reincarnation, teaches a sovereign non-attachment which is ultimately incompatible with too close a concern with the details of secular life. Moreover, its organization is far indeed from the monolithic, theocratic ideal which is Islam's, and gives no scope for enforcing an over-all supervision of secular matters. India today is a secular State. Very similar remarks can be made about the Buddhism of Burma, Cambodia, Ceylon, Laos and Thailand. Philosophically and doctrinally it shares the ideal of non-attachment to the things of this world which an unendingly long view of history and a firm belief in reincarnation render essentially illusory. For Hinayana Buddhists the true religious life is lived apart from the world, in the monasteries; the details of secular social organization are therefore of secondary importance, and change in them is not necessarily intolerable. Daw Mi Mi Khaing's article below adds practical evidence of this state of affairs.

For Christianity and Islam the situation is otherwise. Both monotheisms, both based upon revealed scriptures, they are both also exclusive religions with histories of the persecution and fighting of heretics and unbelievers. Unlike Hindus and Buddhists, neither Christians nor Moslems regard the experience of earthly life as an illusion, both (in most of their forms) maintaining that a truly religious life can be lived in the world. For each this necessarily argues a very close concern indeed with even the smallest details of everyday secular life. But Christianity is both more flexible in its interpretation of scripture (many forms of Christianity allowing also for new revelation through the Church) and less all-embracing in its organization than Islam. Christian doctrine, even at the height of the temporal power of the Church, has always looked upon the State as a separate entity, a necessary concession to human sinfulness, not as a means to attain the other-worldly purposes of life which are the business of the Church. Thus change is allowed for, and a separation between secular and sacred maintained. But this is not so in Islam. There, in theory at least, there can be no distinction between sacred and secular, with the result that not only the life of the individual but the whole of society, the State, the army, all things are subject to specific prescriptions issued by the Lord, and issued once for all, through His Prophet.[3] In such a system any social change is necessarily difficult to accommodate. And the

[3]This exposition follows that of Grunebaum, in *Islam, Essays in the Nature and Growth of a Cultural Tradition* (1955).

roles and statuses of women, being laid down in the Holy Koran, are at least as immutable as anything else. We have no need to feel surprised at the greater conservatism of Pakistan.

Our hypothesis is, then, that the general freedom of women to engage in activities outside their homes, their holding the franchise, their holding public office, and their political consciousness are connected with (among other things) one or more of the following sets of factors: first, a non-restricting traditional family structure and division of labour (what we mean by this will be made more clear in the fourth section of this essay); second, a history of prolonged anti-colonial (or possibly other) political struggle in which women played a full part; third, a religious system which can accommodate at least a fair degree of social change.

Table 8A and 8B are set out for comparison. They demonstrate (8A) the

Table 8A. Women's emancipation in Burma, India, Pakistan, Singapore, Thailand

	Burma	India	Pakistan	Singapore	Thailand
Traditional family and division of labour non-restricting	+	–	–	–	+
Women's participation in prolonged anti-colonial or other political struggle	–	+	+	–	–
Dominant religion relatively tolerant of change[1]	+	+	–	+	+

Table 8B

	Burma	India	Pakistan	Singapore	Thailand
(a) Early franchise	+				+
(b) Franchise with independence		+	+	+	
Relatively many women in political office	–	+	–	–	–
Relative freedom to engage in activities outside the home (present day)[2]	+	Increasing	Increasing only slowly	Increasing	+
Relative political awareness of women[3]	–	+	?	–	–

+ = presence of trait. – = absence of trait. ? = data not adequate.

[1] The table distinguishes between Islam on the one hand, and Hinduism, Buddhism, etc., on the other. This is obviously an oversimplification.

[2] Educational standards of women, and degree of economic development are assumed to be constant. This is obviously not true to the facts (see below).

[3] 'Relative political awareness' is a subjective estimate based mainly on the estimates made in the articles which follow, and first-hand experience of the Chinese groups.

different incidence of these three factors in the five countries we have discussed so far, and (8B) the relative distribution of the four aspects of women's emancipation which we have distinguished.

Some of the variations are fairly clearly concomitant. Experience of political struggle and degree of political awareness appear to vary together; so, too, it seems do family structure and the relative ability of women to engage in activities outside their homes; Pakistan differs from all the rest in type of religion, and from those with similar kinds of family structure in the relative slowness of her women to enter employment. None of these correlations occasions any surprise, but setting them out side by side does help to make them clearer.

Let us now tabulate what we know of the other countries of our region in a similar way (see Tables 9A and 9B). Our readers can then, if they wish, further test our whole analysis against their readings in Part II of this book.

We confine our detailed discussion of these tables to the data from Ceylon, Indonesia (Java), and the Philippines.

It might have been expected that the women of Ceylon would have been granted the vote only after the attainment of national independence, but in fact it came in 1931—the first in Asia. Just under thirty years later Ceylon produced the world's first woman Prime Minister. Neither of these two 'firsts' could have been predicted from the facts recorded in Table 9A, nor, indeed, from Mrs. Siriwardena's picture of the life of Ceylon women. But they are somewhat misleading. Great though Mrs. Bandaranaike's achievement is, her position is partly a legacy from her deceased husband; and the early granting of the franchise was due to the then British Colonial Government's decision to take advantage of the 1931 revision of the constitution in an attempt to draw in women's personal interest in such matters as the incidence of maternal mortality, at that time very high. The fact remains that there is a very big disparity between the very few who have achieved highest position or do show political awareness and the general many in Ceylon.

It should go without saying that this kind of disparity exists everywhere, and by no means only in the East (or only among women). Our discussion of India and Pakistan, for example, has been seriously lopsided because we have concentrated upon the upper and middle classes. It remains our general impression, however, that even comparing similar social classes, Ceylon's politically advanced women are proportionately fewer than India's. We connect this with the fact that they have not had to struggle either for national independence or the franchise.

What of Indonesia? For the sake of simplicity (and for no other reason) we have confined our tabulation to those parts of Indonesia (Java, for example) in which simple (nuclear) family households (father, mother, unmarried

Table 9A. Women's emancipation in Cambodia, Ceylon, Indonesia (Java), Laos, Federation of Malaya, Philippines, Viet-Nam

	Cambodia	Ceylon	Indonesia (Java)	Laos	Federation of Malaya	Philippines	Viet-Nam
Traditional family and division of labour non-restricting	+	–	+	+	+	+	–
Women's participation in prolonged anti-colonial or other political struggle	Post-1945	–	+	Post-1945	–	+	Post-1945
Dominant religion relatively tolerant of social change	+	+	–	+	–	+	+

Table 9B

	Cambodia	Ceylon	Indonesia (Java)	Laos	Federation of Malaya	Philippines	Viet-Nam
(a) Early franchise		+				+	
(b) Franchise granted with independence	+		+	+	+		+
Relatively many women in political office	–	–	–	–	–	–	–
Relative freedom to engage in activities outside the home	+	–	+	+	–	+	+?
Relative political awareness of women	–?	–	+	–?	–	+	+?

+ = presence of trait. – = absence of trait. ? = data not adequate.

children) are the usual type, and women's property rights are guaranteed not only by Islamic law but also by traditional local custom. About 85 per cent of the people of Indonesia are Moslems, but even so Javanese family structure has not been fundamentally altered, and Javanese women retain a great deal of the traditional freedom to engage in activities outside the home which we have come to expect from the previous examples of Burma and Thailand. The difference between Java and Pakistan in this respect is extreme. (Incidentally, it provides an excellent demonstration of our earlier argument in favour of the greater sociological significance of family structure than religion, while underlining also the astonishing durability of family structure in the face even of Islam.) Family structure and recent political history being what they have been in Java—the Dutch withdrawal in 1949 having been preceded by a long and bitter anti-colonial struggle in which women played a full part with men—the present situation as recorded in Table 9B follows our expectations.

The Philippines gives us the most striking example of rapid advance for women on all fronts. Here is a country where the traditional equality between the sexes that we have learnt to expect from the simple family system (and which Robert Fox also reports) was partially removed, though only for the upper classes, by 300 years of Spanish rule, only to emerge with great vigour in the last half-century under the United States Government's policy of equality of opportunity and free education. This last, which does not appear in our tables, was as we have seen, more widespread earlier than in any other country in our region, and there is no doubt it was crucial. Certainly the achievement of Filipino women in education, business, social welfare and the professions has been remarkable; they are in general well organized and politically aware—so much so that at the lower levels of political life, particularly during election campaigns, their voice is said to affect substantially the political climate of the whole nation.

If both recent government policy and traditional family structure have been favourable to women's emancipation in the Philippines, religion has been a conservative influence which probably most Filipino women have welcomed, at least as regards its refusal to countenance divorce. In the last resort, too, all forms of Christianity are committed to accepting the full equality of women with men. As for the training ground of long anti-colonial struggle, that too has not been lacking, for Filipino women took an active part in helping to overthrow Spanish rule, as well as against the United States occupation in its early days and in the resistance to the Japanese in the Second World War. Thus from our present point of view women in the Philippines may be said to have had everything on their side—the only ones in our tables to have three 'plus' signs in the first series.

Perhaps we have already spent too long on what at this stage can only be a preliminary discussion of some of the factors which may have contributed towards the apparent ease and rapidity of the general political emancipation of women in South and South-East Asia over the last thirty years or so. If we have concentrated particularly upon family structure, upon the history of national independence and, though less strongly, upon religion, it is not because we believe that these are the only matters of significance, but because we do think them peculiarly important. This applies most especially to the first set of factors, family structure, and our readers are asked to look upon the analysis we have just been making as a kind of preliminary sketch for the fuller treatment of this subject which occupies the next section of this chapter.

But now, what of the second question we posed at the outset of this section? What are the practical results of women's participation in political life—we do not mean their 'success' or otherwise in the usual feminist sense, but the results in everyday life? What are the effects of their being in office, of exercising the right to vote?

As for women in office, or even in any kind of full-time or policy-making role in political life, it is frequently and correctly remarked how few they are in any country in the world. Our tables show a typical state of affairs. Even in the Philippines, since 1941 when the first woman entered the House of Representatives there has been but one woman chosen in every election, and only one in the Senate. Even the situation in India may not be long-lived; indeed there is a curious set of facts from the analysis of the last general election in India[4] which shows that those areas and constituencies in which the standard of women's education was highest returned fewest women members, even produced fewest women candidates—but we need more study and much more comparative material to make sense of this phenomenon. The fact is that nowhere in the world are there many women in high political position.

This is, of course, in one sense nothing more than a reflection of the general paucity of women in the upper ranks of most other kinds of employment. It is probably to be explained largely in a similar way—that is, by the lack of equal educational opportunity, the inhibition of appropriate experience and inculcation of inappropriate attitudes, the practical difficulties of combining both domestic and outside responsibilities, and so on. But where posts which entail policy-making and the exercise of power are concerned, that is not all. Women do in fact remain at a disadvantage in appointment to leading and managing positions in almost all kinds of occupation (except those which employ solely female labour, and sometimes even

[4] Published in *The Status of Women in South-East Asia* (Longmans, 1954).

there)—and in politics. As we have said, politics is in the last resort a matter of power, and, by and large, power remains a male prerogative. Despite the very great variations which undoubtedly exist between individual countries, we would expect Eastern and Western women to be in much the same predicament here. It is not for nothing that Mrs. Pandit—and she must know—has written of herself as a woman in a man's world.

In countries where the seclusion of women has been traditional, life is often exceedingly difficult for those few women who have emerged into this man's world. Even in those (rather few) Western countries where the free mingling of the sexes in social life is common, one often hears a woman of ambition and talent complaining of the difficulty of keeping abreast with her male colleagues into whose informal social life she cannot easily enter. And it is through informal social contacts that much significant professional and political business is conducted. An Indian or Pakistani woman may find this same situation far more difficult, the separation of the sexes having been traditionally so marked that there may at the outset appear to be virtually no respectable social patterns available for her and her male colleagues to model their professional relationships upon.

Professional women and women politicians in Asian countries without the tradition of seclusion are likely to find themselves in much the same situation as Western women, or perhaps rather more so, owing to the rather greater separation of the sexes in ordinary social intercourse. In many cases, as Daw Mi Mi Khaing and Daw Ni Ni make us understand so warmly, this is a situation which is accepted with grace, even welcomed. But it does not make for the advancement of women in new political roles.

But we must remember the distinction we drew at the beginning between holding political office and exercising the franchise. All the available evidence goes to show that enthusiasm for the role of voter is at present a characteristic of South and South-East Asian women in general. It would obviously be as unwise to assume that every illiterate village woman who casts her vote does so with complete understanding of all the issues at stake as to assume the same thing for every illiterate village man. Descriptions of the first national elections in India tell of some women who appeared to pay exactly the same reverences to the ballot boxes as to the Hindu altars in their own homes. But they voted. Indeed they flocked to the polls. Yet there was no compulsion. And in the towns at least there is evidence that their votes were often cast quite independently: women did not necessarily vote as their husbands did. They discharged their duties as citizens in their own right.

What are we to make of these things?

First, it is again obvious but necessary to point out that voting is not a full-time job. Occurring once and then not again for a matter of years, and taking the minimum of time to perform, voting in a national election creates no problems for domestic organization. Polling day can be, usually is, regarded as a holiday, a welcome break in daily routine, not an interruption. Reciprocally, the actual casting of the vote has virtually no effect upon traditional roles.

But what about its implications? We know already that wives do not always vote the same way as husbands even in the most conservative areas of our region, and even where patrilocal extended families with a 'patriarchal' type of organization have long been traditional. A vote is an individual matter. It cannot be doubted that this must have some effect—long term in most cases no doubt, and additional to many other modern influences, but nevertheless significant—upon the structure of families and the traditional roles of women in them.

But this is one of the topics of the next section of this present chapter, to which we must now direct our attention.

TRADITIONAL INSTITUTIONS: FAMILY ROLES AND THEIR MODIFICATION

Only two social tasks are everywhere inescapably sex-linked: the begetting and the bearing of children. Apart from these infinite variety is possible, though as far as we know all social systems do in fact make other sex linkages more or less rigidly. Men can make excellent child-minders, but in the absence of artificial feeding babies have to be suckled, so it is more convenient for child care to be a female occupation; cooking, cleaning and other domestic jobs can be done by people of either sex, but it is more economical to give them to those who are already anchored to the home by the small children. It is probable that such simple principles as these underlie the almost universal practice of handing over child care and household work to women. Further than this, as the well-known studies by Margaret Mead have demonstrated, generalizations about what are the 'right' or 'proper' or 'universal' or 'natural' roles of men and women simply will not take us. Variations exist even between the different social groups and classes of a single country, still more from one country to another. No matter how much it conflicts with popular belief, we have to agree that there was not a single traditional 'Oriental' conception of women's role and status any more than there was a single 'Western' one.

In this section of our essay we first suggest certain explanations for the differences which have long characterized the traditional interpretations of the roles of 'wife', 'mother' and 'daughter' in different parts of South and South-East Asia, and then consider some of the effects of modern innovations.

The significance of traditional kinship systems

We have several times referred to the significance of family structure, but we have not yet set out what we understand by this term. At the same time, it should have been quite clear that there are several different types of family structure to be found (and traditionally) in South and South-East Asia. In order to relate these differences to their sociological contexts, and to understand their significance for our subject matter, we must make a brief foray into the general theory of kin relationships.

Under 'kin relationships' or 'kinship' we include all social relationships which can be plotted on a family tree (genealogy, pedigree). These obviously include family relationships, relationships by marriage (affinal relationships), by descent, and so forth. Within the general category of kinsmen so defined there are nearly always certain particular groupings which are known in English as 'families'. We use this word to refer to a group of people related by marriage and descent (including adoption) who customarily live together and share a common household budget. The family, then, in our present usage, is simply the domestic unit of relatives, and we do not use the word in any other sense. Thus it refers to a hybrid concept, defined partly by genealogical relationship, partly by residence and partly by the economic criterion of shared consumption. All three criteria are essential.

The first, however, is elastic. Although groups of this general nature exist practically everywhere in the world, it is well known that the genealogical ties between their members are by no means always the same. So we can distinguish formally between the simple family (also known as the 'nuclear' family, the 'biological' family, etc.), which comprises father, mother and unmarried children, and various types of compound family. Compound families consist in effect of a number of simple families linked together either by the further marriages of (usually only one of) the spouses (polygamy), or by bringing in the spouses of adult children, or both. The first method gives rise to the polygynous family (father, mothers, unmarried children) or the polyandrous family (fathers, mother, unmarried children), which is rare; the second to various types of extended family (a three- (or more) generation family) of which the patrilocal version is the most common in our region. In the patrilocal extended family married sons stay with their fathers and bring their brides home to join them with the result that the group comes to include father, mother, unmarried daughters, sons, sons' wives, sons' children. Such a family may also be polygynous. Matrilocal extended families, in which brides stay with their mothers, though predominating locally in parts of Malaya and Indonesia (and elsewhere), are not widespread in our region.

The term 'joint family' does not appear in this classification. We find it more useful to restrict this to legal rather than sociological use. As a term which has special connotations wherever Indian legal codes apply, it is not strictly relevant elsewhere.

It seems likely that other things being equal the traditional status of women has often been rather higher and their roles often less restricted in simple than in compound forms of family structure. Within a simple family the wife is subordinate to no other woman, and because of the sexual division of labour her occupational status *vis-à-vis* her husband is likely to be complementary rather than inferior. Moreover, the hands to do all the necessary work being few, a wife is likely to have to take a part in management and policy-making for the group as a whole. This is especially probable in a subsistence economy, or among small-holding agriculturalists, or in cottage industries, where the family itself is the unit of production, or in small-scale family trading business. All our contributors are agreed that the traditional status of women within the family has been relatively higher, and their activity less restricted, in the lower socio-economic classes in, say, India, Pakistan, Ceylon or among the Chinese, than in the upper classes. People with lower incomes could not usually afford to build up large extended families or to maintain several wives, and their families were, therefore, usually of the simple type; at the same time they were likely to be gaining their livelihood in ways which required the wives' as well as the husbands' economic contribution.

The traditional ideal of the extended patrilocal family (often polygynous) which existed in these countries was, generally speaking, realized only by the relatively well-to-do. Among them virtually no adult married woman could avoid a period of subordination to her mother-in-law, and very many women (young widows, wives of younger sons, for example) could hardly have been able to look forward to attaining any sort of position of real authority in the home. At the same time the economic contribution which women made to the family's livelihood in the upper economic classes was negligible. The sharing of tasks and interests between the sexes was likely to be at a minimum. When to this was joined, as in all these countries it was, a set of values which required the more or less complete seclusion of a respectable man's female relatives, and their very early arranged marriage, it is obvious that these traditional extended family systems set narrow limits to the number and scope of the roles available to women, and often denied them power even at home. The traditional family structures of India, Pakistan, Ceylon and China thus present us with a paradox in that in certain senses women whose fortune it was to be poor enjoyed higher status than those who were rich.

In Burma, Thailand, the Philippines and most parts of Malaya and Indonesia this did not apply. There traditional families at all socio-economic levels were simple families. We have already noticed that these—especially the first three

—are the countries in which proportionately more women have entered paid employment and received higher education. Can we assume that this is because of their simple family structure? We think that there is a close connection, but that the argument is not quite so simple as that.

We earlier used the phrase 'other things being equal'. They seldom are. Family systems are subject to non-family pressures which may well be strong enough to modify their influence. We have already put forward some of our arguments against those writers on the position of women in Asia who have emphasized only the religious pressures, but we do not deny that the influence of religious and ideological systems can be very great. So, too, we must consider the influence of occupational systems and systems of stratification, of political and legal systems, and of the wider kinship systems in which families themselves are embedded. As we have already discussed religion and politics—and will have to mention them again—we will deal here mainly with socio-economic, kinship and legal matters.

We have just mentioned the significance of a family's means of livelihood. In simple families which are themselves units of production, a wife's (mother's) position is inevitably fairly strong. But this may be reversed if the source of livelihood is one which employs the husband separately and takes him away from home, as has been the tradition now for a long time in most parts of the West. If, further, as in the contemporary and nineteenth-century West, prestige is derived largely or even partly from economic achievement as such, there may be a tendency to denigrate domestic work at home—i.e., 'women's work'—which is not economically priced. At the same time domestic work, being a form of manual labour, has little prestige on its own account. The abundance of domestic servants which existed in nineteenth-century Europe made possible the emergence of the 'lady' whose freedom from domestic chores was regarded as an index of her husband's social and economic success, and not at all as an opportunity to gain education and enter the world of occupations outside the home, from which indeed the prevailing sexual division of labour long continued to exclude her.

In such circumstances the situation of middle- and upper-class women in Europe (the Americas and other areas of European settlement overseas had their special differences) was remarkably similar to that of their sisters in the patrilocal extended family systems of India, Pakistan, Ceylon and China.

Legally, too, their position was similar. A hundred years ago the status of a married woman in England was as stated by Blackstone: '. . . the very being and legal existence of the wife is suspended during marriage, or at least is incorporated in that of her husband. . . . But though our law in general considers man and wife as one person, yet there are some instances in which she is considered inferior to him and acting by his compulsion.' Only in 1882 were married English women given the full right to the enjoyment, management and disposition of their own property. In 1923 they were allowed to claim divorce on the same grounds as men, and in 1925 permitted equality at law with their husbands in the guardianship of their children. The doctrine that a man and his wife are one person and that person the husband is not dead even in the England of today.

There is an interesting study waiting to be made of the comparative influence of differing economic systems and legal codes upon family structure in the West, but this one example will have to suffice here to show the effect occupational and legal factors may have. By the nineteenth century—and for a considerable period previously—the simple family system of England was almost as strongly biased in favour of male dominance as any patrilocal extended family system.

We have already seen that this latter system where it existed in India, Pakistan, Ceylon or China, went with a division of occupation which kept family women at home. The legal status of wives, too, though not identical in each place, was compatible with their social inferiority. In all four countries women were traditionally regarded as perpetual legal minors, whose affairs must be conducted for them by others; divorce, if permitted at all, was harder for women to obtain than men; guardianship of children (except when they were very young) rested with the father and his male kinsmen; inheritance rights of daughters were either limited or non-existent. Our contributors from these countries give ample illustration of the practical effect of these limitations, and tell us as much again about the modern changes that are being made. To these we shall return.

What of the legal position in the simple family areas of Burma, Thailand, the Philippines, Malaya and Indonesia? Here daughters traditionally inherited equally with sons; guardianship of children was usually a matter for mutual convenience; divorce—though certainly easier for men in Moslem Malaya and Indonesia—could be initiated by either party; adult women—though with disabilities in Moslem areas—were not regarded as minors. The differences are striking indeed.

To try to explain them solely in terms of family structure, however, would be to beg the question. This is where we must look to the wider kinship system in which family structure itself is enmeshed, and with which local customary law is always closely connected. Setting aside the somewhat special case of Ceylon for the moment, we can state formally that the difference between the predominating kinship systems of India, Pakistan, Viet-Nam, China on the one hand, and Burma, Thailand, the Philippines, Laos, Cambodia, Malaya and the simple family areas of Indonesia (we have in mind mainly the Javanese) on the other, is that whereas the former are patrilineal the latter are what we shall call radial systems. In the next few paragraphs we explain what we mean by this difference and the ways in which we believe it to be crucial for our subject.

When an English-speaking person talks of 'my relatives' he has in mind all those who could be placed anywhere on his own family tree. Each kinsman and kinswoman in the total aggregate of relatives can be imagined as occupying a point on one of the circumferences of a series of concentric circles centred upon the speaker (to whom anthropological jargon usually gives the nickname 'Ego'). The only thing such points necessarily have in common is some kind of radial relationship with the centre of the circles—Ego. This radially reckoned collection of relatives on both sides and in all lines is usually termed Ego's kindred. His kindred includes, of course, his family, but where as a family is by definition a corporate group (sharing at least residence and a common budget) a kindred is not. Membership of a kindred does not, therefore, entail responsibilities towards all the other members jointly, but simply connects one in a particular way (the way of kinship) with a series of individuals. Whether or not one uses these connections is usually a matter for personal choice, but it is commonly found that people do make use of them for support in illness or other trouble, on ceremonial occasions (such as a family wedding or funeral), and for raising loans, making business contacts and so on.

Every people we know of reckons kinship radially like this. A very large number of peoples, including most Western and South-East Asian peoples, use no other method. The result is that for them families and kindreds, as we have defined them, are the only recognized aggregates of kinsfolk. Such kinship systems are usually termed 'bilateral' or 'non-unilineal'; in some ways the term 'radial' which we have used here is more useful. A pure type of radial system would give equal weighting to males and females, with the result that the monogamous simple family, living separately, would be usual and such kin-linked matters as rights of inheritance would be equally held by both sexes.

Equal balance of this kind does appear to exist in our region among the Iban and the Land Dayak peoples of Borneo, for example, aboriginal peoples whom we have not mentioned before. It is less in evidence among more sophisticated peoples, but very nearly exists among the Burmese, the Filipinos and some others. The kind of upper- and middle-class English system we have just discussed is today approaching the pure type of radial system after a prolonged period of weighting on the male side (probably to be ascribed partly to ecclesiastical and legal influences derived from the patrilineal systems of Judea and ancient Rome); there is some evidence that some lower-class English systems are, or have been, slightly biased towards the female side. The connection between these differences on the one hand, and differences and changes in the distribution of various kinds of property and in mobility, occupational status, and political, legal and religious pressures on the other, requires much more detailed discussion than we can give it here.

But it certainly has a bearing on our subject matter; for it is obvious that the more nearly a radial system of kinship approaches to the pure type, the more equally balanced are the rights and duties, and with them the roles and statuses, of men and women. The countries of our region in which radial systems predominate are Burma, Thailand, Cambodia, Laos, the Philippines, Borneo (which we have not mentioned previously), Malaya and parts of Indonesia. These are, as we should now expect, the simple family areas, and we have already argued some of the consequences for women of this. We can now see that they are also likely to be the areas in which women have equal rights to inherit and own property. And this is so.

But not all these radial systems are of the pure type. The effect of Islam in Malaya and Indonesia, for example, has been to introduce a certain male bias; Robert Fox argues that more than three hundred years of Spanish rule had a somewhat similar effect upon the upper-class systems in the Philippines, now thrown off in so far as legal status is conceived, but lingering still in attitudes; where polygyny exists outside Islam, too, as to some extent, though decreasingly, among the Thais and, still less, the Burmese, an element of male bias is inevitable. (In Laos, on the other hand, the custom of living with or near the wife's parents may impart some female bias, such as has been suggested also for certain areas of working-class England; but a tendency to live nearer the wife's rather than the husband's kin if both are not equally nearby is also reported from Java and elsewhere. It seems likely to be more a matter of practical convenience than of basic family structure. But we shall return to this point again.)

A detailed working out of the various differences between these several radial kinship systems of South-East Asia and their influence upon the reciprocal status and respective roles of men and women in the family and beyond is outside the scope of this essay, but enough has been said to demonstrate their significance. The chapters which follow—particularly Daw Mi Mi Khaing's on Burma, the Hanks' on Thailand and Robert Fox's on the Philippines—provide ample illustration. A glance at the contrast presented by the predominantly patrilineal systems traditional in India, Pakistan and China will make the point even clearer.

In these countries, as in many others, the predominant kinship systems are somewhat more complicated. In addition to the radial reckoning of all relatives, there is the custom of emphasizing certain kinds of relatives—those linked by common descent in the male line—more than others. In most Western countries, there is a custom—historically fairly recent—of using surnames. Though there are variations in their employment, Western surnames are usually handed on from fathers to their sons and unmarried daughters. Women do not transmit surnames to their children. In other words, in so far as the surname in the West is inherited, it is inherited unilineally (i.e., through one parent only)—and indeed patrilineally (i.e., through fathers). It is likely that this fact has helped to introduce some of the male bias we have noted in Western radial systems. (It is noteworthy that there were no surnames in traditional Burma or Thailand, that the Filipino ones were introduced by the Spanish, and that the method of naming after the father used in Malaya and Indonesia is strictly Islamic.) But Western surnames, though they do mark off patrilineally related kin from others, are not in fact much more than useful identification marks. In traditional India, Pakistan, China, the principle of patrilineal descent was taken much further.

Above all, it was a framework for the formation of kin groups of a kind unknown to purely radial kin systems. This may be seen in its clearest form in traditional China. The Chinese use surnames patrilineally inherited by both sons and daughters (traditionally a Chinese woman did not take her husband's surname on marriage). But these were more than mere identification labels. Strictly speaking, it was held that all bearers of the same surname were ultimately descendants of the same distant common ancestor, and as such they were forbidden to marry one another. In its widest extension (stretching over more than 2,000 miles of territory and possibly several mutually unintelligible dialects) a Chinese surname group could contain many hundreds of thousands of individuals. They could clearly never form a fully corporate group, and indeed their only shared activity was the general interdiction on intermarriage; but even this goes far beyond the requirements of a 'surname group' in radial reckoning Europe. Locally, however, those who bore the same Chinese surname could recognize and trace the details of their common ancestry, and did in fact often form a close-knit corporate unit. In south-east China (the original homeland of most of the Overseas Chinese in our region) it was common to find a whole village occupied solely by members of one such local surname group (and their wives) who organized local surname temples, schools and so on, and regarded themselves as a largely self-contained unit against all the world. To such groups as these, gaining their membership by shared and traced unilineal descent from a single common known ancestor, social anthropologists give the name 'lineage'. (If, as in this case, descent is derived from fathers, the group is a patrilineage.) Unilineal reckoning does not supersede radial reckoning; it is merely additional to it; so a unilineal kinship system is also radial and can, therefore, form at least three different kinds of kin grouping: families (which may be of varying composition), kindreds and lineages. (The word 'clan' is usually reserved for wider unlineal groupings in which common descent is not actually traced but merely believed in. The widest Chinese surname groups we have just described would be examples.)

Now, in such a system as this, one overriding interest of the lineage is to perpetuate the male line. Daughters are inevitably less valued (though not necessarily less loved) than sons because they cannot help in this—worse, they leave on marriage to become active contributors to the growth of other lineages. Women in the local group are therefore either young unmarried girls or outsiders brought in as wives, essential for the production of new recruits for the lineage, but not themselves birthright members. It is not surprising that they should be regarded as of lower status than adult males who alone are full members. Obviously compatible with this state of affairs is the institution of polygyny—making the higher production of sons per father possible, but necessarily subordinating some women. Closely connected, too, is the ideal of building up a patrilocal extended family so that property, inherited by sons alone—daughters get a marriage portion which does not break up the estate, but no more—may be held together as long as possible. Again, it is only to be expected that in such a system divorce should be very difficult, if not impossible, and widows and their children should be under the control of the deceased husband's brothers or other male kin. All these things, which we have already noted, are documented in the articles by Ann Wee and Foong Wong below.

In traditional India (we are now writing of the days before the partition of the subcontinent between two separate States) the predominant types of kinship system were not altogether dissimilar from the Chinese. Without either the concept of the surname or the local single lineage villages of South China, most kinship reckoning in India nevertheless emphasized the male line and used it as the framework of family groupings. Like any other patrilocal extended family, the usual Indian 'joint family' (to give it its commonly used legal appellation) comprised in effect a small patrilineal core of males (which could be called a small patrilineage) together with their wives and children. On marriage the sons (full members) remained, the daughters moved out to make their contribution to the continuation of a different patriline. Property, especially if it consisted of real estate, was ideally kept undivided, being held jointly (not severally) by all male members of the group, relinquished rather than transmitted by those who died and entered into rather than inherited by those who were born. Women held rights to maintenance only.

Again it is obvious that such a system sets a premium on polygyny, and against divorce and the remarriage of widows, controlling women in the interests of the group—in effect, of the men—and denying them full property rights or the guardianship of children. In other words it necessarily places them in the position of minors.

It is interesting to note that whereas in the radial system of the Javanese (Indonesia) Islam appears to have imparted a male bias, in the patrilineal system of India it worked to some extent the other way. For under Islam a daughter is entitled to inherit property (though a lesser share than a son), polygyny is limited, and divorce and the remarriage of widows are permitted. Thus it was that upper-class Hindu women, who in many parts of India experienced the full influence of patrilineal kinship institutions backed, as Romila Tharpar shows us, by religious sanctions, were in several respects more restricted than their Moslem counterparts. (But, as we have already argued, Islam can impose a stronger control than Hinduism, and when modern changes began to flood in upon India, Hindu women often profited by them earlier than Moslems.) As for the radial systems of Java, the relatively slight male bias introduced by Islam seems to have been far less than the male dominance which existed in eighteenth- and nineteenth-century Europe, let alone in the patrilineal systems of India. Islam itself, of course, like Judaism, arose in a predominantly patrilineal area where the subordinate status of women was taken for granted.

We have now enough material to try to classify traditional (by which we mean, say, the eighteenth- and nineteenth-century) kinship systems of our area. We can place them in a graded series, stretching from the almost pure radial systems of aboriginal Borneo and traditional Burma through the slightly more male-biased radial systems of Laos, Cambodia, Thailand and the Philippines, and the Moslem-influenced radial systems of Malaya and Java to the more or less strictly male-dominated patrilineal systems of Moslem India, Hindu India, Viet-Nam and China. Though the exact order requires much more careful inquiry, we can set out the series tentatively as follows:

	Borneo
	Burma
	Laos
	Thailand
Radial	Cambodia
	Philippines
	Java
	Malaya
	Ceylon
	Moslem India
Patrilineal	Hindu India
	China

Ceylon, which we have so far omitted, occupies a kind of intermediate position. Traditional Ceylonese kinship was complex, but in general it appears to have been reckoned radially and to have allowed the inheritance of property by women. However, at least in areas where irrigated land was in short supply, a strong effort was made to meet the difficulties of land division which this would entail by restricting it in practice and building up extended patrilocal families, or, it seems, developing polyandry.

Our readers are invited to compare this graded list with the tables we have presented earlier, and to bear it in mind when reading the articles which follow. We believe that the facts recorded in our tables and the articles of our contributors together support our present hypothesis, which is, simply, that the reciprocal statuses of men and women are likely to be more nearly equal, and their respective roles less rigidly demarcated, among people who emphasize the radial rather than the unilineal reckoning of kin relationships.

Matrilineal reckoning requires fuller treatment than we can give it here. It occurs sporadically in our region, notably in Minangkabau (Sumatra, Indonesia) and Negri Sembilan (Malaya) and elsewhere, but is predominant in none of our countries. Briefly our argument would be that whereas a woman is likely to have a higher lineage status in a matrilineal system than in a patrilineal one, it does not follow that she has a higher status than a man. The point about matriliny is not that women are the recipients of inherited rights and positions (they often are not), but that these things can be transferred only through mothers. The analogy is with the genetic transmission of certain kinds of haemophilia (bleeding disease) which are found only in males but inherited only through females. Although the fact that her children are members of her own lineage group and not his may give a woman a certain measure of independence of her husband in a matrilineal system, her lineage status *vis-à-vis* her brothers may well be low and her roles relatively circumscribed. Our hypothesis is not affected.

Kinship and change

What of modern changes in traditional kinship? In general we see them tending in the direction of pure type radial systems. We have already remarked this tendency in the West, where, it is important to remember, eighteenth- and nineteenth-century systems of kinship, radial though they were, were much more male-biased than most South-East Asian ones. There is every reason to suppose that the essentially similar influences which are at work in the East will have similar effects.

One set of influences which we have not so far considered is the legal. Legal changes are discussed by many of our contributors, notably Romila Tharpar and Ann Wee. The ending of polygamy, the raising of the ages of consent and marriage, the granting of inheritance rights to widows and daughters, and so on—these and similar provisions are aimed directly at raising the status of women. They will have an indirect influence in the same direction too, for they are in effect attacks upon the principle of patrilineal descent and the patrilocal extended family. The degree to which legal changes are effective in practice is said to be small as yet. It is likely to grow.

It will grow because other changes are tending the same way. Anything which gives women the status of full adults in their own right before the law, allows them to own and manage property, gives them access to occupations and contacts outside the home is an attack on strict patriliny. Our contributors show us more than enough examples, and mention in their turn nearly all the innovations we have discussed earlier. We shall dwell upon only one: urbanization.

Professor Karim's is the most decided of our contributions on this subject. Women, he tells us, are much freer in the towns than in the villages of Pakistan. Why?

The reasons usually given are many. They include the contrast between the greater conservatism of villages, where everybody knows everybody else and no one dares to break customary conventions, and the relative anonymity of city life; the break-up of extended family living which the shortage of housing often brings about; the greater opportunities for employment, education, 'Westernization' and so on. Most of these points are valid though their weighting must vary greatly from place to place. It is unfortunate that detailed studies of what really happens when, for example, the members of a strictly patrilineal type of family and kinship unit come to town are so few.

One of the fullest is Maurice Freedman's book on *Chinese Family and Marriage in Singapore* (London, 1957). This makes it quite clear that one of the most significant concomitants of living in Singapore has been the virtually complete loss of the southern Chinese lineage system and the almost complete disappearance of polygynous extended families of the traditional type. Stephen Morris (in an article in the *British Journal of Sociology*, 1958) has recorded the somewhat similar disappearance of the legal joint family organization among the Indian and Pakistani immigrants in the towns of East Africa. Can we take it that this kind of thing is typical not only of immigrant communities overseas—obviously cut off from their home ties—but also of modern urbanization in general? It is our suggestion that we can—and that the evidence of our contributors supports us.

We must first distinguish between two conceptually different things: the custom of stressing the patrilineal line in reckoning kinship on the one hand, and the existence of exclusive corporate groups of patrilineal kinsmen on the other. What we wish to draw attention to is the effect upon these two things (in practice usually closely connected) of two particular aspects of modern urban life: first, economic relationships, and second, the legal and administrative framework in which they operate.

What a person in a modern town wants is a job, or a commercial or professional contact of some kind. To rely solely on one's patrikin for this would be as obviously foolish as to ignore them if they could be useful. One exploits any and every connection, or better still series of connections: one's acquaintances, friends, friends' friends, co-members in any and all sorts of organization, and, of course, all possible kinsmen. Neither in India nor China was it usual for people to rely on their relatives alone, even traditionally or even in the rural areas, and certainly not on their patrilineal relatives alone; but where matters of essential livelihood were concerned and income was derived from land they were usually more important. Where income is derived from employment in non-traditional occupations, from commerce, and the professions, as it is in a modern town, this is no longer so. There, radial linkages—in addition to non-kin ties, of course—are more valuable because they are more numerous and wide-spreading.

It is probable that commercial businesses and indeed any undertakings that require wide personal contacts (politics, for example) have always had this kind of effect for those who practise them. Be that as it may, we suggest here that in so far as the reckoning of kinship is concerned an economic system such as we find in most modern towns adds weight to radial rather than merely unilineal methods.

This might not necessarily weaken the use of patriliny for group formation, however, as the long continued existence of patrilocal extended families in many trading communities shows. A more direct attack upon patrilineal groupings appears to come from the legal and administration and the provision of certain social services—especially Ann Wee both have something to say on this topic, in addition to the points we have already raised. Our present comments are confined to economic matters.

The traditional South Chinese patrilineage never had much economic importance. Its practical *raison d'être* was closely bound up with the management of relationships with a particular form of local administration and the provision of certain social services—especially education—for its members. Neither of these tasks is necessary in the modern city of Singapore, or, indeed, in any well-run modern city. Even the substitutes for local lineage organization which developed in the early days among Singapore Chinese are now largely redundant.

Different factors can lead to somewhat similar results for the traditional patrilocal joint family of India and Pakistan. It should be obvious that in writing of this we do not have in mind the poorer sections of the population but the rather better-off who in traditional times would have built up extended families based solidly on joint property. Their modern counterparts are the people who now go ahead in business, the professions and the higher salaried positions. But it is hardly possible for any of these occupations to be run as a joint family enterprise today.

It is true that a pair of brothers may be partners, or a father and his sons form a company, and that various forms of so-called 'nepotism' may be discerned in the allocation of salaried posts; but none of these things is necessarily an indication of the persistence of the joint family in the strict legal sense, or even of the custom of living together in extended families. After all, similar 'familial' links can be found in similar concerns throughout the world, including many places where there is no tradition of extended family living or joint family property at all. Moreover—and this is the point—the legal and administrative framework of modern economic institutions is a modern innovation, developed originally in the West, different in principle from that of the joint family. This is obvious for institutions employing salaried workers, but is no less true for partnerships or companies whose members hold shares (for shares are owned severally not jointly), and they can be withdrawn.

Thus, to use the distinction drawn by Maine, the modern relationship between partners is contractual, the traditional relationship between members of a joint family was one of status. Once this change has been made, and property is no longer jointly held, the peculiar legal structure of the joint family—which we insisted earlier was its distinguishing mark—is destroyed. What is left may well be some kind of extended family dwelling group, bound by strong ties of affection and feelings of mutual dependence and obligation, which find expression in mutual assistance of all kinds and also in continued co-participation in family ritual observances. But these things alone do not constitute a 'joint family' in the strict (i.e., legal) sense. Furthermore, as our contributors show us, once the element of legal jointness has been removed, the component units of an extended family often set up separate households, though, of course, there is continued visiting, mutual assistance, and sharing in family rituals and ceremonies (as, indeed, there is between related families in radial kinship systems which have never developed extended family organization at all). It is interesting to note too—as Morris did in East Africa—how often at the present time business partners are in fact not patrilineal kinsmen at all.

We conclude, then, that the economic, administrative, and legal systems of modern towns are such that while they lend weight to radial (and non-kin) linkages they also undermine the importance of patriliny as a principle in the formation of corporate groups. The full working out of these tendencies is likely to be a slow process; at present all stages of the change are still to be seen. Moreover, by no means all towns are 'modern' in the respects we have picked out, and even in truly modern towns traditional occupations continue to be organized along largely traditional lines. Nevertheless, we claim that the trend away from patriliny is plainly built in to modern urbanization.

Indeed we go further and suggest that it is built in to modern economic systems in general. It is only because in our region towns are in effect still the only centres of modern economic organization that this appears to be an urban phenomenon. It will spread.

It is likely, of course, that however rapid economic development proves to be pockets of traditional economic structure will linger for a very long time, much as small-holding ('peasant') farming and family trading businesses still continue in the modern West. As far as kinship organization is concerned, however, this will make little difference to our prediction, for, as we have already seen, such small-scale enterprises as these were not usually organized in extended family units anyway, nor did their members pay much attention to lineage organization where this existed, either. In any event, the majority of the population is likely to be caught up in the developing modern systems, and as these will also be those of the well-to-do they will set the standard.

What will this standard be? We have argued a general tendency in the direction of a pure type radial system of kinship. Our earlier argument leads us to expect two interrelated concomitants of this: first, the general appearance of simple ('nuclear') family units, and second, the more equal balance of status and role between the sexes.

But other modern developments are working in the same direction. Urban housing, the need for mobility of labour, 'Westernization'—all require the simple family; modern world opinion demands the raising of the status of women. So, too, does modern economic growth which probably depends, even more than on the increasing employment of women as well as men, upon an increasingly numerous and discriminating set of consumers. Because of their special position in the family, wives and mothers are potentially society's most active buyers; but as long as the status of women is relatively low, and their role relatively restricted, the full effect of this particular spur to economic growth will not be felt.

Our previous hypothesis was that the relative statuses of men and women were likely to be more equal and their respective roles less rigidly demarcated in societies which emphasized radial rather than unilineal methods of reckoning kinship. If we have now established that one of the particular effects of modern change in general is the strengthening of radial and the undermining of unilineal relationships, we can put forward the further hypothesis that modern socio-economic development favours the greater equality of the sexes—and not only in South and South-East Asia.

THE RELATIVE EAST OF CHANGE: THE QUESTION OF COMPATIBILITY

It will appear to many of our readers that we have left the most obviously important aspects of modern changes until last. If it is a fact that women everywhere spend most of their time on domestic tasks, then surely the things that really matter to them as individuals are the layout of their houses, their access to water supplies, their furnishings, pots and pans, and methods of cooking, the kinds of clothes they and their families wear and how these are made and mended and washed? And surely when a family moves to town, or a village improvement scheme gets under way, or imported cloth and processed foods replace the home-made varieties, these are just the matters that change most quickly and easily?

Of course this is largely true. We have touched upon it in our discussion of modern communications. If we do not describe it further here it is because we do not feel it necessary to anticipate what our contributors can and do tell us so much more expertly from their own first-hand experience.

In any case, the extent to which such strictly technological changes, vitally important though they may be in affecting almost every aspect of daily life, lead actually to changes in the respective roles of men and women is problematical. Is the division of labour between the sexes affected by, say, the fact that cloth is now imported and no longer woven at home, or cooking done on a gas stove instead of a charcoal *chatti*?

Potentially much more important for role change than changes in the techniques of domestic work are changes in its organization. We have frequently referred to the indirect contribution to these which the 'enabling' nature of some technical innovations makes. Sometimes there is a direct connection; the design of living accommodation in a tenement block in, say, Singapore, which makes impossible the traditional separation between the men's and the women's quarters of a Malay house is an example. Sometimes role changes are connected with the adoption of new medical or hygienic measures; for instance, Javanese husbands who traditionally played a responsible and important part at the birth of their babies are now shooed out of the way by modern medically trained midwives. More often, however, role changes within the family seem to stem from such changes in the family's own structure and organization, as we have been discussing in the previous section of this essay.

A simple family is a very different work group from an extended family. Because only one adult of each sex is present, even the most rigid traditional sexual division of labour cannot always be maintained. We have argued that this fact helps to raise the status of a wife and extend her activities; but there is another set of factors we have not considered.

Experience of the 'isolated' simple family in the West—removed from all kin, unable to rely on neighbours for help, and without domestic servants—shows it to be only barely a viable unit, especially if (as is usual) the husband is employed away from home. As long as all goes well, no one is ill or incapacitated, and the children are fairly widely spaced out, this domestic unit can be self-contained—given hard work and sensible management on the part of the wife; but sickness, too many children too close to one another, the additional work caused by the presence of, say, an invalid mother or an elderly father-in-law, any of these things can make it impossible to manage. The development of social services, the custom of putting old people into institutions, and the determination to control birth spacing and numbers in the West should be seen in the light of this organizational fact at least as much as in purely economic or psychological terms.

Moreover—and this is a point we wish to stress—there can be no doubt that one of the factors which today make further change in the respective roles of Western men and women difficult is the relative isolation of the simple family, for this necessarily creates a practical incompatibility between the role of wife-mother and the role of worker outside the home—at least during the years of child bearing and child rearing. Are we therefore faced with the paradox that the predictable spread of the simple family, which we have argued augers a less restricted set of social roles for women and their improved status, carries within itself also the denial of these things?

There are, in fact, various possible solutions. They include the widespread development of specialized domestic services, whether commercially or through governmetal agencies, the employment of household servants, and, of course, the removal of 'isolation'. The first has hardly been fully worked out anywhere in the world as yet, though the social services in certain European countries go a long way towards it. It seems likely that if increasing economic growth makes increasing demands for women workers such services will be widely extended. At present they barely exist anywhere in the Orient.

In most parts of South and South-East Asia, however, household servants are still easily available, and the isolation of the simple family is also far from complete. In the traditional simple family areas of Burma, the Philippines, Indonesia and so on, it is usual for a couple to set up house after marriage near one or other (often both) of their parental homes, with the result that practical assistance is always at hand—as it is also for the so-called 'matrifocal' clusters of families found in many settled areas of, for example, working-class England. But we do not need to dwell on these matters. Our middle-class contributors are all well aware that in this respect changes of role are easier for them than for their Western counterparts today; they are also much concerned for the future of their daughters and grand-daughters in the coming years, when household servants may well be hard to find and families may well be both simple and scattered.

Mrs. Subandrio's article is of particular interest in this connection. A woman of great achievement outside the home, she is also the wife of Indonesia's Foreign Minister and a mother in a Javanese simple family. She has several ways of dealing with the practical business of organizing this apparently rather complicated series of roles. There are household servants; there are commercial suppliers of excellent cooked meals; there are close relatives nearby on whom she can rely but to whom she is not at all subordinate in the running of her own home. The result is that in fact her several roles are not incompatible.

She herself makes another point. Nowadays, she tell us, sons as well as daughters are being taught to take their share in domestic work. If this means that a Javanese man can, without loss of dignity, perform what are usually considered women's tasks it is of more than practical significance, for it implies a flexibility of attitude towards the sexual division of labour which is not found everywhere in our region—or in many parts of the West—and which where it exists must help to make some modern changes relatively easy. By contrast, a rigid sex-typing of occupations can make change difficult, for it may lead to such a close identification of occupation with sex that it becomes impossible for a man to perform 'women's work' without loss of 'manliness', or for a woman to perform 'men's work' without diminution of 'femininity'. These are usually not strictly practical but what we have earlier called ideological incompatibilities. Our previous argument might lead us to expect greater flexibility in this respect in the traditionally more purely radial —and simple family—kinship systems, of which Java's is certainly one. But there are other factors too.

It is sometimes suggested that it is relatively easier for women to enter paid occupations in the new nations of the world than in the West simply because most occupations there are too new to have been given any rigid sex-typing as yet. If there is no tradition of, for example, modern medicine at all, so the argument runs, then there can be no traditional sexual allocation of the role of doctor. Similarly, if women are prominent in pharmacy, for instance, as they are in Viet-Nam, this is because pharmacy is a new occupation without any traditional sex linkage.

There may be something in this argument, but it ignores the possible carry-over from traditional occupations which were similar if not identical with modern ones (after all, healing is not a new art), and fails to notice that the sexual division of labour in many a new nation often follows that current in the Western nation which has most influenced it. Pharmacy is popular among women in France as well as Viet-Nam; employees in textiles are predominantly female all over the world; transport and communications work is strikingly masculine in most parts of both East and West; the majority of pre-university teachers are women in the United States of America as well as in the Philippines. On the other hand there are important divergences from this pattern. Typists and secretaries, in the West so often female, are in our region predominantly male, and most countries of South and South-East Asia can show large numbers of women working in unskilled tasks on construction and road building which in the West are performed either by machines or exclusively by men.

These last two examples, however different from modern Western practices, are closely similar to those of the nineteenth century when, as in the modern East, secondary schooling—essential for office work—was still primarily for boys, and the harder manual work had not yet been legislated out of the hands of the poorer women. Fashions as to the belief in compatibility between certain occupations and the 'natural' physiological and personality characteristics of the two sexes vary historically as well as geographically.

There is one further problem of compatibility which is crucial to our subject matter. It arises from the family role of men, which despite our earlier protestations we have so far almost entirely neglected. In most of the countries of our region—probably most in the world—the chief nurturing role within the family is a female one. Men may take part in it, or not. But there are other roles equally necessary which are predominantly male. Two in particular, the roles of chief breadwinner and of holder of authority and power, are discussed very fully by our contributors below. Closely allied with them is a third: the role of status giver. Almost everywhere in the world a family's prestige and status are judged according to the prestige and status of its senior male members. This is probably because in most societies—and our region is no exception, as we have seen—men take a larger part in the occupational, political, religious and legal systems of society at large, and thus have the main responsibility for their families' relationship to it, and are seen as their representatives.

It appears to follow that a woman—certainly a married woman—is allotted the prestige and status of her husband (in a simple family; her father-in-law in an extended family). A social system which permits married women to participate in occupational, political, religious and legal roles outside the home may thus create considerable difficulties if such women are then allocated prestige and status in their own right. What if the status of husband and wife are incompatible? What if the wife stands higher than the husband

—to whose status shall the family be allocated?

Social systems which do not permit women to compete with men at all certainly avoid this problem. In other words they obviate any possible incompatibility between the status of husband and wife (father-in-law and daughter-in-law) by postulating an absolute incompatibility between the roles of men and women. We have already argued that such rigid sex-typing as this makes change particularly difficult. We suggest that the social system traditional to Pakistan was of this kind. Other systems allow women to compete in certain occupations only—as actresses, for example, or in other kinds of entertainment in which they can have a prestige ranking in their own right, but at the expense of being altogether *déclassées* in the 'respectable' world of the regular (male) stratification system. Several Western countries have fallen into this category at certain periods of their history; so also, we suggest, did traditional China, Japan and probably India at certain periods. Change in such countries will not be easy, for women must face the charge of being not only unfeminine but also disreputable. (The example of Florence Nightingale comes to mind immediately.) Once fairly launched, however, women may well find change less difficult in such a system, for at least the walls have been partially breached.

A third method of dealing with the problem is to allow women to enter freely into most occupations, leaving questions of status and prestige to be settled in a different sphere altogether—as in Burma, for example, where men have prestige built in to their manhood and recognized in their superior religious status with which women by definition cannot compete. A rather similar system seems to obtain in Thailand, and probably also in Cambodia and Laos. Most occupational changes here are likely to be relatively painless, at least as long as the religious system holds its prestige. But there is one exception. Because status (in our usage) is necessarily associated with power it can never in fact be a purely spiritual attribute. It is not an accident that, despite their long tradition of relatively unrestricted access to occupations outside the home, Burmese, Thai, Cambodian and Laotian women have not entered political life in any numbers or really competed for authority in any sphere.

Our contributors make it perfectly clear that this situation is gladly accepted along with the religion which entails it; it is a religion which also holds out prospects of future rebirth in masculine form and does nothing to limit the very wide choice of secular occupations in this life which the kinship systems of these countries permit. By contrast, the Republic of the Philippines, with a similar kinship system and a similarly wide choice of occupations outisde the home, but with Roman Catholic Christianity instead of Theravāda Buddhism, is one of the few countries of our region which has produced a strong feminist movement.

It is not suggested that these three ways of trying to meet the problem of avoiding ambiguities in allocating family status exhaust the sociological possibilities, but they do illustrate the main differences in our region.

A complication enters the picture when a man's prestige (if not his status), and therefore the children's, depends in part upon his wife's assisting him in his career, especially in its public social aspects. Hitherto this has been largely a Western phenomenon. Dr. and Mrs. Hanks have interesting things to say about its adoption in Thailand, where women have up till now played roles in the secular and non-political world in their own right, and left questions of status largely to their husbands. The Hanks see this piece of 'Westernization' as a threat to women's personal independence, and predict a revulsion from it once Thai women fully appreciate what is happening. In other words, they see Western women as being considerably less independent than their Thai sisters.

The arguments we have put forward above prepare us not only to agree with this view, but to maintain that it holds good for several other aspects of the mutual roles and relationships of men and women and for several other parts of South and South-East Asia as well.

We shall not recapitulate the various points this essay has tried to raise. We have made some tentative sociological analyses in general terms, using mainly the concepts of role and status. We should, however, be the first to insist that role analysis alone cannot be exhaustive, and further, that even the fullest sociological analysis alone cannot give complete explanation. It is for our readers to decide, from the detailed studies of particular countries and the personal documents which follow, how far our present essay goes towards this desirable ideal.

* * * * *

Note 1982

Because some recent studies of the status of women (particularly but not exclusively in Western countries) have claimed that many of the basic problems that women have to contend with in modern societies are connected with the prevalence of the nuclear type of family structure, I would like to clarify the point of view that I took on this subject.

As I saw it, two different levels of argument were relevant here: one I shall call jural, the other practical. It appeared to me that the comparative sociological evidence from the papers in the book *Women in the New Asia* indicated that the societies in South and South-East Asia in which the nuclear family existed as the traditionally preferred form were usually societies in which the inheritance of rights to property passed through and to both males and females. (For reasons that are made clear in the text above, I termed such systems 'radial' systems. They are more usually known in the literature on kinship as 'non-unilineal' or 'bilateral' systems.) *Prima facie*, I argued, the jural position of women in a society with such a system of inheritance was likely to be relatively 'better' than in a society with a purely patrilineal (agnatic) system. (The paper considers matrilineal systems, which are rare in the region, only briefly.) If this is so, then in any society the existence of the nuclear family as the traditionally preferred form (whether or not it is also the statistically most usual type) can be used as an *index* of the likelihood of relatively 'higher' female status. This argument is pursued in the essay, and examples given. I also point out that there is no guarantee that the intrinsically egalitarian nature of a non-unilineal system which I was postulating would not be overridden by other factors, and I quoted the example of traditional (i.e. eighteenth- and nineteenth-century) England as a case in point. Thus at the jural level I did not argue that the statistical prevalence of the nuclear family indicates gender quality, but I did and do maintain that where that form of family exists as the traditionally preferred (normative) form of domestic unit it is reasonable to investigate whether or not there is a non-unilineal system of inheritance and with it the probability of the relatively higher status of women that I assumed their claim to property rights would confer.

A second jural point is connected with women's freedom to engage in activities outside the home. The paper argues that there is likely to be a difference in the jural situation of women (and in the related pressures of morality and public opinion) as between patrilineal and non-unilineal ('radial') systems of kinship such that the societies in which women have traditionally been rather more free to engage in income-producing activities outside the home are those with radial systems. In other words, in our region the same set of societies which affords inheritance rights to women is also likely to allow them opportunities for at least some degree of independent economic (and possibly political) activity, and, as we have seen, these are also the societies which show a traditional preference for (as well as a preponderance of) nuclear family structures.

At the purely practical level I saw the issue as turning on the availability or otherwise of domestic help. It is often argued that in this matter the extended family offers advantages that the nuclear family cannot, and on the face of it this would appear to be obvious enough. But the argument is frequently clouded by failure to define clearly what is meant by 'extended family'. As used in my paper here, the term refers to a patrilocal unit; that is, one in which sons continue to reside in their paternal home after their own marriages while daughters marry out (ideally into similar patrilocal domestic groups containing their husbands' parents, brothers and unmarried sisters). However, such patrilocal extended families do not usually (and certainly not normatively) exist in the societies of western Europe or those derived from them and the term 'extended family' as used in sociological writing about such societies refers most frequently to something very different—namely, the circle of close relatives living near one another but not usually sharing the same dwelling. In such circumstances, the domestic groups are still nuclear families but they are able to rely upon—and give—practical assistance and support because the parents and unmarried siblings of one or other (or both) of the spouses are living nearby as are their married brothers and/or sisters and probably other kin as well. The distinction between these two uses of the term 'extended family' is perhaps implicit in my paper, but I certainly did not discuss it fully and I fear this may have led to misunderstanding. Both types appear to offer their adult female members rather similar advantages in the matter of readily available (unpaid) mutual domestic assistance. It is certainly true that women in the so-called 'isolated' nuclear family, living at a distance from the close kinsmen of either spouse, are at a serious disadvantage in this respect unless, of course, they can make use of some kind of paid or publicly provided help. It is also the case that the widespread occurrence of such isolation seems to be a concomitant of modernization which both enables and in a number of ways may be said also to require it. It should be added that young married women in patrilocal families are often oppressed and exploited by their mothers-in-law, a disability which does not arise (at least never to the same extent) in the neolocal-but-neighbouring domestic units of the second type that appears to offer the optimum solution to the practical problems of everyday life for most women—a conclusion which leads one to suppose that the position of women in this sense is 'better' in societies in which this type of family arrangement predominates statistically. In the region covered by this book these would be mainly in Thailand, Burma, Laos, Malaysia, Indonesia and the Philippines—just the same set of societies that we have already picked out as affording women a higher status on jural grounds and (not by accident) the set in which the nuclear family was the traditional normative pattern too. Significantly this pattern is beginning to predominate and is becoming more and more preferred in the modernizing sectors of a number of societies whose traditional normative patterns used to be patrilocal—India, the overseas Chinese, Pakistan, for example.

The following table summarizes the argument and augments the information given in the figures on pages 215, 220, and 225 above:

Likelihood (other things being equal) of	Patrilocal extended family		Nuclear family with nearby kin		'Isolated' nuclear family	
	Relatively wealthy	Relatively poor	Relatively wealthy	Relatively poor	Relatively wealthy	Relatively poor
(a) Women owning property rights	0	0		(if any exist)		(if any exist)
(b) Women holding jural capacity to pass on property rights	0	0				
(c) Women becoming full members of husbands' families	?	?				
(d) Women contributing to production inside home	0?		0?		0?	
(e) Women contributing to domestic income from activities outside home	0	0	0?		0?	
(f) Availability of domestic help						0

APPENDIX

Contents of *Women in the New Asia*

PART I

Men, women and change: an essay in understanding social roles in South and South-East Asia (*by Barbara E. Ward*)

PART II

Burma: balance and harmony (*by Mi Mi Khaing*)
Patterns of social change in a Burmese family (*by Ni Ni Gyi*)
The life of Ceylon women (*by B. S. Siriwardena*)
Men's and women's roles in India: a sociological review (*by S. C. Dube*)
Our changing life in India (*by Sushilla Nayer*)
Three generations in my Calcutta family (*by Jyotirmoyee Sarma*)
The respective roles of men and women in Indonesia (*by Hurustiati Subandrio*)
Yesterday and today in Laos: a girl's autobiographical notes (*by Banyen Phimmasone Lévy*)
Men and women in Malay society (*by Michael Swift*)
Changes in the position of Malay women (*by Hashimah Roose*)
Changing patterns of an East Pakistan family (*by A. K. Nazmul Karim*)
Combining marriage and career in Karachi (*by Amna Gani*)
Men and women in the Philippines (*by Robert Fox*)
A career-housewife in the Philippines (*by Angelina Arceo-Ortega*)
Chinese women of Singapore: their present status in the family and in marriage (*by Ann E. Wee*)
A Chinese family in Singapore (*by Foong Wong*)
Thailand: equality between the sexes (*by Lucien M. Hanks, Jr. and Jane Richardson Hanks*)
My life history in Thailand (*by Pramuan Dickinson*)
A woman of Viet-Nam in a changing world (*by Le Kwang Kim*)

PART III

The history of female emancipation in southern Asia (*by Romila Tharpar*)
Population characteristics of South and South-East Asia (*by T. E. Smith*)
Appendix: Family planning in South and South-East Asia (*by Barbara Cadbury*)

12. Women and Technology in Developing Countries*

The tide of technological change—represented by labour-saving household devices, employment in factories, the conveniences of the towns into which people are migrating, increased education, and medical advances, particularly the Pill—is increasingly emancipating women in the developing countries from ancient ways of life which were characterized by heavy feminine burdens of toil. Yet, paradoxically, these instruments of liberation are at the same time causing many women to be chained more tightly than ever to their domestic duties.

At one level of argument the title of this article embodies a fallacy. Technological developments do not necessarily discriminate between the sexes any more than between colours, creeds or social classes. Changes in methods of transport and communication, increased control over epidemic diseases, availability of mass-produced goods, etc., are not intrinsically sexually selective. Already one cosmonaut has been a woman, and women are everywhere drivers of automobiles and aeroplanes, surgeons, precision workers of all kinds, computer operators and so on. Thus, even in its most dramatic aspects, the technological revolution is not an exclusively male preserve. We are all in it together.

Nevertheless, the prevailing division of labour between males and females inevitably brings it about that in most parts of the world there are certain aspects of technological change which, potentially at least, are of more direct significance for women than for men. Domestic organization is everywhere primarily a female responsibility. While changes in it certainly do affect men, too—and may indeed draw men into domestic chores more frequently than has been customary in the past—their effect upon women is always direct and often profound. Though less spectacular than flights to the moon or organ transplants, the developments in everyday matters (such as transport)

*Originally published in *Impact of Science on Society*, Vol. XX, No. 1 (1970). © Unesco, 1970. Reproduced by permission of Unesco.

and the invention of new domestic appliances (such as refrigerators, rice-cookers, electric irons and the like—not to mention the Pill and other contraceptives) have had, or will have, a far more revolutionary impact upon domestic life and relationships and so, in the long run, upon the attitudes and values of both men and women almost everywhere.

THE EFFECTS OF TRANSPORTATION

A study of the changing roles of women in Asia, published by Unesco in 1963,[1] gives some vivid illustrations of the impacts of modern transportation on the lives of women in developing countries. A Thai woman gave a graphic description of the ways in which ordinary travel has changed since the end of the nineteenth century. A journey which took her grandfather two months on elephant-back and her father two weeks by train and on foot could now be accomplished in a few hours by fast car. An Indian writer in the same volume pointed out that modern means of transport have been one of the most liberating influences even upon women in full *purdah* (seclusion). And two women from countries as far apart as the Philippines and Ceylon explained in almost identical words how driving their own motorcars made it possible for each of them to combine successfully the roles of housewife, mother and professional educationist.

These writers were all highly educated representatives of their countries, and relatively well-to-do. However, the revolution in transport has affected less privileged women almost as much. For one thing it makes emigration possible, and is a kind of 'enabling clause' for urbanization. Where in the past the migration of workers, as in southern Africa for example, was mainly a man's affair, and women were left behind often for years at a time to carry on the home as best they could (with all the hard labour necessary for mere subsistence in a tribal society), the coming of relatively cheap and convenient mechanical transport makes the movement of whole families a fairly simple matter.

Recent migratory movements, like those from the Caribbean or the Indian sub-continent to the United Kingdom, though spear-headed by men, have very quickly included women and children as well. Here is a sphere in which 'modernization', which in its earlier stages was often entirely disruptive of family life, is proving far less so as it develops further.

At the same time, of course, more women than ever before are 'seeing the world'. It is still true that women travel away from their homes less frequently than men. Even today, my own village in south-western England contains

[1] Barbara E. Ward, *Women in the New Asia* (Paris: Unesco, 1963).

several women who have never visited London and two who have never even been as far as the county town thirty miles away. None of the men has been so stationary. But these stay-at-home women are all over sixty years old. The younger ones have all travelled, some of them very far afield indeed. For good or ill they have made new personal contacts, seized new opportunities for education and employment, and have married men who in their grandmothers' days would have been considered 'foreigners'. Similar changes are taking place all over the world.

THE SPREAD OF EDUCATION

But travel is only one part of the modern system of communications. Not only people, but goods and ideas too, are being distributed more and more freely. The spread of books, newspapers and the telephone, radio, cinema and television marks a whole series of social revolutions. In education, the arts and entertainment, their influence is obvious, producing new knowledge, new concepts, new and modified social attitudes, new ways of passing time and new openings for employment. The volume already referred to points out that the husbands who refused to countenance the education of women because their wives might learn to send and receive love letters from other men foresaw only a very restricted few of the complex transformations that improved communications would bring.

One of the most striking accompaniments of that side of technological change which is connected with the spread of modern education has frequently been a widening of the intellectual gap between women and men, and—even more damaging for those it affects—between parents, especially mothers, and their sons. At its most drastic this latter gap may involve an almost complete breakdown in communication. The tragedy implicit in such a situation probably never affected very many families, and will in any case affect fewer and fewer as the numbers of educated girls increase, but there are still some women in Africa and Asia whose sons were sent to schools in Europe so young that they find it almost impossible to talk with their mothers in their native tongue when they return home.

Although the generation gap is seldom as wide as this, nevertheless during the years in which modern schooling is just becoming universal it is inevitably very great. Moreover, because the education of girls lags everywhere behind that of boys, women are likely to remain the greater sufferers for at least a long time to come.

The educational discrimination between the sexes affects relationships within the same generation, too. Marriages which break down because of incompatibility in this sense are not few. Any discussion of modernization which ignores problems of this nature (and they are many) would be seriously incomplete.

Even though it continues to lag behind, however, the education of women has probably been by far the most important factor in bringing about changes in their role and status all over the world in the last fifty years. It is education, moreover, that helps make it possible for women to take advantage of the many technological developments that can provide them with better material goods and save them from hard and time-consuming physical labour. Women who cannot read or keep accounts cannot successfully cope with urban life, public transport and modern kinds of shopping; nor can they understand the printed instructions which accompany so much of modern merchandise. Literacy gives them access not only to books and newspapers and letter-writing, but also—and much more important—to bus and train services, modern shops, and a whole new range of goods and services.

THE PRODUCTS OF TECHNOLOGY

The goods and household equipment that are now available are contributing to other aspects of the domestic revolution. Cloth, which in many places and until very recently had to be hand-woven (even, as in much of South-East Asia, hand spun) can now be bought by the yard; sewing machines speed the making up into garments, and even provide a source of income; mass-produced enamel, aluminium and plastic pots and pans are to be found all over the world; soap, cosmetics, medicaments, surgical plaster, even comfortable and hygienic sanitary towels, are on sale almost everywhere. For people who live in towns foodstuffs, once all laboriously planted, weeded, harvested and processed by family hand labour—largely female—are now available ready-wrapped in the stores. Even in villages the preparation of food has in many places been made much easier by the introduction of electricity and piped water.

These things do not by any means exist everywhere in the world as yet, but they are surprisingly widespread, and where they do exist their effect upon women's lives can hardly be exaggerated. For example, there is a fishing village in Hong Kong (typical of many others), which I first visited in 1950. At that time all the fishing-boats were wind-driven, slow and at the mercy of the very uncertain weather of the South China Sea. All the fisher families lived entirely on their boats, owning no property whatsoever ashore. The village contained no radio, no piped water, no electricity, no latrine. Only two of the fishermen's children went to school and both of them were boys.

By 1966, all but one of the boats had been mechanized, and each had a radio. Many fishing families had moved their older members, most of their women and all their younger children into newly built houses on the land. There was a new school, with three trained teachers and more than a hundred fisher-pupils, including all the girls between the ages of 7 and 15. There were also a splendid latrine and three stand-pipes with a never-failing supply of sweet water. In addition, there was a new maternity and child welfare clinic in the nearby market town, at which all the babies for the last five years had been born (previously all births had taken place on the boats, at sea).

In 1968 the generosity of a charitable trust in New Zealand made it possible for the villagers to purchase a small but adequate generator which gave them their electric light. Within six months every house had an electric iron, an automatic rice-cooker, and at least two electric fans to set beside its radio. One enterprising shopkeeper was selling iced drinks from his electric refrigerator, and there was talk of installing television.

In less than twenty years the women of this village have experienced a technological revolution which has improved their and their children's health, increased their expectation of life and given their children the chance of a good education. It has also improved their personal income, for now, for the first time, they have a good deal of leisure which most of them use to earn extra cash by making plastic flowers at home for a Hong Kong factory.

The women themselves say that the changes they value most are those which have brought better health and the chance of an education for their children. They also mention their appreciation of having more leisure and less everlasting hard work. They are quite well aware of the advantages technological change has brought to their own lives, discuss it clear-mindedly and often, and are busily looking forward to opportunities of buying still more electrical equipment.

On the other side of the world, in Mexico, changes almost as far-reaching have taken place in the same period. The key technological innovation in the villages there was a very simple one: the introduction, about fifteen years ago, of a mechanical method of grinding maize.

Maize, as used for making the flat, pancake-like *tortillas* which are the staple food, must first be soaked in water and then ground daily. Up till about 1950 most village women had to rise every day before dawn and trudge off to the natural rocks which were their grinding places. Grinding was done by rolling the maize between an upper stone held in the hands and the living rock. For an average household this took two or three hours—sometimes longer—and it was tiring work. Today the housewife simply takes her bucket of soaked maize along to the local mill, usually situated in a small shop. There she joins her neighbours in a friendly gossip until her turn comes round, and then the job is done for her—quickly, cleanly and cheaply.

The housewife also has piped water in her village now. She probably owns a sewing machine and—like her counterparts in the Hong Kong village—an electric iron, a radio and often a television set. She is still a very busy person and many aspects of the material conditions of her life would appear intolerable to a contemporary villager in a fully industrialized country. Nevertheless, her life is already vastly different from her mother's. Her daughters will undoubtedly see further changes, too.

THE SURGE TO THE TOWNS

The examples of change cited above—which stand for many—involve villages. However, it is obvious that the effects of technological change are still more apparent in towns, especially in the great metropolitan cities which have been developing at an unprecedented rate on every continent during the present century. It is here that the full impact of modern technology upon everyday living is experienced. Here are the centres of manufacture and distribution of material goods, and here are such large concentrations of population as to make at least some supply of services essential.

The surge to the towns, which is one of the major characteristics of our time, is to be explained as much by the 'pull' exerted by all these attractions as by the 'push' from an overpopulated countryside, for even where the countryside is not overpopulated (in Thailand, for example, or many parts of Africa) the towns continue to attract an apparently endless stream of rural emigrants. The reasons for this are made clear in the following true cases.

Two girls from the Hong Kong fishing village described above have married townsmen. One of them lives with her husband and three children in a small one-room apartment, measuring about 12 feet square, in a recently built block on an estate containing several thousand identical apartments. The family shares communal lavatory and washing facilities, but does all its cooking, ironing, mating, homework, sewing and sheer living in the one room, surrounded in the building by others with whom the family had no previous acquaintance and enveloped always by a volume of noise that has to be heard to be believed.

This woman has asserted over and over again, both spontaneously and in answer to direct questioning, how happy she is to have escaped from village life. Here, she says, everything is convenient. She and her husband own a refrigerator, two rice-cookers, an electric iron, a small electric heater (Hong Kong can be cold in the winter) and a television set. The water taps and flush toilets, though shared with others, are only a few yards away. A street market, shops and a small restaurant are at her door. The apartment block also houses a primary school, a clinic, a welfare officer and a social club. The rent is very cheap.

The other girl is less lucky. She lives in a squatter's hut half-way up one of Hong Kong's steep hillsides. Made of wood and beaten-out kerosene tins, the hut is far from weatherproof, and in the rains the earthen floor becomes a pool of mud. There is no toilet. The nearest stand-pipe for water is half a mile away, and except in the dry season it is easier to fetch water from a near-by (very doubtfully clean) stream. The three children are well dressed but dirty. So far she has managed to find a school place for only one of them. Her husband is intermittently unemployed.

Despite all this, this woman, too, frequently declares her firm conviction that she is far better off here than in the village. Pressed for a reason, she points to her electricity supply (probably illegally installed), her two rice-cookers, electric iron, fan and heater, and the sewing machine with which she makes a little extra money. On being informed that she could also have all these amenities in the village nowadays, she explains that life here in town is far less hard work than it ever was in the village, that town shopping is convenient, public transport useful, and the local welfare clinic on the spot. Finally she adds that she has far more leisure in town.

These two case histories are included in order to draw attention to the fact that modern technological innovations make it possible even for people living in what by most standards would be considered insupportable conditions of squalor and overcrowding to consider themselves much better off than they would have been in traditional circumstances. That there are enormous numbers living in towns (and villages) today who do not have access to the goods which would make them feel like this is true. The brutalities of acute poverty and actual hunger are still real enough. None the less, it remains true that more people, in absolute terms, have more goods than ever before, and that many of these goods liberate women in particular from at least some of the back-breaking work that has been their usual lot, and that more of the people so affected live in urban than in rural areas. Women to whom goods of this kind mean not just prestige but also less fatigue, better health and greater leisure are usually quite clear in their minds on this point. Generally speaking they want to live in town.

It is in towns, moreover, that women are more likely to find employment, though it seems likely that unlike men, who go to the towns to seek work, most of the migrant women who take employment in the cities of the world do so rather as a response to the economic necessity they find pressing upon them after they have arrived. And when wage-earning in town takes places, its effects are far-reaching, for it is likely to be in a non-traditional occupation, will probably be connected with modern technology and will bring with it far-reaching changes in domestic roles and in outlooks. Women working in modern textile mills, for example, or in a big store, business office or educational establishment, have to keep to fixed hours and their pay is usually based on hours worked. Because they have prior obligations to housework, catering, cooking and, above all, children, most women find this both difficult and tiring.

It is sometimes argued that the organizational problems that outside work poses for women are more easily dealt with in countries where the large, extended family exists, or where domestic servants are still easily available. This is probably true, but it does little to help the majority of working women who in any country come from the poorer sections of the population among whom both extended families and domestic servants are rare or non-existent.

Even among the upper classes in such countries the problems are becoming fairly large. With more and more varied employment available and wages rising, the attractions of factory work prevail easily over the few perquisites of domestic service. At the same time, the move towards 'going separate', that is setting up independent simple (nuclear) family households is very marked.

I have heard highly educated Asian women debating in worried tones the same problem that worries their Western counterparts: now that at last we are educated and emancipated we find ourselves chained more securely than before by the sheer demands of domesticity. For such women one can predict an increasing resort to modern domestic gadgets.

The technological revolution, with its educational and other 'modernizing' corollaries, first frees some women from total immersion in the domestic sphere, then in freeing others begins to confine the first group again. Finally by producing still more technological equipment of a domestic nature, it may help to redress the balance it has itself destroyed.

THE NEGATIVE ASPECTS OF TECHNOLOGICAL CHANGE

Sometimes the impact of technological change has been unmitigatedly depressing to standards of living. This was very frequently the case in nineteenth-century Europe, for example. It was the basis of Dickens's attacks upon English society, and of much of the work of Engels and Marx, to mention only three of the most influential writers.

Relatively secure in their Western welfare states, with their remarkable new washing machines, detergents and deep freezes, bourgeois Western writers try to believe that such things cannot happen any longer. The world is supposed to have learnt its lesson; industrialization is expected to proceed in an orderly fashion, taking due care of the human relationships and the human wants of the workers. Yet in every continent there are back streets and shanty towns which, despite everything said above about the ways in which they can be made supportable, are a disgrace to civilization. A very large proportion of the hundreds of thousands who flock into towns live there below the poverty level. How can one decide whether or not they would have been better off if they had stayed in their villages? Put very simply, industrialization and urbanization still can, and very frequently do, depress as well as elevate standards of living.

Modern technological developments can have their Luddite effects too. Cottage industries (in which women are able to take a full part mainly because they involve work at home) are especially vulnerable. The story of the nineteenth century English hand-loom weavers is well known: how, under their possibly imaginary 'General Ludd', they fought against their displacement by power looms, resulting in widespread unemployment, lower wages and shoddier goods. Exactly similar reactions have occurred all over the Orient.

It does not take the full force of large-scale foreign competition to drive small peasant industry out of business. The impact of local technological change can be just as dramatic, as the following illustrates.

Until about fifteen years ago the Melanau women of Sarawak, in East Malaysia, enjoyed a somewhat unusual economic and social independence because their individual contribution to the processing of the Melanau's single export crop, sago, brought them in a regular cash income. Then, about 1955, an enterprising Chinese invented a mechanical means of refining sago. Within a very few years the need for women's employment had almost entirely disappeared—and there was nothing to take its place. The Melanau women gained enforced leisure, and lost their incomes; relief from toil meant also loss of independence.

The facile optimism which sees nothing but good in the increasing pace of technological advance is as obviously ill-founded as the equally facile pessimism which sees nothing but bad. Their circumstances being so different, Melanau and Hong Kong village women would be hardly likely to see eye to eye on this matter.

MEDICAL ADVANCES AND BIRTH CONTROL

There is, however, one field where the impact of modern technology upon the lives of women appears, on the face of it, if not unmitigatedly good, at least very widely welcome. This is the field of health, where medical advances have brought many improvements. Probably the most important of all medical advances is birth control, which is undoubtedly one of the crucial factors to be considered in any assessment of the effects of modern technology upon women. For the first time in human history there is the possibility of freedom from the physiological and social effects of the more-or-less continuous round of pregnancy, parturition and lactation which, with numerous miscarriages and the ever-present chance of death in childbirth, has been the lot of the vast majority of women between the ages of 15 and 50 since the human race began.

Moreover, the babies that are born are likely to survive. This, too, is crucial. A modern Westerner reads the pathetic inscriptions on the numerous tiny graves of past centuries which are scattered throughout the old burial grounds of Europe and North America with pity; most Asian, African and South American women would read them with a sympathy born of experience. One of the most striking differences between conversations with women in most of the so-called developed countries and most of the so-called developing countries today is that in the former one can ask: 'And how many children have you had?' whereas in the latter you ask: 'How many have you raised?' Increasingly as the former question becomes safer to ask in the developing countries—and this is happening—the roles of wives and mothers there will be marked by a new freedom from fear.

These are matters of peculiar personal concern to women. Their impact upon the structure of domestic relationships and thence upon the whole fabric of society itself is barely to be seen as yet. All that can be said at this stage is that the effects when they do become apparent are likely to be very considerable, unprecedented and, because of differing domestic circumstances in different parts of the world, various. And they will not be confined to women.